TWELVE BASKETS FULL

And they took up twelve baskets full of the fragments, and of the fishes.　　　MARK 6:43

Blessed shall be thy basket and thy store. . . . if thou shalt harken unto the voice of the Lord.
DEUTERONOMY 28:5, 2

TWELVE BASKETS FULL

by Margaret T. Applegarth

author of *Moment by Moment,*
Men as Trees Walking, etc.

HARPER & ROW, PUBLISHERS
New York, Evanston, and London

CONTENTS

TWELVE BASKETS FULL

1

TWELVE BASKETS FULL

And they took up twelve baskets full of the fragments, and of the fishes.   MARK 6:43

Christian history is actually one long record of twelve baskets full, all because somebody said: *"Master, there is a lad here!"* and that boy rushed home to shout: "Just wait till you hear what I and Jesus did today!" With a mother asking indignantly: "Do you mean to tell me that 4,999 grown men grabbed a lunch basket away from a little fellow your size?"

"No! no! Mother, it wasn't like that at all. I gave it!"

"You *gave* it? But, what on earth made you do that? Weren't you hungry, or what?"

"But don't you understand—I wanted terribly to give it. There was everybody starving to death, so I just went over to Andrew and said: 'See this lunch my mother fixed for me? Well, you can have it if you want it!' So the next thing I knew Andrew was saying: 'Master, there's a lad here!' And all of a sudden we were all simply *family*—Jesus loving each of us as if there was only one of us, and all of us loving Him back; share and share alike. The way you do, yourself, when you cook something special, and simply have to carry it down the street in this very same basket to someone you love. *That way!*"

"Oh! Yes, I see now how it was!"

But the rest of her life she always used to stop and stare at her own straw basket hanging up on its old peg in her pantry, while she whispered three enchanted syllables: "Twelve? Twelve!

1

Twelve!" Seeing in the interwovenness some symbol of her son's unselfish sharing, remembering too the simple way it started: "Master, there is a lad here!" Every neighbor for years to come was going to hear her twice-told tale: how—on a morning like any morning, on a day like any day—she had filled the little basket; at the last minute adding one more small loaf, one more little fish, simply because the boy had been growing by leaps and bounds lately; and when he went traipsing all over the countryside, following that Man, who knew how far he might go? Who, indeed? When her boy's sharing would cross every border line in Christendom, get written into four gospels, get translated into a thousand tongues, telling the unfailing mystery of God's providing hand able to use one mother's meager meal to feed five thousand hungry persons . . . seated by fifties . . . on the green grass.

Christian history is a record, then, of other stories starting the same way, the gospels gathering up twelve baskets full of details, so that nothing be lost.

"Master, there is a lad here" (Mark 9:14-29; Luke 9:37-45); a dangerously disturbed boy, a perfect nuisance in the neighborhood, wreaking havoc on himself and on his family. The disciples, being prayerless, were powerless. But the Great Physician knew the only cure for delinquents. How the neighbors must have marveled to see the little fellow so sane and sensible again.

"Master, there is a girl here" (Mark 5:21-24, 35-43; Luke 8:41-56); a dangerously sick daughter, with Jairus pinning all his hopes on the Master's miracle touch. But by the time Jesus reached the house, the child was reported dead, mourners were lamenting loudly, and neighbors laughing Jesus to scorn when He said she was only sleeping. Didn't they know death when they saw it? But how calm He was as He put everyone out of the room but the parents. How gently He took the little girl's hand as He said: "Get up, my little darling!" She got up at once. ("For she was twelve years old," the Bible adds in its beautiful footnote fashion.) How sensibly the Lord of heaven and earth and history said to the mother: "Now give her something to eat!" Knowing

twelve-year-old appetites. Afterward, when she went walking up and down the street in her gay young way, did the neighbors say: "Did you ever see the likes of her?" But that was because they were too local to have heard of the equally remarkable recovery of the Syrophoenician woman's daughter. ("Imagine His doing all that for a mere Gentile! Why on earth did He bother?")

"Master, there is a tragic girl here with a demon" (Mark 7:24-30). The mother was Greek, with a heart so anxious and a rapartee so swift that Jesus was touched by her outsider's faith in His power: already she was seeing her child in her mind's eye, well —whole—walking! And He made it come true.

"Master, there is a child here." Over and over the disciples were overheard clamoring for place and position; and Jesus would quietly place a child in their midst: "Of such is my Kingdom! Whoever receives one such child, receives me." Adding: "For truly I say to you, whoever gives you a cup of water to drink because you bear the name of Christ, will by no means lose his reward."

Only a few years ago, over in Africa, Mabel Shaw was teaching this verse to her kindergarten class, when suddenly she realized this was pretty thick theology for tiny tots. But later that same day, sitting at her window, Miss Shaw noticed some strange coolies come into the mission compound to fling themselves down for rest under the shade trees, after laying aside their heavy burdens. At the same time she saw a surprising sight —all her small black kindergarten babies hurrying toward the well to fill their little drinking cups. Balancing these on top of their heads, in proper African style, they formed a careful procession across the compound toward the unknown coolies. Kneeling in front of them, they offered the cold water with charming politeness. The men were completely astonished, but spontaneously shouted in gratitude: "The children of the King! The children of the King!"

"Master, there are some infants here," and a dozen disciples

driving away such unbusinesslike babies as beneath their Lord's notice; but He roundly rebuked them: "Let them keep coming and coming and coming! Never stop them! You seem to have no least idea how important children are going to be in my Kingdom, tomorrow."

Martin Luther discovered this, centuries later: "How wise of God to keep renewing His Church every twenty years with this new generation of members." Each with a stewardship of small sharings to result in twelve baskets full. Was it only incidental, do you think, that there turned out to be a basket apiece for each disbelieving disciple? Did he, too, take his home, conscious whenever he saw it: "Think what I and Jesus did that day!" For each man could recall how the increase kept coming only as person by person had reached in and found enough for his need, and then watching anxiously to see how his neighbor might fare. In each man's caring, the sharing grew.

"Master, there is a girl here"—born of a Christian bondswoman and an Irish chieftain, churning butter in her father's pantry over sixteen hundred years ago. Vivid and energetic and generous, she would make twelve ordinary pats of butter and a larger thirteenth one to give the passing stranger, for the sake of the Saviour; not to mention twelve usual loaves of bread, plus a larger thirteenth loaf. She had a little song for singing as she churned or baked:

> O God, bless my pantry!
> Pantry which the Lord has blessed, never be lacking in aught.
> O Mary's Son, my Friend, come and come into my pantry,
> Let there be abundance ever on the board for Thee.

Thousands of Irish peasant girls and princesses came under St. Bridget's teaching; and across these sixteen centuries clergymen of her church still cherish the prayer she made at one of their early training conferences:

> I would like the angels of heaven to be among us.
> I would like full baskets for charity.

I would like rich treasures of mercy.
I would like cheerfulness to reign over us all.
I would like Jesus to be present.
I would like the three Marys of the gospel to be with us.
I would like myself to be a rent-payer to the Lord.

"We do not have enough to go around among so many!" No disciple ever yet had enough. There does not seem to be enough even now to save the world and the Church. But our Lord is still saying: "Feed them! And see what happens!"

This *Twelve Baskets Full* shares only a few of the fragments of what has happened.

In a child's lunch basket, a mother's thoughts.

Japanese proverb

When a child goes away from home, he carries his mother's hand with him. Chinese proverb

There is as much in our Lord's pantry as will satisfy His bairns. . . . Hunger on: for there is meat in hunger for Christ: go never from Him, but fash Him with a dishful of hungry desires till He feed you.

Samuel Rutherford; from a Scottish prison, 1630

I saw a stranger yestere'en:
I put food in the eating place,
Drink in the drinking place,
Music in the listening place;
And in the sacred name of the Triune
He blessed myself and my house,
My cattle and my dear ones.

And the lark sang in her song:
Often, often, often, goes the Christ in the stranger's guise,
Often, often, often, goes the Christ in the stranger's guise.
Ancient Gaelic Rune of Hospitality

2

THE APPLE IS BITTEN AGAIN

Through covetousness shall they with feigned words make merchandise of you: whose judgment now for a long time lingereth
not, and their damnation slumbereth not.   2 PETER 2:3

It is highly proper for a stewardship book to open with a chapter
stating that Christian history is one long record of twelve baskets
full, all because one person in 5,000 was willing to share what he
had for the good of others. It is equally proper for the second
chapter to state that Christian history is also one long record of
forbidden apples which men have been tempted to eat, and did
eat, thus producing the perpetual deficit in which the Lord's
work is always being carried on—people having squandered
paradise for the lure of one particular apple.

But suppose the boy who gave his lunch basket should become
a scientist. Some day he may sit in front of the fact of this
forbidden tree to study it. What on earth makes it so desirable?
He will observe how the trunk of it stretches upright from earth
toward heaven in two parallel lines. He will note that a serpent
loops two loops insinuatingly around the trunk. He will jot in the
margin a question mark: *Why should this resemble a dollar*

sign—$? Trunk and serpent? Serpent and trunk? With the love of money the root of all evil? And an insinuating voice forever making merchandise of a man: "Eat it—it can't hurt you!" "Buy it—it will make you live longer, look younger!" "Charge it—pay later on our easy installment plan!" "King Size—twice as big, longer-lasting!" "Get the wider handsomer De Luxe Model—the kind the Jonses installed!" "Ask for the Large Size Economy Package at your grocer's today!" "Cheaper by the dozen!" "Your nose knows!" "Now you too can afford our super-duper sensational bargain—one day only! Come early and avoid the rush. Doors open 9 a.m. sharp."

No matter how earnestly the consumer may pray: "Lord, I want to want *not* to want these things the advertisements want me to want," he lives in a state of siege all day. Practically everything he hears, sees, tastes, touches, and smells tries to sell him something. When George Bernard Shaw sat down in front of this perpetual apple he said: "There are only two tragedies in life. One is not to get your heart's desire. The other is—to get it."

For in order to get it, last year consumers in this country spent:

$37 billion in consumer credit plans, with their excessive interest charges;
$44 billion on food in supermarkets;
$12 billion on meals in restaurants;
$10 billion on automobiles;
$ 9 billion on liquor;
$ 5 billion on tobacco;
$ 4 billion on women's clothes;
$ 1½ billion on jewelry;
$ 1½ billion on candy;
$ 1 billion on baby-sitters;
$500 million on dogs.

When Ralph Waldo Emerson sat down in front of such an overtempting apple in his day, he noticed: "It is pitiful the things by which we are rich—a matter of coins, coats and carpets, a little more or less stone, wood or paint; the fashion of a cloak, or hat; like the luck of the naked Indians, of whom one is proud in the possession of a glass bead or a red feather, and the rest miserable in the want of it. . . . If N. has a breakfront desk you want one, of course, but a bigger, richer, more glamorous one."

More recently an Oriental student sat down in front of our national dollar sign, saying: "American life is so complex. When I first looked on the floor, I saw a carpet, which makes you need a vacuum cleaner, and for this you need electricity, and for this you need a hydro, and for this you need the T.V.A., and for this you need capital, and part of this capital comes from taxes, but —you don't like taxes!"

No wonder our Lord said: "Show me a penny!" and suggested simply that what was due to Caesar should be paid to Caesar, and what was due to God, to God. For at dusk on the Sabbath the head of a Hebrew family had to ask himself three things: Have you tithed? (paying the temple taxes). Have you prepared the *erub?* (put out the proper utensils for the Sabbath meal). Have you lighted the lamp? And even his shekel held a great message —on one side were the words: *"Jerusalem the Holy,"* with a chalice known as the pot of manna; on the other side was a three-petaled lily: "I will be as the dew unto Israel; he shall grow as the lily."

But Carl Sandburg reminds us of our own meaningful coins:

> In God We Trust: it is so written.
> The writing goes onto every silver dollar.
> The fact: God is the great God who made us all.
> We is you and me and all of us in the United
>   States of America.
> And trusting God means that we give ourselves,
>   the whole United States of America to
>   God, the great One.
> Yes . . . Perhaps . . . is that so?

Surely this belongs on the usual Bulletin some Sunday morning when the sermon is to be on stewardship. And, if the treasurer could be properly persuaded, how tempting to attach a dollar greenback beneath the poem on the same Bulletin, in order to prove what religious motives our own forefathers had in designing this bill. For they put a pyramid inside a circle to symbolize the unbreakable strength of this nation under God. Three-in-one. But the pyramid is an unfinished symphony, as the space near the top shows. And that *Eye of God*—think what a clarifying responsive reading could appear underneath it:

Minister: The Lord is in His holy temple, His eyes behold, His eyelids try, the children of men. (Psalm 11:4)

People: My substance was not hid from Thee, when I was made in secret, and curiously wrought in the lowest parts of the earth. Thine eyes did see my substance, yet being imperfect; and in Thy Book all my members are written, when as yet there was none of them. (Psalm 139:15-16)

Minister: If I have seen any perish from want of clothing, or any poor without covering . . .

People: If I have made gold my hope, or said to the fine gold: "Thou are my confidence"; if I have rejoiced because my wealth was great, and because my hand had gotten much,

Minister: This were an iniquity to be punished by the Judge,

People: For I should have forgotten the God that is above. (Job 31:19, 24-25, 28)

Prayer (in unison): Have Mercy, O Lord, upon all forestallers, and upon all who seek undue profits or unlawful gains. Turn Thou the hearts of them that live by cunning rather than by labor. Teach us that we stand daily and wholly in need of one another. And give us grace by hand and mind to add our proper share to the common stock. Through Jesus Christ our Lord. Amen.

from Queen Elizabeth's Prayerbook, 1559

There is, of course, still more to capture the imagination in this dollar bill, for the Latin phrase *"Novus Ordo Seclorum"* speaks of *"a new order of the ages"*; and *"Annuit Coeptis"* dwells on the fact that *"God has blessed our undertakings."*

Still looking at the pyramid, it might be appropriate to recall the boastful inscription on an earlier one in Egypt: "I, King

Saib, built this pyramid. I, when I built it, covered it with satin. Let him who cometh after me, and says he is equal to me, cover it with mats."

Pitirim Sorokin, who has spent his life at Harvard, sitting down in front of dollar signs and studying altruistic and selfish love, tells about the day when Cleopatra gave a bountiful banquet for Mark Antony, and bewildered her guests by showing an enormous pearl of absolute perfection. Guest after guest held it with awe, for it was valued at three-quarters of a million dollars in our money. But when they handed it back to her, she dropped it into a glass of vinegar, waited while it dissolved, and then drank it disdainfully.

It is one thing to notice how God walks through history, calling: "Adam, where art thou?" wanting man to acknowledge how inconsequential it is to trade a temporary apple for a permanent paradise. It is quite another thing to notice that Jesus also walks through history, calling: "If any man will come after me let him deny himself, and follow me." Not an abundance of things. But self-denial, His hallmark. And a far harder plus than loving your neighbor as yourself. Quite obviously the Good Samaritan could have stopped sooner—that oil in the wound, that ride on his beast, that inn, that extra promise to the innkeeper, all these were spiritual compulsions beyond the line of duty. "BE KINDER THAN NECESSARY" was the motto on Sir Wilfred Grenfell's medicine chest through all those lonely Labrador years, a daily reminder of whom he was the representative. It seemed like an isolated life. But not at all! He became for all of us like Chaucer's Doctour of Phisick: "A verrey parfit praktisonour—in al this world ne was there noon like"! And everyone knew what he meant when he wrote: "The only real heathen and heretics are the purely selfish. It is for our own sakes as well as theirs that we desire their conversion. For while they are losing all life has to give, we are losing the share they might contribute."

To find this irreducible minimum is the real reason for this book. All sorts and conditions of men have been finding "great peace in a little busyness," as Geoffrey Chaucer wrote. They have sat down in front of the dollar sign and seen the two straight lines of the trunk extending from earth toward heaven, with the serpent insinuating itself in two loops, trying to make merchandise of men.

In 1774 John Woolman wrote in his Journal: "I saw that a humble man, with the blessing of the Lord, might live on little; and that where the heart was set on greatness, success in business did not satisfy the craving; but that commonly with an increase of wealth, the desire of wealth increased." And he became so "baptized into the feelings of the people" that he could be this kind of storekeeper: "I found it good for me to advise poor people to take such things as were most useful and not costly." Of whom *Fortune* magazine could say, in 1949: "*His life of business has the same quality as the lives of the saints.*"

In India lived the Christian from whom Gandhi drew inspiration, Charles F. Andrews, radiant happiness shining from him. And on his study table were words carved in Greek from Matthew 5:47: "*What do ye to excess?*" For as C. F. always explained: "Have you given to the extreme limit of love? Christ seeks deeds not words. If the Christian faith has no power to restore or re-create the human will leading on to deeds of unselfish service, then it stands self-condemned."

To live with this lyrical lilt is not impossible. For as William James wrote in his last chapter of *The Varieties of Religious Experience* it brings an assurance of safety and peace, a preponderance of loving affection: "We and God have business with each other; and in opening ourselves to His influence, our deepest destiny is fulfilled."

The more she yaf awey,
The more, y-wis, she hadde alway.
                                    Geoffrey Chaucer

Adam lay inbounden,
Bounden in a bond;
Four thousand winter
Thought he not too long;
And all was for an appil,
An appil that he took
As clerics finden
Written in their book;
Blessed bee the time
That appil taken was.
Therefore we must singen
Deo Gratias.
       Fifteenth-century carol

      O why did God,
Creator wise, that peopled highest Heaven
With spirits masculine, create at last
This novelty on earth, this fair defect
Of nature, and not fill the world at once
With men as angels without feminine,
Or find some other way to generate
Mankind? This mischief had not then befall'n.
     John Milton, *Paradise Lost*, 1663

You can count the apples on a tree, but you cannot count
the trees in an apple.
       African proverb

3

THE GREEKS HAD A WORD FOR IT

I am debtor both to the Greeks, and to the barbarians, both to
the wise, and to the unwise.   ROMANS 1:14

The moment a Christian goes to church he talks Greek. And
this is as it should be, with nothing whatever upsetting about it.
Plato used to say: "Whenever anyone gives something too big to
something too small to carry it—too big sails to too small a ship,
too big meals to too small a body, too big powers to too small
a soul—the result is bound to be a complete upset." But the
Christian has had nineteen centuries to learn his Greek, and he
tosses off his elaborate vocabulary with perfect ease, all the way
from *"doxology"* through *"hymn," "choir," "chorus," "amen,"*
"Bible" and *"angel,"* into the deeper intricacies of *"episcopal,"*
"methodist," "baptist," "presbyter," "ecclesiastical," "eucharist,"
"bishop," "theology," "anthropologist," "geologist," "evangelist"
and *"economist."* Stumbling over the last two, perhaps none too
sure if he is either of them, until William Tyndale explained (before being burned at the stake in 1536 for daring to let Greek
speak "ye modir tonge"): "Euangelio, that we cal gospel, is a
greke word, and signifyth good, merry, glad and ioyeful tydings,
that maketh a mannes hert glad, and maketh hym synge, daunce
and leepe for ioye."

Such singing, dancing, and leaping for joy is considerably more
of an effort for any *economist,* as even the Greeks themselves
found true. Listen to Socrates in his speech to his judges, just

13

before they condemned him to death (for Impiety, of all things! How he must have rubbed them the wrong way):

I will obey God rather than you, and as long as I have breath I will not cease from exhorting you. God has sent me to attack this city, as if it were a great horse sluggish from its size, which needs to be roused by a gadfly. I think I am that gadfly. Are you not ashamed of caring so much for money and for reputation and for honor? Will you not think about wisdom and truth and how to make your soul better? I shall reproach you for indifference to what is most valuable and prizing what is unimportant. I shall do this to everyone I meet, young or old, for this is God's command to me. . . . O men of Athens, of what are you thinking, that you give all your time to the getting and spending of money, while you neglect your own children to whom you must leave it all some day?

No wonder the old Christian world recognized the likeness of Socrates to Christ, or that once Erasmus said: "Holy Socrates, pray for us!" But in the midst of all his spontaneous talking, occasionally Socrates prayed for himself; then the essence of the man showed clear: "Give me beauty in the inward soul; and may the inner and the outer be at one. May I consider wisdom to be wealth, and let me have only as much gold as a temperate man and only he can bear and carry. This prayer, I think, is enough for me." It was 399 B.C. when the Athenian judges gave hemlock to this brave spirit, who had said: "Our venture is a glorious one! The soul with her proper jewels—which are justice and courage and nobility and truth—in these arrayed she is ready to go on her journey when her time comes."

Plato is known to us for his statement that "an unexamined life is not worth living"; and we respond to his vision of the ideal *Republic:* " 'In heaven,' " I replied, " 'there is laid up a pattern of the Eternal City which he who desires may behold; and beholding, may set his own house in order. But whether such a one exists, or ever will exist in fact, is no matter, for he (the wise man) will live after the manner of that city, having nothing to do with any other.' "

This constant preparation for beauty and common courtesy was understood by scholars and slaves alike: "Men come to be builders by building, harp players by playing the harp; exactly so, by doing just actions, we come to be just; and by doing brave actions, brave." Such was Aristotle; and now Epictetus, the lame ex-slave:

Dare to look up to God and say, Deal with me for the future as Thou wilt, I am of the same mind as Thou art; I am Thine: I refuse nothing that pleases Thee. Lead me where Thou wilt; clothe me in any dress Thou choosest. Is it Thy will that I should hold the office of a magistrate, that I should be in the condition of a private man, stay here or be in exile, be poor, be rich? I will make Thy defence to men in behalf of all these conditions. . . . The universe is but one great city, full of beloved ones, divine and human, by nature endeared to each other. . . . If thou wouldst make a man happy, add not unto his riches, but take away from his desires.

These early Greeks not only influenced our language but also fascinated our church fathers. We have spoken already of Desiderius Erasmus and his admiration of Socrates; in his *Praise of Folly* (which did so much to pave the way for the Protestant Reformation) Erasmus tells of the day when Plato was entertaining some friends in a room where there was a couch richly covered with a superb rug. Diogenes came in from the street, very dirty as usual, got up on this couch and walked around on the rug, saying: "I trample on the pride of Plato!" To which Plato mildly replied: "But with greater pride, Diogenes!" For it is not enough to adapt from Greek the word "economist" without sensing what disciplined human history is wrapped up in the practicing of it.

By the period when the gospels came to be written, it was the Greek writer Luke who knew the exact Greek term to use for our Lord's word "steward": "*oikonomas*"—"Who then is the faithful and wise steward whom the master will set over his household to give them their portion of food at the proper time?" (Luke 12:42).

"Oikos" means an occupied house: so that it is easy to picture this economical housekeeper as the manager of his household. Which puts the word down anybody's street. Not too big to upset the too small person, as Plato feared. Not a university professor's word; not one for a thesis, nor a Ph.D. degree. Not a politician's word. Nor one for the United Nations. Nor one for brokers and bankers. But the everyday Christian's everyday word for his own careful management of God's House, God's Business on earth, God's Budget. A Monday-through-Saturday word for the Christian who cares and shares. A Sunday-to-Sunday word for the Christian who spends and lends to the Lord. A term with dignity and duty in it. And, charmingly enough, the French New Testament uses the same phraseology: *"un économe fidèle,"* so that the kinship is even more universal. To quote Euripides: "When once I had seen the truth, there was no drug I could take to unsee it, and lose again what I had seen."

For although the Greek world seemed to be the largest thing on earth just then, Christianity was larger; and everything else has been relatively small since this stewardship of the loving-kindness of God took hold of a man and his purse. Everybody everywhere had always known that there was something that made men kin. Something more substantial than things, more upsetting than size. They wrote all this kinship into old proverbs. They longed for it in ancient prayers. But only in Jesus Christ's men has this perfect economist-housekeeper emerged, occasionally. But whenever he appears on earth a new Tertullian has always cried: *"See how these Christians love another!"*

"From the murmur and subtlety of suspicion with which we vex one another, give us rest. Make a new beginning, and mingle again the kindred of the nations in the alchemy of Love, and with some finer essence of forbearance and forgiveness temper our minds." (Aristophanes, 400 B.C.)

INDEBTEDNESS

When Zeno was asked what a friend is, he answered:
"Another I!"

I have within me within my soul, a great Temple of
Justice.

Euripides, 480-406 B.C.

> *I care for riches to make gifts*
> *To friends, or lead a sick man back to health*
> *With ease and plenty. Else small aid is wealth*
> *For daily gladness; once a man be done*
> *With hunger, rich and poor are all as one.*

Euripides, 480-406 B.C.

Like the hyacinth which the shepherd tramples under-
foot upon the mountain, but which yet blooms purple
and fragrant on the ground. Sappho, 600 B.C.

We are but stewards of what we falsely call our own;
yet avarice is so insatiable that it is not in the power of
abundance to fill it. . . . Economy is in itself a source of
great wealth. Seneca, A.D. 65.

Not to be covetous is money; not to be a purchaser is
revenue. Cicero, 106-43 B.C.

Spend your brief moment according to nature's law, and
serenely greet the journey's end as an olive falls when it
is ripe, blessing the branch that bare it, and giving thanks
to the tree that gave it life.

Marcus Aurelius, A.D. 121-180

There is necessity to sail, but no necessity to live.
Pompey to frightened mariners in a storm, 67 B.C.

*When a poor man stands at your gate, the Holy One
stands at his right hand. . . . If I am here, then everyone
is here. . . . He that gives should never remember, he
that receives should never forget.*
                                    from *The Talmud,* A.D. 408

*That which is given once is received back a thousand
times. . . . I met a hundred men on the road to Delhi,
and they were all my brothers. . . . A giver sails uphill
in a ship. . . . Even Buddha was once a cart-horse and
carried the loads of others.*   Hindu proverbs

*If a man think well of you, make his thought come
true. . . . There is a window from heart to heart. . . .
He gives double who gives unasked.*
                                    Arabian proverbs

*All the wood for a temple does not come from one tree.
. . . One kind word will warm three winter months. . . .
Think of your own sins the first part of the night while
you are awake, and of the sins of others the second part
of the night while you are asleep.*   Chinese proverbs

*Benevolence is the most honorable dignity conferred by
heaven, and the quiet home in which a man shall dwell.*
                                    Confucius, 500 B.C.

*Not to help someone in distress is to kill him in your
own heart. . . . All food is God's. . . . The wonderful and
the impossible have collided.*   African proverbs

*Go with mean people and you will think life is mean.
Then read Plutarch, and the world is a proud place,
with heroes and demigods standing around us, who will
not let us sleep.*   Ralph Waldo Emerson, 1803-1882

4

THE MOST COLOSSAL GIVEAWAY
PRIZE ON EARTH

For all things are yours, whether Paul or Apollos or Peter, or the
world, or life, or death, or things present, or things to come; all
are yours; for you are Christ's; and Christ is God's.

1 CORINTHIANS 3:21-23

Probably you watched Gino Prato on TV, and held your breath
as he answered incredible questions correctly, earning $32,000
on the air, and a $10,000 job afterward, plus a free reunion with
his father in Italy (after a thirty-three-year absence), and a
standing ovation at La Scala Opera House in Milan—and you
said in astonishment: "Now who would have thought the little
fellow had it in him?"

Probably you saw Mrs. Alice Morgan, with her quizzical
seventy-year-old face all screwed up in thought, as she answered
difficult investment questions correctly, also earning $32,000, and
giving it to her church in Bristol, Connecticut, to pay off the
mortgage on the parsonage; at which you may have said: "But
I didn't think the little woman had it in her!"

Probably you also saw the small ten-year-old Leonard Ross answering correctly about which stock sold for what, and in which year, thus earning $100,000; and no doubt you said, breathlessly: "Who would have thought the little chap had it in him?"

Probably you heard how the lovely Marisa Zucchi won half of Italy's top $8,000 TV prize, then had to decide whether to risk losing all she had gained by trying also to win the other half of "Leave or Double": dissolving into tears herself (and all her audience with her) as she sobbed No! No! not with *la madre* so sick at home—*una febbre! l'inflammazione!*—in need of every *lire, presto!* Probably you envied the sequel: an ex-king equally moved by beauty in tears, sending his certified check to cover the other $4,000. For although this was by no means your favorite king—Farouk of Egypt—still you probably thought: "Oh, to move somebody that way! Oh, to find a fat prize in my mail, too!"

Yet at this very moment, piled high on your doorstep, lies the most colossal giveaway prize on earth from the King of heaven and earth. Towering up and up in the air so tall that your neighbors stand around, thunderstruck: "Who would have thought this little Christian had it in him?" But St. Paul wrote the letter specifying your winnings in staggering details:

"All things are yours, whether of Paul . . ."

But suddenly you hesitate to bring into your house such a startling set of prizes from Paul, for the very first item sounds too cold and callous for comfort: "And Paul stood by consenting." Consenting while they laid a young man's clothes at his feet. Consenting while the mob stoned this young man to death. Consenting as your ancestors consented when Indians were slain and shoved further and further West from their birthright heritage in the East into less and less desirable territory which nobody wanted (yet). Consenting, as you yourself consented, when Americans pushed Japanese out of their houses and businesses into Relocation Centers, during the war. Consenting, as you may be consenting, when Negroes are being persecuted, threatened, stoned, bombed, and burned out of their homes for wanting only what the Constitution promises . . .

"No! No! I'm not a bit like that!" you may shudder. "Paul has given me too poor a prize to accept, publicly." But wait a minute! Will you take in, privately, his truly tremendous things, then? His glorious blinding light on the way to Damascus? It is all yours! Yours to see sharply, suddenly and vividly God's design for your days—caring for His churches; bolstering up the ruined ones; maintaining a spiritual glow. Be sure to take in Paul's famous basket, and practice dangling dramatically over the city wall, yourself—with Christianity hanging in mid-air in your town, too, until you convince the reluctant that yes! you were right; then take Paul's travel books and journey on to all sorts of ship-wrecks, stonings, imprisonments, forty stripes save one. He took it in his stride. And don't forget to take into your house Paul's thorn in the flesh. He hated it, too, as you will. He prayed to lose it, as you will pray. But three times God said: "My grace is sufficient, Paul, my strength is made perfect in weakness." Take that in also; and learn how to live beautifully with a thorn. For there can be roses, later.

Then, of course, his lively pile of love letters lie stacked outside your door. As old Dr. Oliver Wendell Holmes used to say: "As long as there are postmen, life will have zest!" And these are strictly personal; for you alone. Read them breathlessly. Note whom he loved—and why. Note where he went—and why. Note what he did—and why. Lay down your own neck for some great cause, as Priscilla and Aquila did. Support some suffering souls, as Phoebe did. Invite some foreign visitor to share your home, as Lydia did. Ask him back again, even after he lands in jail. All very risky? but note how redemptive! Note also Paul's stewardship of skill in earning a living, without complaint—of time, wasting no moments on minor matters—of treasure, cheerfully giving everything away to bring Christ's Kingdom sooner. Then take in, too, dangerous doors! "Effectual," he calls them, "with many adversaries." By this time you may ask in alarm: "This isn't my idea of a PRIZE!" But you must have skipped Paul's love letter to the Philippians where he plainly states: "Forgetting those things which are behind, I press toward the prize of the high calling of God in Christ Jesus." That settles it! God's powei working with you, through you, in you; as it did in Paul.

"All things are yours . . . whether of Apollos . . ."

Apollos has left you ability to win friends and influence people. Buttonholing and telling. Getting up on platforms and telling. Meeting new acquaintances and telling. Seeking people specially and telling. Helping lame ones over stiles and telling. For the stewardship of speech is the syllable-by-syllable sentence with sparkle, and the Spirit quickening you.

"All things are yours . . . whether of Peter . . ."

His presents may be a perfect nuisance in your life: that old fishing boat now yours for a pulpit to preach the Lord's sermons from; his family yours—each littlest old lady calling forth your more affectionate attention, now that his mother-in-law is yours; his somewhat ridiculous boastings are yours; his peterings-out are yours; his brash questions also yours: "Lord, we have left all to follow Thee, what then shall we have?" His three denials are yours, all because a miserable serving-woman's twitting was too much to take. His going afishing, to get away from it all, is your escape too. His running pell-mell to the empty tomb; his exhilaration after the resurrection is yours. His threefold affirmations (canceling out the three denials) are yours: "Yea, Lord, Thou knowest I love Thee." His rousing sermon at Pentecost—yours; and another three thousand strangers still to be added to the church daily. His three dreams on a rooftop while praying are yours: "Rise, Peter, rise and eat! Nothing God has ever made is unclean." The three knockings at the front door are yours, and that Voice saying: "It's all right, Peter, go on down; *I have sent them!*" His daring venture of eating at the same table with outsiders, sleeping under their roof, taking them into his church, is your next venture also. And best of all, his shadow is yours— his blessed shadow which fell on the sick and healed them whenever he went down their street. The stewardship of personality: turned redemptive. So poor he had to say: "Silver and gold have I none"; yet so rich that he could add: "but such as I have, I give: rise up and walk!" And a man, lame from birth, leaped up with joy. Yes, you may have trouble with Peter's prizes; but at least need never plod along at the same poor old dying rate, now that his shadow has fallen on your street and on you.

"All things are yours . . . the world . . ."

Although you may never really hear it there is a litany of land and sky and air forever ringing in our ears: it is wonderful to walk the earth to the beat of it. For the world is yours—

All its 25,000 miles in circumference is yours.

All its revolving sun, moon, and stars are yours.

All its laws of growth and of gravity, all its laws of light and sound, all its laws of high tide and low tide are yours.

All its chemistry, physics, and geology are yours.

All its atmosphere—with fourteen pounds of air pressing down on every square inch of your body to keep it safe—is yours.

All its oceans and seven seas and lakes and rivers are yours.

All its mountains and valleys and templed hills are yours.

All its forests, orchards, and vineyards are yours.

All its fields white unto the harvest are yours. But you have a stewardship in this lending from the Lord: not to squander trees or let fields turn into dust bowls.

All its gold and silver and copper and uranium are yours. But you have a stewardship in this lending from the hand of God: not to use earth's resources to destroy earth's children.

All its railroads, airplanes, ships and automobiles are yours. But you have a stewardship of concern for the use of man-made tools from God-given sources, not to jostle nor slaughter the family of God on your broad highways.

"All things are yours . . . life . . ."

All this wonderful, throbbing, breathing, quenchable force inside you is yours for threescore years and ten, since life is yours.

All its 90,000 births a day, its childhood, adolescence, maturity and senility are yours.

All its two and a half billion peoples and kindreds and tribes are yours.

All its languages, tongues and dialects are yours.

All its cannibals, headhunters, dictators, assassins and thieves are yours.

All its emperors, presidents, governments and millionaires are yours.

All its professors, teachers, students, illiterates and idiots are yours.

All its doctors, nurses, diseases, hungers and thirsts are yours.

All its invalids, deaf, dumb, blind and lame are yours.

All its preachers, its 872,000,000 Christians and the unsaved are yours.

All its blood and sweat and tears are yours.

All its joy and bliss and creativity are yours.

An almost intolerable stewardship—that a Christian should be someone to whom God entrusts all these fellow men? No wonder the neighbors stand out on your sidewalk, saying: "I didn't think the little creature could cope! But look quick—do you see what I see?"

"All things are yours . . . death . . ."

All its wonder, dread, beauty and release from pain are yours.

All its safe lying down to sleep at night and safe waking up in the morning are yours.

All its little rehearsal for eternal life are yours.

All its immortality in the "many mansions" are yours.

All the angels, archangels, and the great cloud of witnesses are yours.

All the understanding of things never understood, all the wonder, love and praise of adoration are yours.

All the peace that passes understanding is yours.

"All things are yours . . . things present . . ."

All the status quo is yours.

All the Cold War is yours.

All the Middle East situation is yours.

All Apartheid in Africa is yours.

All segregation in the United States is yours.

All race prejudice is yours.

All poverty, slums and juvenile delinquency are yours.

All music, art, poetry and beauty are yours.

All churches, charities, hospitals, asylums, libraries and public parks are yours.

All the United Nations, Church World Service and American Friends Service Committee are yours.

"All things are yours . . . things to come . . ."

All peace on earth and goodwill among men are yours.

All international Christianity is yours.

All integration and nonsegregation are yours.

All life, liberty and the pursuit of happiness are yours.

All quietness and confidence forever are yours.

"All things are yours . . . for you are Christ's! and Christ is God's!"

A climax so magnificent that you understand why Paul painted for you his illuminated text: "For God, who commanded the light to shine out of darkness, hath shined in our hearts, to give the light of the knowledge of the glory of God in the face of Jesus Christ. But—we have this treasure in earthen vessels, that the excellency of the power may be of God and not of us."

And you know, too, why Peter left you this invisible portrait for your mind's eye: "Whom not having seen, we love!"

Here, great God, today we offer
 Of Thine own to Thee;
And for Thine acceptance proffer,
 All unworthily,
Hearts and minds, and hands and voices
 In our choicest melody.

Jesus! our only Joy be Thou,
 As Thou our Prize wilt be;
Jesus! be Thou our Glory now
 And through eternity.

    Bernard of Clairvaux, 1091-1153

While we deliberate, He reigns; when we decide wisely,
He reigns; when we decide foolishly, He reigns; when
we serve Him in humble loyalty, He reigns; when we
serve Him self-assertedly, He reigns; when we rebel and
seek to withhold our services, He reigns—the Alpha and
Omega, which is and which was and which is to come,
the Almighty. William Temple, 1881-1944

Eternal and most glorious God, who hast stamped the
soul of man with Thine Image, received it into Thine
Revenue, and made it part of Thy Treasury, suffer us
not so to undervaluate ourselves, nay, so to impoverish
Thee as to give away these souls for nothing, and all the
world is nothing if the soul must be given for it. Do this,
O God, for His sake, who knows our natural infirmities,
for He had them, and knows the weight of our sins,
for He paid a dear price for them, even Thy Son, our
Saviour Jesus Christ. Amen.

    John Donne, 1573-1631

5

CHARITY IN A COLD CLIMATE

Besides those things that are without, that which cometh upon me daily, the care of all the churches. Who is weak, and I am not weak? Who is offended, and I burn not?

2 CORINTHIANS 11:28-29

Sooner or later the moment comes in history when every man's work stands revealed, exactly as Paul wrote: whether it be of gold or silver or precious stones, or wood, hay, stubble—the fire will reveal it.

Much as Louis XI once gave Boulogne to the Virgin, in a pious moment, but kept the revenues for himself; which, when people learned of it, made the gesture seem singularly empty. Much as St. Jude's-on-the-Square gave an annual bazaar to raise its missionary quota, making this the social event of the season. The women always had the time of their lives preparing for it, and all might have continued in this pleasant pattern if the denomination had not sent them as a speaker a breeze out of Bantu-land named Beulah. Beulah was black and observant, and in the end turned out to be thoroughly upsetting. Although through the business session she sat as silent as a statue carved from teakwood, the planes of her dark face highlighted in the sunshine, the primitive pattern of her dress equally eye-catching. Members could not keep their eyes off her: how much of these gay preliminaries did she understand? What did she make of it all? Whereas she was actually putting two and two together; and adding a Third whom they were omitting.

27

The president was in top form: "I have been reading about us in *The Nation!*" she began, holding up her copy. "A writer named Stanley Rowland, Jr., says that nowhere but nowhere is the church more popular than in the suburbs. But he fears that the main mood of a suburban church is much like a fashionable shopping center: on weekdays people shop for food, on Saturdays for recreation, and on Sundays people shop for the Holy Ghost—preferring their preacher to keep as gentle and ghostlike as possible, not stirring them up about the revolutionary world they live in, or the needs at the ends of the earth. So I said to myself: 'Does this describe St. Jude's-on-the-Square?' And knew at once that the answer was no! no! no! Not with our Big Bazaar coming up next month when we will care for the ends of the earth at one fell swoop, as it were; and especially not with Beulah here to address us today, which puts the world right on our doorstep! But before Beulah speaks, I believe that each of our Bazaar chairmen has certain last-minute requests to report. Who first?"

The Home-Made Baked-Goods Chairman was on her feet at once: "Bring me cakes to match my mountains! Bring me pies to match my plains! And even if you think you can't bake, ladies, just buy a box of jiffy-mix, shake it open and bring me the result. Remember that the result can produce something in hungry Africa as spectacular as Beulah, here! Won't that be worth a few moments in your kitchen? So remember—the more cakes and pies and cookies, the more Beulahs!"

The Apron chairman said Mrs. Johnson had taken the words from her month; aprons did not need to be coveralls, nowadays, but sweet little frivolous dabs would sell well, too—silly and saucy for Sunday night suppers and bridge parties. At this the Bridge Table chairman was on her feet: "Come now, Mrs. Taylor, that's my province—we plan to have at least ten tables of Bridge, for the bored; at a dollar a head, think what a lot of good that will do at the ends of the earth! So tell your friends who hate Bazaars to come along, anyhow, and play the time away."

The Dance chairman sprang to her feet: "There will be dancing in the gym at twenty-five cents a dance. So do urge the young couples to come. All the latest peppy steps. And a small refreshment bar with gingerpop to cool them off. Think what a million dollars could do at the ends of the earth!"

The Grab-bag and Fish-pond chairman broke in: "And bring the children! They'll fall in love with missions when they see the big surprises they can fish up from our pool at five cents a throw. Or a pull from the Grab-bag at ten cents a try! You will want to try it, yourselves, ladies—you have no idea what absolutely darling surprises you may get."

After much laughter and suspense-raising announcements, the president had a happy inspiration: "Beulah," she said, "before you speak, don't you have some favorite hymn we could sing? I saw you thumbing through the hymnal; then we could stand and stretch ourselves; and perhaps someone near the windows would open them, please, and let in some fresh air."

In her deep rich voice Beulah said, instantly: "To the glory of God, Number 199, please!" So everybody sang: "*I love to tell the story of unseen things above*," before Beulah spoke.

When she was introduced she stood quietly: "In my country," she began, "we no sing for stretching or for let in fresh airs! We sing only for adore Father God. For tell Him 'Thank You, thank You very much!' So just now, Father God He talk stiff to me, like in Africa when I stupid. 'Beulah,' He say, and He sad, so sad, 'these St. Jude lady, they just *play-acting*! Like those marketplace childrens piping, nobodies dancing; childrens mourning, nobodies crying. Very sad. These St. Jude lady, does they loving my Son Jesus, His story? Not like my Son Jesus, He love. He really poor. Born stable. Never no place for lay down head. He hungry, like it hurts. He die on cross, like it hurts. He give all what He got, like it hurts. My Son Jesus, He real Bread-of-Life. No cake-mix, in a jiffy. Thirty-three years is long time my Son Jesus spending and caring. Beulah, you ask these St. Jude lady—suppose you got friend you lovealot. She got birthdays coming up. You like give nice presents, but no want pay own money from pocket. What

shall do? So give card parties. Dollar a head. Yes? Why not? Got
eight dollar, easy. So sent nice presents. But friend not happy.
She wag the head, she beat the breast: 'Where is these love you
used to got, that other ladies must buy these present for me?'
And friend, she weep. So sad. So lonely on birthdays: 'Where is
these love went to?' she asking all time. So sad. So lonely.' "

Not a pin dropped in St. Jude's-on-the-Square. There was
anguish on the lovely planes of Beulah's dark face.

"Father God talk stiff in my ear just now. 'Beulah,' He say,
'these is work bad for rest my family in these town. Beulah, you
seeing Baker-shop across Square? Beulah, will these baker making
money on Bazaar-day? No! all cake sitting on shelf all day. All
pie sitting on shelf all day. Little cookie, just sitting. Nobody
wanting. Lady they buying St. Jude all day. Baker he losing
money for support St. Jude missions all day. These cake not
"*Home Made*," like signs say—lady no taking eggs and cracking
him. No taking flours and measuring him. No taking milks and
pouring him. No taking sugars and measuring him. Lady just
take jiffy-mix box. Jiffy in pan! Jiffy in oven! Jiffy, done! No
"*Home Made*"—factory made, Beulah.' Father God, He fussy
over truth-tellings. So Father God He finally saying: 'Beulah, you
telling these St. Jude lady your own story. Then maybe they
seeing Bazaar is cheap ways of loving.' "

The ladies of St. Jude's sat in a dreadful sort of silence, watching that earnest dark face illumined with new tenderness.

"O.K., Lord, I telling. I born girl baby, like maybe you guessing.
In Africa, nobody wanting. Family throwing me in jungle for
dying. All day. All night. Black baby, she crying. No fish-pond
for saving. No grab-bag for helping. No dollar a head card party.
No twenty-five cents dancing. Baby lying. Crying. Dying. But
Father God got somebody in Bantu-land like Son Jesus. Like
Apostle Paul. *Shipwreck?* Yes! Never mind. *Stone?* Yes! Never
mind. *Prison?* Yes! Never mind. *Spear?* Yes! Never mind. Just
going finding these baby girl. Just picking up. Feeding. Hiding.
Caring. Out of own pocketbook! Loving. Teaching. Thirty years

these loving going on. Then one day sending these saved one over ocean to St. Jude's-on-the-Square, for telling St. Jude lady these Bazaar are play-acting. Father God He needing more bigger loving out of more bigger pocketbooks. Father God still working miracle for more blacker baby! So Father God He talking stiff to these St. Jude lady. These dresses you got on, you making *Baker* buy him for you, or you paying from own pocketbooks? These funny little business on the head, you make hat from cake-mix? or husband paying from pocketbooks because they loving you? Father God, He wanting these loving too. His Son Jesus, He wanting these loving. Bazaar not loving. Not frivolous Sunday supper apron, all ruffles. But big warm wraparound lovings. A God-so-loving-the-world-like-He-loving-baby-Beulah. *That* loving! Father God now saying: 'Sit down, Beulah. I through talking stiff.'"

So Beulah sat down.

And St. Jude's-on-the-Square sat, also. Nobody had the ghost of an idea what on earth to do next. But apparently Father God told Beulah. For quite softly she started humming her favorite hymn, with all St. Jude's joining joyfully: "I love to tell the story because I know 'tis true, it satisfies my longings as nothing else could do."

Possibly you have heard that out of their own pocketbooks St. Jude's quite easily quadrupled all the proceeds from all the Bazaars they had ever had. They had "shopped for the Holy Ghost." And He had made intercession for them with groanings that could not be uttered.

> *Agonies are one of my changes of garments.*
> *I do not ask the wounded person how he*
> *   feels. I myself become the wounded person.*
> *My hurt turns livid as I lean on a*
> *   cane, and observe. Or again,*

The disdain and calmness of martyrs,
The mother of old, condemned for a
    witch, burnt with dry wood, her
    children gazing on;
The hounded slave that flags in the
    race; leans by the fence, blowing,
    covered with sweat.
The twinges that sting like needles his
    legs and neck; the murderous
    buckshot and the bullets,
All this I feel, or am.
I am the wounded slave, I wince at
    the bite of the dogs,
Hell and despair are upon me, crack,
    and again crack, the marksmen,
I clutch the rails of the fence, my
    gore drips.

Walt Whitman, 1819-1892

By loving hearts the cloak is shared and the loaf is
shared and the work and the penny are shared. The sor-
rows and the prayers and hopes are shared. By loving
hearts they are shared, and by the fulfillers of the com-
mandment. By desperate man and by his servant in
Christ they are shared . . . To what new country do they
rush forward—these two hand in hand, with the winds of
God behind them, and before them, in this dark night,
the shining of a bright and morning Star?

Jean Kenyon MacKenzie, Africa, 1920

And of some have compassion, making a difference.

St. Jude, verse 22

6

TIME IS OF THE ESSENCE

Who knowest but that thou art come to the kingdom for such a time as this?   ESTHER 4:14

Queen Esther caught the tragic urgency in Mordecai's question and realized there was not a moment to lose: time was of the essence. But it is wise to read further in her story and find that she also had what it took: "Very well, I will go in to the king, which it is not lawful to do, and—if I perish, I perish!"

History hinges on such pluck and such promptness.

Dickens opened his *Tale of Two Cities* with the same sort of time bomb ticking alternately:

It was the best of times, it was the worst of times, it was the age of wisdom, it was the age of foolishness, it was the epoch of belief, it was the epoch of incredulity, it was the season of Light, it was the season of Darkness, it was the winter of despair, we had everything before us, we had nothing before us, we were all going direct to Heaven, we were all going direct the other way—in short, the period was so far like the present period, that some of its noisiest authorities insisted on its being received, for good or for evil, in the superlative degree of comparison only. There were a king with a large jaw and a queen with a plain face, on the throne of England; there were a king with a large jaw and a queen with a fair face, on the throne of France. In both countries it was clearer than crystal to the lords of the State preserves of loaves and fishes that things in general were settled forever. It was the year of our Lord one thousand seven hundred and seventy-five.

33

And Dickens added that likely enough, rooted in the forests of France grew trees—already marked by the Woodman, Fate— to be sawn into boards to make a certain movable framework with a sack and a knife in it, terrible in history. And, in the farm-houses near Paris, rude carts, which the Farmer, Death, had already set apart to be his tumbrels of the Revolution. With Charles Darnell to end the story with another deliberate case of: "If I perish, I perish."

Famine? or bread?
Money? or mercy?
Mammon? or God?
Witholdings? or outpourings?

Everybody comes to the Kingdom for such a choice as this. Keep pushing back into history and Wordsworth will look across the English Channel at the French Revolution, writing: "Milton, thou shouldst be living at this hour!" But back in his own day, Milton had seen in his mind's eye another terror, in the wholesale massacre of Waldensians from France, escaping into Italy, so that Milton also wrote a poem: "Avenge, O Lord, Thy slaughtered saints."

And why were there Waldensians? Because of that amazing moment in the year 1170 when Peter Waldo, a rich cloth merchant of Lyons, began giving away his wealth to those in need; other rich men also followed his example, giving up all their property and becoming known as "The Poor Men of Lyons." They traveled all over France preaching the gospel of Jesus Christ with such power and simplicity that they were excommunicated by the Pope—since they preached in opposition to the enormous possessions of the Pope's clergy.

At about this same turbulent time, between the years 1180 and 1226, a fashionable young Italian—living a life of folly in Assisi— suddenly shocked and shamed his wealthy family by giving away all his goods and dressing in a coarse brown peasant's tunic, tied with a rough rope. Known as "The Little Brother of the Poor,"

Francis of Assisi went up and down the byways of Italy seeking to insure that anybody meeting him by chance might have a spiritual adventure. In the perfect purity of his beautiful life the whole world still finds the truest imitation of Christ. It was Il Poverello who said to the men who began following his new Rule: "*We know as much as we do!*" When the bishop of his church protested against his giving away everything, Francis answered: "But if we have goods, we must have arms to protect them; for it is from possessions that quarrels come." For he too was born into the kingdom for such a time of ecclesiastical worldiness in high places.

Two hundred years later, and Girolamo Savonarola was rocking Italy. Of his own conversion he said: "A word did it!" But in disturbing frivolous Florence he used many words, and had a "Bonfire of Vanities" to burn up their fashionable follies. When the Pope sent a messenger from Rome offering to make this firebrand a cardinal, to quiet his eloquence, Savonarola looked at the scarlet cap and said scathingly: "I desire neither hats nor mitres, be they great or small; I desire nothing save what God gives to His saints—death: a crimson hat, a hat of blood is what I desire."

It was what he received, of course; for no man faces ease who can *pray* as he did: "Lord, we pray not for tranquility nor that our tribulations may cease; we pray for Thy Spirit and Thy love, that Thou grant us strength and grace to overcome adversity," or *say* as he did: "Would you rise in the world? You must work while others amuse themselves. Are you desirous of a reputation for courage? You must risk your life! All this is paying in advance. Observe the other side of the picture: the bad things are paid for afterwards."

Therefore when the moment to perish came that day in 1498, the Pope's delegate stepped up to the edge of the flames and shouted so that all Florence might hear: "I separate thee from the Church!" But out from the center of that fearful fire God's fearless man raised his voice also: "From the Church Militant, but not from the Church Triumphant!"

Such is the stuff of history—ever repeated, never forgotten. No mighty movement has ever been started but somebody somewhere has seemed matched for that hour. Back in the days when Wordsworth was looking across the English Channel at the horrors of the French Revolution, sensing this same Terror about to sweep England, wishing Milton were alive to say something scathing, a far better man than Milton was doing something so timely that he swept this English Terror from error into fervor for Almighty God. Men called John Wesley a "Bible eater." But there was that dark date when he found himself shut out forever from all the established churches in England because he had become too free a *Bible talker!* Either he had to be dumb or preach out in the fields, the streets or the cemeteries, wherever mobs of working people could congregate to devour his messages eagerly. His habitual decorum laid aside, he dared choose the odium of outdoor preaching—and thus save England! But note this prayer in his first Covenant Service at Spitalfields in 1775:

I am no longer my own but Thine; put me to what Thou wilt, rank me with whom Thou wilt; put me to doing, put me to suffering; let me be employed for Thee, or laid aside for Thee; exalted for Thee, or brought low for Thee; let me be full, let me be empty; let me have all things, let me have nothing; I freely and heartily yield all things to Thy pleasure and disposal; and now, O glorious and blessed God, Father, Son and Holy Spirit, Thou art mine and I am Thine; and the covenant which I have made on earth, let it be ratified in Heaven.

This was talk which the common people heard gladly. It made them forget the excitement wrapped up in their industrial revolution for the far deeper excitements wrapped up in John Wesley, watching him with enthusiasm. At one time in his life he fasted every Wednesday and Friday until after three in the afternoon, saying: "Mortification is still an indispensable Christian duty. Whatever increases the strength and authority of your body over your mind, however innocent it may be, that thing is sin to you." This bothered the British; but blessed them, too.

With equal common sense he looked at his followers and said:

"Make all you can, save all you can, give all you can; do all the good you can, in all the ways you can, to all the souls you can, in every place you can, at all the times you can, with all the zeal you can, as long as you can." Everybody everywhere understood every word of it, especially when they began adding up his own record: 250,000 miles on horseback or in a buggy over primitive roads in all kinds of weather. Did some British mathematician figure out that this total distance was equal to ten trips around the earth? No wonder he could say: "The whole world is my parish!"

He preached 40,000 sermons. Figure that out, too—in three-score years and ten, only 25,550 days; think, therefore, of the sermons per day; often as many as four, when travel used up too many days and "time was of the essence." Moreover he was a writer with 400 books to his credit, and his sermons and Journals fill twenty-five volumes. From the printing of which he went into debt several thousands of pounds. Looking at those who disagreed with his methods his reminder was Christian courtesy personified: "Though we cannot think alike, may we not love alike? May we not be of one heart, though we are not of one opinion? My only question at present is: 'Is thine heart right as my heart is with thy heart? If it be, give me thine hand!' "

A lady once asked him: "If you know the Lord would come at midnight tomorrow, how would you spend the day?"

"Madam, I would spend it just as I intend to spend it. I would preach tonight at Gloucester, and again tomorrow morning. After that I would ride to Tewkesbury, preach in the afternoon, and meet the Society in the evening. I should then go to Friend Martin's house, as he expects to entertain me. I would converse, pray with the family, retire to my room at ten o'clock, commend myself to my heavenly Father, and wake up in glory."

"Every man," says Jacques Maritain, "must purify the springs of history in his own breast." No wonder that through John Wesley's dedicated moments, other Englishmen could purge out the Terror in their midst.

Mark Twain has a wonderful story about how the Mississippi River cut through a narrow neck of land one night, so that a Negro who went to sleep in Missouri woke up to find that the land he lived on was now east of the river—part of Illinois, so that lo! this made him a free man. Just such a miracle made the first Methodist missionary in America! For John Stewart was a Negro from Virginia, free-born, to be sure; but such a slave to liquor that he had sunk so low in servitude to strong drink that only the next bottle in the next saloon governed his waking thoughts; until that marvelous moment when a Methodist sermon woke him from his sleep of death into a complete conversion in Marietta, Ohio. The year was 1815. And the congregation may have smiled up their sleeves to see this ignorant Negro actually start off very soon to convert the Indians! Nobody gave him a penny. Nobody ordained him. He just obeyed that impulse, and went first to the Delaware Indians living along the Muskingum River, then on to Wyandotte Indians. Fortunately another Negro joined him, for Jonathan Pointer had lived long enough among Indians to speak their language, and could therefore act as interpreter. From such preaching came a religious awakening; and from such an awakening the Methodists also began awakening on the other side of the river, as it were: stirred themselves into wondering why they should not collect money and organize a national Methodist Missionary Society. Which was done in 1819. For time is of the essence when God begins using the foolish things of this world to confound the wise.

Just as a later Esther came to the kingdom for such a time in the eighteenth century when the red-haired Barbara Heck landed in New York, disturbing the city with news of the Wesleyan movement, started the John Street Church, then moved on to Canada. Along the highway near Prescott, Ontario, the inscription on her tomb tells her story:

BARBARA HECK PUT HER BRAVE SOUL
AGAINST THE RUGGED POSSIBILITIES OF

THE FUTURE AND UNDER GOD BROUGHT
INTO EXISTENCE AMERICAN AND CANADIAN
METHODISM. BETWEEN THESE HER MEMORY
WILL EVER FORM A MOST HALLOWED LINK.

In Boston another monument tells what one totally poor and totally unknown abolitionist could do to hit slavery a long, hard, last blow. For in 1831, without a single dollar in hand or a single subscriber in view, William Lloyd Garrison took some paper and some printer's ink, which he had on hand, and published the first issue of *The Liberator*. Then he sold his bed and slept on the floor, in order to buy more paper to keep printing later issues. He ate so little that he grew as slim as his pencil. Meanwhile the hostile forces on the opposition side ostracized and vilified him; once even dragging him through the streets of Boston with a halter around his neck. *But—The Liberator* kept on appearing; Bostonians kept on reading; *and*—slavery was abolished. Moreover both sides of his monument witness to his imperishable stand: "MY COUNTRY IS THE WORLD. MY COUNTRYMEN ARE MANKIND" (his masthead on *The Liberator*); "I AM IN EARNEST, I WILL NOT EQUIVOCATE, I WILL NOT EXCUSE, I WILL NOT RETREAT A SINGLE STEP, AND I WILL BE HEARD."

For the full record of why his voice in New England was crucial just then, it is well to remember also the widow of General Nathanael Greene inheriting his large cotton plantations in Georgia, and conceiving the clever idea that maybe something might separate cotton seeds from the fiber: "Eli, why can't you add pins to do it?" Catherine Littlefield Greene suggested to Eli Whitney, giving him funds to work out her invention. So Eli added the pins. Mrs. Greene added up royalties. But no lady in history ever added an aftermath which produced more profound political and social mathematics—unhappily reviving the dying institution of slavery, remotely causing the Civil War, and completely changing the status of women from that day to this. Since weaving came out of the home the moment New England men saw a cheap substitute for linen: all to be had by demanding more and more cotton from more and more slaves; with more and more factories as soon as more and more rivers could be dammed up to turn more and more spindles, with more and more women tending more and more looms at lower and lower starvation wages. (At $3.75 per week as a minimum; $8, as a maximum.) Mr. Garrison's copies of *The Liberator* threatened all sorts of pocketbooks in all sorts of places: God's moment in the conscience of men! Much as the brother of our Lord, writing (James 5:1-15 Moffatt translation):

Come now, you rich men, weep and shriek over your impending miseries! You have been storing up treasure in the very last days; your wealth lies rotting, and your clothes are moth-eaten; your gold and silver lie rusted over, and their rust will be evidence against you. . . . See, the wages of which you have defrauded the workmen who mowed your fields call out, and the cries of the harvesters have reached the ears of the Lord of Hosts. You have revelled on earth and plunged into dissipation; you have fattened yourselves as for the Day of slaughter; you have condemned, you have murdered the righteous—unresisting. . . . Do not murmur against one another, brothers, lest you be judged; look, the Judge is standing at the very door!

In Lillian Hellman's play, Autumn Garden, *one of her characters says that there are no big moments you can reach until you've made a pile of smaller moments to stand on!*

> When, as a child, I laughed and wept,
>   Time crept.
> When, as a youth, I dreamed and talked,
>   Time walked.

When I became a full grown man,
Time ran.
And later, as I older grew,
Time flew.
Soon I shall find, while travelling on,
Time gone.
Will Christ have saved my soul by then?
Amen.

Inscription on door of grandfather clock in Chester
Cathedral

The Golden Age is in my heart today.
Who are you, anyone, who can remain
unmoved when the light breaks upon you?
Who can say it is just as well to see as not to see?
Who can ever be the same child or woman or
man again after the day has broken?
Who can admit there is anything else in the
world after this has come to the world?
I brushed aside all obstructions from my
doorsill and stepped into the road;
And though so many cried to me, I did not turn back;
And though I was very sorrowful at having
to leave my friends behind, I did not turn back;
And though the ground was rough and I
was overtaken by fierce storms, I did not turn back;
For when the soul is started on the soul's
journey it does not turn back.
Can you go on with your old life as if
nothing had happened?
The whole universe has happened;
All of love in all of life has happened;
All your forgotten kinship to the
people has happened;

All the terrible thirst for justice
   has happened;
All the sad things have happened
   in gladness at last;
And all the things out of place have
   happened in place at last;
And all old enmity has happened in
   friendship at last;
The Golden Age is on my soul today.

Author unknown

7

SUNDAY-GO-TO-MEETING CLOTHES

The daughters of Zion are haughty, and walk with stretched necks and wanton eyes, walking and mincing as they go. . . . In that day the Lord will take away the bravery of their tinkling ornaments, their bonnets, the changeable suits of apparel, and the mantles, and wimples, and the crisping pins, the glasses and the fine linen, and the hoods, and the veils.   ISAIAH 3:16, 18, 22-23

Is Isaiah describing last season's Easter Parade, perhaps? Designed by Christian Dior, perhaps? Although what is "Christian" —at Easter—about Christian women in Christian America spending four billion dollars last year on clothes? Centuries ago, Isaiah also called attention to a stewardship of spending: "Wherefore do ye spend money for that which is not bread? and your labor for that which satisfieth not?"

A text to which Matthew, the tax collector, added a footnote from the Sermon on the Mount, when our Lord Himself asked the same sort of question: "And why take ye thought for raiment? Consider the lilies of the field, how they grow; they toil not, neither do they spin; and yet I say unto you that even Solomon in all his glory was not arrayed like one of these. Wherefore, if God so clothe the grass of the field, which today is, and tomorrow is cast into the oven, shall He not much more clothe you, O ye of little faith?"

Such *little faith*, dressed up in Sunday-go-to-meeting-clothes, was conspicuous back in Chaucer's Canterbury parade, also (1340-1400):

> A good wif was ther of biside Bathe—
> In al the parrishe wif ne was ther noon
> That to offrynge bifore hir sholde goon;
> And if ther dide, certeyn so wrooth was she
> That she was out of alle charitee.
> Hir coverchief ful fyne weren of ground—
> I dorste swere they weyden ten pound—
> That on a Sonday weren upon hir heed.
> Hir hosin weren of fyn scarlet reed,
> Ful streite y-teyd, and shoes ful moyste and newe;
> Boold was hir face, and fair, and reed of hewe.
> She was a worthy womman al hir lyve.

Chaucer's passing reference to the Good Wif's offering is as modern as next Sunday morning, when many another Good Wif may also feel "out of alle charitee" if another contributor in the same pew puts more into the collection plate. In the later sixteen-sixties, notice Samuel Pepys writing in his immortal Diary: "I did give 10 shillings and no more, though I believe most of the rest did give more, and did believe that I did so too."

This comment is hardly complete without his consciousness of his clothes:

January 1st. (Lord's day). I rose, put on my suit with great skirts, having not lately worn any other clothes but them.

10th. This day I put on my new silk suit; the first that ever I wore in my life.

14th. To the Privy Seale, and thence to my lord's; where Mr. Pin, the tailor, and I agreed upon his making me a velvet coat and cape, the first that ever I had.

22nd. This morning, hearing that the queen grows worse again, I went to stop the making of my velvet dress till I see whether she lives or dies.

30th. To my great sorrow, find myself 43 £ worse than I was last month; which was then 760 £, and now it is but 717 £. But it hath chiefly arisen from my laying out in clothes for myself and my wife, viz: for her about 12 £ and for myself 55 £, or there-about.

Having made myself a velvet cloak, two new cloth skirts, black, plain both, a new shag gown trimmed with gold buttons and twist, with a new hat, and silk tops for my legs, and many other things; being resolved henceforth to go like myself. And also two perriwigs, one whereof cost me 3 £ and the other 40 s. I have worn neither yet, but will begin next week, God willing.

29th. (Lord's day). This morning I put on my best black suit, trimmed with scarlet ribbons, very neat, with my cloak lined with velvet, and a new beaver, which, altogether, is very noble, with my black silk knee canons I bought a month ago. (Diary, 1669)

If clothes make the man, then what a worshiper Samuel Pepys was; and no wonder that as such frivolity increased, Isaac Watts could call a hymn: "Against Pride in Clothes"; writing:

> Doth vain discourse or empty mirth
> Well suit the honors of our birth?
> Shall we be fond of gay attire
> Which children love and fools admire?
>
> What if we wear the richest vest,
> Peacocks and flies are better drest.
> This flesh, with all its gaudy forms
> Must drop to dust, and feed the worms.
>
> The tulip and the butterfly
> Appear in gayer coats than I:
> Let me be dressed fine as I will,
> Flies, worms, and flowers exceed me still.

Try singing this to the time of "Old Hundredth" and you can sense the disapproval sinking into your consciousness. As Peter Cartwright wrote of the Methodists of his day: "The members were very plain in dress. They wore no jewelry, no superfluous ornament, or extravagant dress of any kind." John Wesley, on meeting a widow in deep mourning two years after her husband had died, said to her: "What, madam, have you not forgiven God Almighty yet?" Another Methodist preacher wrote, as late as 1854: "My soul is deeply pained, O Lord, what will become of Thy Church? Several of our members wear earrings; some of them wear finger-rings. Lord, pity them!"

By the time that Matthew Vassar started Vassar Female Academy in Poughkeepsie, two hooks seemed plenty for each young lady: one for her Sunday-go-to-meeting dress, and one for her weekday homespun. But a four billion dollar women's clothing bill shows that American women today have gone circling back to the days of Isaiah, the Good Wif of Bathe, and Samuel Pepys. Easter advertisements paint pictures of this glamorous new You in the pew: "Our Easter bonnet, madam, will make you the focus of all eyes in church next Sunday" . . . "Our super-Easter suit will set you off as you have never been set off before" . . . "Our Easter gloves will make the touch of your hand an unforgettable experience" . . . "Our Easter shoes will make you feel as if you were walking on air" . . . "Our Easter undies will make you feel like a million dollars" . . . "Our Easter corsage will tell the world that somebody loves you!"

And Somebody does.

For you He created every flower that blooms, every stalk of wheat that grows, every grape that ripens on every vine, every berry on every bush, every vegetable in every kitchen garden. For you—the wool on every sheep, the silk from every silk-worm, the cotton from every plantation. Yet above all, and in all, and through all, the one unspeakable Easter Gift without which food and raiment are meaningless; and Easter itself, emptiness.

The only obvious conclusion is that the sole motive for Easter is the making of a new You: "If any man is in Christ Jesus he is a new creature." "You are the body of Christ, and members in particular." "Put ye on the Lord Jesus Christ." "As God's own chosen, be clothed with compassion, kindliness, humility, gentleness, and good temper. . . . And above all you must be loving, for love is the link of the perfect life." So that, sitting in your pew next Sunday, how little your new suit or gloves or shoes or bonnet matter! But suppose the new You had Easter hands inside the Easter gloves, doing all the tender things the Saviour did. Taking bread and blessing it and breaking it, and sharing it with the hungry. Holding the Scriptures, opening them, finding the place, explaining what the passage means to you. Taking little children in your arms and blessing them. Touching sick bodies and nursing them into new health. Restoring souls more redemptively than any gloves ever manufactured. All because the Master promised you such "greater works" as your stewardship of sharing. A modern Dorcas. Although as you think of her you may say to yourself: "But how homesick in heaven! Without all those stitches to take in time!"

As for *feet*, Mr. Standfast in *Pilgrim's Progress* painted the perfect picture: "I have loved to hear my Lord spoken of; and wherever I have seen the print of His shoe in the earth, there I have been delighted to place mine also." It means the stewardship of the second mile; or the third; or the fourth. Even up to the eighth—for rather recently an Indian woman crossed her entire reservation, carrying a pottery vase she had made as a good-by gift for the missionary going on furlough. As he traced the exquisite old tribal patterns, he said gratefully: "And to think that you walked eight miles to bring it to me, and will have the same eight miles back!" Her brown face showed surprise: "*But the walk is part of the gift,*" she explained. To show that she had known all along what a vase involved. ("How beautiful are the feet of them that bring glad tidings, and publish peace.") No shoe store in town can furnish a new You with this tirelessness: it is part of an unpayable debt and a lavish overflow of goodwill.

Above all, Easter is the season when a new hat is a reminder of a tragic crown of thorns pressed down upon the Saviour's brow by those who—later—simply sat and watched him die. Such sitting happens every Easter. Sitting, and staring; but stylish. The overcoming of this inertia involves a drastic revision of budgets. Could two hooks do? (The Spirit still says unto the churches about those who overcome self-indulgence: "They shall walk with me in white: for they are worthy.")

To the eye of vulgar Logic, what is man? An omnivorous Biped that wears Breeches.
To the eye of Pure Reason, what is he? A Soul, a Spirit, a divine Apparition.
Round his mysterious Me, there lies, under all these wool-rags, a Garment of Flesh, contextured in the Loom of Heaven; whereby he is revealed to his like, and dwells with them in Union and Division; and sees and fashions for himself a Universe, with azure starry spaces, and long Thousands of Years. Deep-hidden is he under that strange Garment; amid Sounds and Colors and Forms, as it were, swathed in, and inextricably overshrouded. Yet it is sky-woven, and worthy of a God.

Thomas Carlyle, 1795-1881

By all means use some time to be alone.
Salute thyself: see what thy soul doth wear.
Dare to look in thy chest; for 'tis thine own:
And tumble up and down what thou findest there.
Who cannot rest till he good fellows find,
He breaks up house, turns out of doors his mind.

George Herbert, 1593-1633

What shame! the silkworm works
And works till he can fly;
While you remain a man
And still on earth will lie.

Angelus Silesius

8

DELIBERATELY BORROWING TROUBLE

Alas master, for it was borrowed.   2 KINGS 6:5

We too have become a borrowing generation.

But who would expect to find the borrowed ax and the immediate need of Elisha's prophets for more room in 893 B.C. (as recorded in 2 Kings 6:1-7) coming true all over again in A.D. 1953 in Pineville, Kentucky, when word got around that not one of the 163 married students in the Mountain Preachers Bible School had a decent home for wife or child, and 700 workers deliberately borrowed trouble by flocking from all over Kentucky and Tennessee, with a few from Virginia and North Carolina, to start building—with 6,000 fascinated observers standing around all day.

Not even Grandma Moses could paint a merrier picture, with men up on roofs nailing shingles; men on their knees banging floors; hammers pounding; boards creaking; with 19 brand-new houses rising in one day; and the tangy scent of fresh-cut lumber everywhere. When the sun came up, they all got down to business. By eight o'clock the floor boards were down. By noon the framework of all the nineteen corner supports of the cottages were up. By three o'clock there were walls. By four o'clock, doors and windows. By sunset, men working on the roofs. The Cumberland Mountains had not echoed to such sounds since pioneer days, when neighbors pitched in to help a newcomer at his house-raising.

This was on such a gigantic scale that the Pineville Bakery decided to bake an enormous birthday cake to help the preachers celebrate; someone in the bakery knew his 2 Kings, for on the icing was the verse: "Let us make a little chamber, I pray thee, on the wall; and let us set for him there a bed . . . and it shall be, when he cometh to us, that he shall turn in thither." Each of the 19 cottages had four rooms and a bath; and the job, done in one day by 700 volunteers from one denomination, shows what imagination and co-operation can do on earth if only enough people deliberately borrow somebody's trouble.

The Reverend A. Ritchie Low made his entire Vermont congregation eager—summer after summer—to borrow a hundred Negro boys and girls from Harlem and the sizzling sidewalks of New York. Most of these children had never seen a daisy growing in a field. They were marvelously polite guests; and, when winter came, Harlem mothers borrowed Vermont children for a return visit, when the little white New Englanders proved much more timid about subways than the black children had been about cows.

Suppose that the entire record of the Kingdom of God on earth is simply somebody somewhere deliberately borrowing trouble? Then the first thing to do is to lay a finger on the map, asking: "Who? Here?"

In Helsinki the women of Finland clubbed together to buy some rooms as a present for Matilda Wrede on her sixtieth birthday—the whole idea having come first from a very poor woman; but the suggestion caught fire and the money poured in. Few women have ever had an apartment given to them as a national gesture of gratitude. And certainly no other woman has ever had one furnished in quite so fabulous a fashion. Such as the cabinet made by prisoners, with her monogram carved at one corner and the Wrede coat of arms on the other: "Because you have such a bad habit of giving everything away!" the men mentioned, smiling.

On her desk lay a metal paper weight in the shape of a fallen log with a broken ax imbedded in it. The convict explained: "The fallen log is the prisoner's hard heart; the ax which has struck straight into the wood is the love of God; but the handle is broken, Fröken Wrede, just as your frail body has been broken in bringing us your message."

Also on the desk lay the penholder which she used for twenty-five years, made for her by a murderer: "This is part of the broken broom handle from the broom which swept the dirt from the prison for eighteen years; but I give this penholder to you, Fröken, asking you to write many, *many* letters to us prisoners, to sweep our brains and our hearts clean." There was a coffee service from the convicts at Sornas prison; and a loving cup with the inscription: "To Her Who Drained Our Cup of Sorrow." There was a wooden bracelet carved by prisoners; on presenting it they showed her how easily it slipped up and down her arm: "The Prisoner's Freedom! The Prisoner's Freedom! That has been the aim of your whole life, Fröken Wrede!"

On her table was a box made out of driftwood from some old ship found on the shore, with a monogram copied from her handkerchief by a very violent inmate, with whom nothing could ever be done by others. Another man gave her a wooden spoon on which he had painted a dandelion: "I could see the brave little thing perking up its head out there in the prison yard. I was always afraid some heavy boot would crush it. At first, you know, it was only two green leaves of hope. Then the bud opened into a yellow flower. How I loved it all the way! Later it became a ball of fluff and the gray wisps of it went flying every-which-way over the whole yard. The reason I painted it for you, Fröken, is because it is a real picture of yourself. You have dared to come here, into sorrow and sin and filth; you have gone from cell to cell all up and down each corridor, all day, and every one of us has received friendliness and sunshine from you."

Finnish prison rules required a prisoner always to look straight into a visitor's eyes without evasiveness. To meet this ruling Matilda Wrede always wore a silver brooch at her throat to catch the prisoner's attention with something which might linger in his mind, for the words engraved on the pin were: ARMO JA RAUHA"—"GRACE AND PEACE." One day a prisoner asked to borrow the pin for an hour, and gave her a duplicate which seemed made out of polished ivory. She held the lovely thing in her hands as the convict told her that no! it was a large piece of bone found in his soup seven months earlier. Instantly he knew that this was what he wanted to make for her; so he bleached it in the sun until the color was exquisite. And this, too, was in those Furnished Rooms which the women of Finland had presented her—each separate object a separate story of a separate cell which a lady had entered fearlessly, her sense of humor contagious; her deliberate borrowing of trouble convincing; the clearness and the pity in her eyes convicting. For a time Matilda Wrede rationed herself to an allowance of four cents a day, the sum given to each prisoner—partly because she wanted to be on their level, and partly because she wanted more to share with them. Already all she had was theirs, as well as a home she maintained for released prisoners, unwelcome or suspected elsewhere in society. When she lay dying she asked those by her bedside: "Is there a happier person than I? Has anyone lived such a rich life before?"

In Germany Pastor Friedrich von Bodelschwingh might well feel that he had! First by taking into a small farmhouse a few incurables, completely crippled in mind and body. Suddenly the one farmhouse was not enough, and he spent his money on building a village of houses which then grew into a city of 12,000 inhabitants, all hopelessly sick—epileptics, neurotics, insane. There was a Theological College, as well, where tramps became Christian "Brethren of the High Road"; and a Reformatory for boys and homeless persons. This lovely little City of Hope, Bethel, covers 1,000 acres, with all the houses picturesquely placed among flower gardens and fruit trees; with safe streets for so many uncertain feet, and its own shops, factories, schools, post office, fire department and power plant.

Although he came from the aristocracy, Pastor Bodelschwingh devoted all his life to the minute details of this immense family. To an unhurried helper he cried: "Please! Not so slow or else they die in the meantime!" Until he died at 79, his entire income went into this largest religious welfare establishment on earth. His son took oversight then, the war years presenting unusual problems since Bielefield was constantly bombed, at Hitler's orders, in a determination to exterminate all the unfit, orders even coming to remove the poorest and the most afflicted—the very ones, of course, whose troubles the new Pastor Bodelschwingh had taken upon himself.

In Africa, is the name too familiar to need any further details of how Albert Schweitzer has been deliberately borrowing trouble? But seen through the twenty-eight-year-old eyes of Olga Deterding, the angle is fresh indeed—for she had been an international playgirl, daughter of a millionaire, who once had $56,000 spending money each year, two sport cars, eleven servants, and a suite at the Ritz Hotel in Paris. But she worked as a nurse without pay in the hospital at Lambaréné, until her recent death, and had written to a friend: "I think this is the only Christian village in the world, everybody works for love." (She did not know of the Bodelschwinghs, so much closer to her European home.) Two other young millionaires also visited Lambaréné, were so much caught by this "reverence for life" that William Mellon—a former banker in Pittsburgh and, at the moment, a cattle raiser in Arizona—decided to study medicine. After graduation, he and his wife searched this continent for some underprivileged, suffering section of humanity, finding it in Deschapelles, Haiti, where their new Albert Schweitzer Hospital has not only absorbed their own $1,500,000 fortune but also all their skill and ingenuity as they, too, heal and teach; and—borrow trouble in behalf of all who need them.

But the really risky borrower was Saly Mayer. Few men have ever matched the superb pluck of this Swiss lace manufacturer who saved nearly 200,000 Hungarian Jews from being deported into Hitler's death camps in Germany. In the spring of 1944 the Nazis offered to trade the lives of these Jews still left alive in Hungary for 10,000 trucks, 800 tons of coffee, 200 tons of tea, 2,000,000 bars of soap. Mr. Mayer represented the American Jewish Joint Contribution Committee; and by a dangerously deliberate game of maneuvering managed to keep his negotiations with the Nazis so long drawn out that the war actually ended before a single one of his Jews had been deported.

Such large-scale borrowing should never discourage small-scale pocketbooks. Consider Bill Brownlow pushing his heavy junk cart for eight years through the streets of Marblethorpe, England, shouting at the top of his voice: "Any rags, any bottles, any rubbish today?"

Sixty-four years old when he started, seventy-two when he had saved up $18,000. At once he started building bungalows for the aged in town; and by the first Christmas had the first six of his houses ready for the first six old men he had chosen to move in with their families, rent free for the rest of their lives. His sole comment: "Twelve hours a day for eight years, pushing the cart around for junk—worth it, wasn't it?"

Or imagine the surprise of two wealthy globe-trotters in Korea when they saw a boy pulling a crude plow with the father guiding the handles.

"Must be mighty poor," commented the merchant.

Their guide nodded: "Right! That is Chi Num and his son. When their church here had to be rebuilt after the bombings, they sold their ox and put the money into the Restoration Fund. So this spring, of course, they must pull the plow themselves."

Both the merchant and the lawyer were speechless. But when

the lawyer reached home he took his kodak picture to his Catholic priest, simply saying: "I have come to double my pledge to our church, and I want you to find me some work in the parish. This Korean has shown me what sacrifice is."

That is why I have thought it necessary to ask these brothers to go on in advance and get your promised contribution ready in good time. I want it to be forthcoming as a generous gift, not as money wrung out of you. Mark this: he who sows sparingly will reap sparingly, and he who sows generously will reap a generous harvest. Everyone is to give what he has made up his mind to give; there is to be no grudging or compulsion about it, for God loves the giver who gives cheerfully. God is able to bless you with ample means, so that you may always have quite enough for any emergency of your own and ample besides for any kind act to others; as it is written,

   He scatters his gifts to the poor broadcast,
   his charity lasts for ever.

He who furnishes the sower with seed and with bread to eat will supply seed for you and multiply it; he will increase the crop of your charities—you will be enriched on all hands, so that you can be generous on all occasions, and your generosity, of which I am the agent, will make men give thanks to God; for the service rendered by this fund does more than supply the wants of the saints, it overflows with many a cry of thanks to God. This service shows what you are, it makes men praise God for the way you have come under the gospel of Christ which you confess, and for the generosity of your contributions to themselves and to all; they are drawn to you and pray for you, on account of the surpass-

*ing grace which God has shown to you. Thanks be to
God for His unspeakable gift!*

2 Corinthians 9:5-15; Moffatt Translation

*Eternal God, who committest to us the swift and solemn
trust of life; since we know not what a day may bring
forth, but only that the hour for serving Thee is always
present, may we wake to the instant claims of Thy holy
will, not waiting for tomorrow, but yielding today. Con-
secrate with Thy presence the way our feet may go, and
humblest work will shine, and the roughest place be
made plain. Lift us above unrighteous anger and mis-
trust, into faith, and hope, and charity, by a simple and
steadfast reliance on Thy sure will. In all things draw
us to the mind of Christ, that Thy lost image may be
traced again, and that Thou mayest own us at one
with Him and Thee, to the glory of Thy great name.
Amen.*

James Martineau, 1805

9

HARDLY SPOKEN OF IN PARLORS

He that giveth, let him do it with simplicity. . . . he that showeth
mercy with cheerfulness. . . . be kindly affectioned one to another
with brotherly love.   ROMANS 12:8, 10

*"Money, which represents the prose of life, and which is hardly
spoken of in parlors without an apology, is, in its effects and
laws, as beautiful as roses"*—Emerson wrote these words; Lo Po

Hong practiced them; Montpelier, Virginia, experienced them; and Columbia University could translate them into Chinese.

For although the famous Lin Yutang once said (long before communism crowded roses out) that there was no Good Samaritan spirit in his native China, obviously he had never heard of Joseph Lo Po Hong in China, nor of the Episcopal Church in Montpelier, nor of the Dean Lung Chair of Chinese Language at Columbia University. Probably never spoken of in the parlors where Lin Yutang visited. But as beautiful as roses, nonetheless.

All over Shanghai Lo Po Hong became known as the Chinese Rockefeller, not only unusually prosperous in business but handsome, and honored by prominent positions—such as Chinese councilor for the International Settlement, president of the Board of Trade, founder of the Central Committee for Refugees.

And, above all, delighting to call himself St. Joseph's Coolie ever since the day he noticed a beggar lying in a Shanghai gutter, dying of disease and hunger. He whistled for a rickshaw to take this outcast to the nearest hospital. But even the rickshaw boy hesitated to carry such a sordid passenger. Enough cash and he was persuaded. However, when hospital after hospital refused this bundle of rags and dirt, the rickshaw boy refused to go another step, dumping the beggar out on the road.

It was then that Mr. Lo Po Hong turned into a Good Samaritan. For he picked up this evil-smelling load, laid him across his own shoulder, carried him to his own home, put him into a clean bed and nursed him back to health as faithfully as if this were a brother. Little dreaming, perhaps, that the next thirty-five years of his life would belong to equally sick and equally poor and equally homeless creatures.

He began by buying a deserted graveyard, with a statue of St. Joseph in the middle of the plot. Then for seven years he went around from office to office of his rich business friends begging money to build St. Joseph's Hospital, the largest in town; yet still not big enough; for next he wanted an asylum for the insane, then a home for the aged, another for the orphans who were wandering the streets like little wild animals. In this energetic and contagious fashion he founded, put up and supported twelve such great charitable establishments, always persuading others to help, but privately emptying his own bank account, and personally caring for all the prisoners condemned to die. People called him the Robber's Chaplain, and he could be seen riding with them in open carts to their execution.

In 1939, when Japan invaded China, he filled another big building with homeless refugees. It was while he was on his way to market, to buy food for this starving family of more than a thousand souls, that a bomb fell nearby and killed him. Several generations of Christian parents and grandparents lay behind this outpouring of brotherly love. The institutions still stand—a lengthened shadow of the man.

In far gentler fashion, Montpelier, Virginia, carries its own Shanghai shadow also. For in 1851 the Reverend Robert Nelson sailed from Hanover County with his family to become an Episcopal missionary in China, where he ministered to the Church of Our Saviour in Shanghai. During his thirty years in China he returned only twice on furlough; and when at home he would preach in the little log schoolhouse in the Montpelier neighborhood. People came in crowds from miles around to hear him tell about Shanghai—too many to sit inside the school, so that they pressed closely around the windows and doorways to catch every syllable of his fascinating message.

On his last return to China, in 1876, he told his Shanghai congregation in the Church of Our Saviour how deeply he longed to see an Episcopal Church built in Montpelier some day. And lo! the *Shanghai* Church of Our Saviour promptly started a building fund for a *Montpelier* Church of Our Saviour in Virginia, a well-to-do Chinese lady giving the first contribution. Land for this new edifice was given by Edward Watts Morris, being part of his own plantation. The church was consecrated in 1882 by the Bishop of Virginia, and used from then until 1928 when disaster came in the burning of the church to the ground. Episcopal papers carried news of this catastrophe overseas, and the moment the Shanghai Church of Our Saviour read it, again a generous contribution was given for the restoration of their Virginia namesake. A Chinese member personally sent two very handsome brass alms basins with a Chinese inscription around their rims which nobody in town could read, of course.

A few years ago, however, when Bishop Tsu of China was speaking in Richmond, he asked to visit this church which his own people had helped to build for Americans. It was a memorable moment for everybody, for as he stood in the lovely little sanctuary Bishop Tsu said: "Let us pray—you saying the Lord's Prayer in English, and I in Chinese."

Perhaps even Lin Yutang might have felt that some of God's Kingdom had come on earth, and some of His will had been done, and certainly His name had been hallowed both in Shanghai and Montpelier. Certainly it seemed more beautiful than even Virginia roses when the congregation heard Bishop Tsu translate the Chinese words on the alms basins, and wondered that they had not known all along that the text would say: "IT IS MORE BLESSED TO GIVE THAN TO RECEIVE."

To close this brief give-and-take chapter comes a Chinese handy man, walking in and out of the front parlor of General Horace Carpenter, a wealthy American who had made his fortune as a Forty-niner out west. This Chinese servant was humble and honest and unusually able. The General became so impressed by Dean Lung's background that he left a generous legacy to his Chinese friend, who was spending his own last years back in his Cantonese village; but, far beyond this, General Carpenter donated one hundred thousand dollars to Columbia University in New York City to endow a Chair in Chinese, in honor of his servant, Dean Lung. So that it is indeed true to quote Emerson: "money which is rarely spoken of in parlors without an apology, is more beautiful than roses," for the students at Columbia often speak of it in classrooms *in Chinese:* and with no apologies, but with eternal gratitude.

There is no other way of serving the gods than by spending oneself for man.

Chinese proverb

Ch'ing, the chief carpenter, was carving wood into a stand for musical instruments. When finished, the work appeared to those who saw it as though of heavenly craftsmanship, and the Prince asked him: "What mystery is there in your art?"

"No mystery, your Highness. And yet there is something. When I am about to make such a stand, I guard any lessening of my spiritual power. I first reduce my mind to absolute quiet. Three days in this condition, and I become oblivious to any reward to be gained, and I become oblivious to any fame to be acquired. Seven days, and I become unconscious of my four limbs and my physical frame. Then, with no thought of the court present in my mind, my skill becomes concentrated, and all disturbing elements from without are gone. I enter some forest, search for a suitable tree. It contains the form required, which is later elaborated. I see the stand in my mind's eye; and then set to work. Beyond that there is nothing. I bring my own native capacity into relation with that of the wood. What was suspected to be supernatural craftsmanship in my work was due solely to this."

from an ancient Chinese book

10

SIX IMPOSSIBLE THINGS BEFORE BREAKFAST

To everything there is a season, and a time to every purpose under
the sun . . . a time to rend, and a time to sew.

ECCLESIASTES 3:1, 7

From time out of mind women have been sitting by windows,
with sewing baskets on their laps—as I sit now; needlework
dropped for the moment, and a certain faraway look in the eye,
almost ancestral; for my great-grandmother did this; and hers,
before her. Although I may think I am thinking, more likely it
is merely feeling—an aimless mood, soothing but unfocused.

Nothing agitating, anyhow, as it was that morning in Wonderland when Alice complained to the queen: "But I find it quite
impossible to believe what you say!" At which her majesty
mumbled: "Well, maybe you do, my dear; but when I was your
age I made it a point to believe six impossible things before
breakfast!"

The daily practice of such sixes could become my own stitch
in time, to make the impossible, possible; and to help me sew a
straight seam through the remainder of the day. Also, ever since
all sorts of shepherds and scholars have stumbled across ancient
Dead Sea Scrolls, centuries old, concealed in caves in Palestine,
it has seemed sensible to excavate this sewing basket, to discover
what Scriptures may be hidden there for me to unearth. Has the
stewardship of six impossible things been entrusted to me all
along, and I unaware? One by one let me pick up these contents,
and obey the impossible things—

1.   *It is not impossible for me to obey the pinpricks of conscience,*
O God!

As the daughter of a preacher there was the picking up of a
certain paper of pins from my mother's sewing basket, years ago.
As it fell open dramatically, I gave one astonished look, then
dashed to the study, calling: "Look, daddy, look! Here's your
congregation; see? Pew after pew of them, sitting in rows with
their hats on! But look out, for they're all awfully sharp at the
other end!"

"They are, indeed," he agreed, and added: "Out of the mouths
of babes and sucklings!" Then he burst out laughing: "Here I
am, slaving over next Sunday's sermon, using Paul's text *'called to
be saints';* and here you are, bringing me saints from my own
sanctuary. Had you noticed that the poor things can only go as
far as their heads will allow them? And would you be willing
to call those silvery plates over their heads halos instead of hats?
On Sunday I'm going to quote from an ancient Letter to Diognetus which says: *'Christians hold the world together.'* The point is,
could we trust this congregation to hold anything together long?
I can see that they might fall out, or get bent, or not want to
stick together, or maybe even prick one another, so that they will
never come back. Anyhow, thank you for the illustration."

The fact is that in church, whenever it is still enough to hear
the proverbial pin drop, it would stun the congregation to find
out that they were being looked over in search of pinheads
dropping out by the wayside, exactly as Paul wrote about
Demas: "Demas has forsaken me, having loved this present world
and is departed unto Thessalonika"—departed unto the Thespians,
late Saturday nights—unto the television viewers, Sundays at
eleven—unto the get-rich-quick hucksters, Mondays through
Fridays.

Never again has a pin been just a pin. But a symbol of a makeshift Christian, here today and gone tomorrow. Paul wrote to
the Romans about them: "Without faith it is impossible to please

Him." Faith which is dedicated and dependable in holding the world together. Not giving pin-money of a Sunday while spending plenty on gimmicks, of a Monday. Rather like Huckleberry Finn who said his conscience was so big that it took up more room than all the rest of him put together. A steward with a conscience over the impossible things, humming in that chair by the window:

> O use me, Lord, use even me,
> Just as Thou wilt, and when, and where.

2. *It is not impossible for me to go through the eye of this needle Thou hast placed in my hand, Lord Jesus.*

Needles can write almost as much history as pens. The way Dorcas had been writing her memoirs all over Joppa. For the moment Peter reached town after her death, all the widows and orphans started showing him her handiwork: "See! She made all these clothes for us the year we lost our money, and do notice the fine stitches—fit for a queen, and we so poor!" From all corners the same sort of praise: "Dorcas made . . ." "Dorcas noticed . . ." "Dorcas gave . . ."

Sometimes I wonder if she was not homesick in heaven in that brief interval before Peter summoned her back. For uselessness is alivelessness. And ceaseless sharing had been her natural habitat; so that it was very heaven on earth to be restored to her old room and her old sewing basket, going once again through the eye of her needle, using all her goods to clothe the poor—every garment practically a sampler, DORCAS: HER DRESS.

Not being much of a needlewoman, sometimes it seems as if Hans Christian Andersen had written my memoir in his brief fairy story about the Darning Needle who thought she was an Embroidery Needle; yet all the time coarse and common, making too big holes in too fine goods. In which case why, oh, why not start making coarse tents over in the workroom with Priscilla and Aquila and Paul, covering the defenseless heads of the homeless, seeing refugees through the eye of my large needle, sheltered in a time of storm?

Precisely this imaginative process gripped the proper Bostonians during the war, when they put on a campaign to *"Cover Copley Square"* with blankets, quilts and afghans. Policemen measured the complete area, and church committees then figured out how many quilts would be needed to cope with Copley Square! Then they persuaded every willing-hearted woman with a needle, big or little, to quilt, crochet or knit. One by one as quilts were turned in, the corresponding area was filled in on a giant diagram publicly placed in the Square. It was like seeing Exodus 35:4-10, 21-26 repeat itself out of Boston sewing baskets doing the Lord's work on earth. For actually every day is Judgment Day, as Jesus proved when He described the shock of even the Safely-Saved who kept saying: "But when did we see *You*, Lord?" The stewardship of my needle, therefore, is a constant stitch in time forever clothing this Stranger.

3. *It is not impossible for me to rend my heart and not my garments, O God.*

My most impossible thing before breakfast may be allowing those two women in the church at Philippi to appall me as they appalled Paul: "I beseech Enodias, and beseech Syntyche that they be of the same mind in the Lord; and I intreat thee also, true yokefellow, *help those women* who have labored with me in the gospel, and with others of my fellowlaborers whose names are in the book of life. Rejoice in the Lord always, and again I say, rejoice! Whatsoever things are lovely, whatsoever things are of good report, if there be any virtue and if there be any praise, think on these things."

Taking scissors out of the sewing basket, I am amused to see that the two circles resemble a lorgnette until I recall somebody's cynical remark that a lorgnette is "a dirty look on a long stick." At once my conscience pricks. For instead of helping those women in my church who scrap and disagree in public, do

I not look through these cynical spectacles at their antics, even going so far as to call up an absentee member: "wait till you hear the latest about those impossible women." Neither lovely! nor of good report! nor of virtue! nor of praise! For with all such cutting gossip I am really answering Paul's question: "Who shall separate us from the love of Christ?" by acknowledging: "*I shall!*" Maybe tribulation will not cut me off from God; nor distress; nor persecution; nor famine; nor nakedness—but oh! the peril of my sword! This cutting edge of my scissors: woe betide the person who comes between.

My scissors rebuke me as I hold them up—lorgnette end or separating end, cutting Enodias and Syntyche down to size. Snipping off a little here; slicing off a section there; dividing; divorcing; putting asunder. This dangerous weapon needs a special sheath—"Let the words of my mouth and the meditations of my heart be acceptable in Thy sight, O Lord, my strength and my Redeemer." Then, realizing what dismal discipline this speech entails, suppose I add: "Such knowledge is too wonderful for me! I cannot attain unto it!"

"Oh yes, you can!" God answers. "With me all things are possible!"

It will be a blessing then to unearth from the basket this treasure from St. Augustine:

O Thou good Omnipotent, who so carest for each of us, as if Thou carest for him alone, and so for all, as if all were one! Blessed is the man who loveth Thee, and his friend in Thee and his enemy for Thee. I behold how some things pass away that others may replace them, but Thou dost never depart, O God my Father, O Thou most supreme, most good, most potent, most omnipotent, most merciful yet most just, most secret yet most present, beauty of all things beautiful, what have I said now, my God, my Life, my holy Joy? Or what says any man when he speaks of Thee? To Thee I entrust whatsoever I have received from Thee, and so I shall lose nothing.

The stewardship of the sheathed tongue and the unused lorgnette, and a woman in a chair by the window, humming:

Lord, speak to me, that I may speak
In living echoes of Thy tone;
As Thou hast sought, so let me seek
Thy erring children, lost and lone.

4. *It is not impossible for me to let Thee mend my Past and my Present with Thy Future, Father.*

Too much church time is spent in rivalries and divisions. The Women's Bible Class too often like a church-within-a-church, a law unto itself, so devoted to its teacher that the Women's Missionary Society and its president and its program are anathema. The organist and the trustees are at odds. The janitor and the Ladies' Aid are not on speaking terms. The Sunday School nobody's pet; always needing something impossible. More chairs. More quarterlies. More teachers. As a person with a needle and a passion for patching things up, I ask: "But which patch goes where?"

Our Lord has the answer, of course: "No man seweth a piece of new cloth on an old garment; else the new piece that filleth it in taketh away from the old, and the rent is made worse" (Mark 2:21).

Chloe is my heroine here. For she had the common sense to make Paul aware of the camp followers in the church at Corinth; his letter to them simply bristles with bluntness: "It hath been told me by those of the household of Chloe that there are dissensions among you, and that some of you say: I am of Paul! I am of Peter! I am of Apollos! And I of Christ! Is Christ divided? Was Paul crucified for you? Or were any of you baptized in the name of Paul?" (I Corinthians 1:11-13).

Obviously Christ is the answer. The original cloth was His, and only He can provide more of the same for patches. The Kingdom is His. The work is His. The results are to be His. "If it be possible, as much as lieth in you, live peaceably with all men." Armed with such patches of peace I look around at my divided world. Split! Schizophrenic! Northerners *versus* Southerners, at the moment. White *versus* Black, pro tem. Communists *versus* Democracies, for decades. Labor *versus* Capital. East *versus* West. Liturgical Churches *versus* Free Churches.

No wonder my private patch seems pretty inadequate. But George Eliot provides a hint: "By *desiring* what is perfectly good even when we do not quite know what it is, and cannot do what we would, we are part of the power against evil, widening the skirts of light and making the struggle with darkness narrower."

From 300 years ago, comes Jeremy Taylor's prayer: "O blessed Lord, in whose garment was variety, but no rent or seam, have mercy upon Thy holy church; and so unite all hearts and affections by the union of faith and charity, that we be not torn into factions and schisms, but being anointed by Thy Spirit from above, may keep the unity of the Spirit in the bond of peace. Amen."

After which an inner light from the Quaker Whittier simply has to be hummed in the chair by the window, to the thrilling Easter tune of "Palestrina":

Forgive, O Lord, our severing ways, the rival altars that we raise,
The wrangling tongues that mar Thy praise, O forgive us.
Thy grace impart; in time to be shall one great temple rise to Thee—
One Church for all humanity, O grant it!
White flowers of love its walls shall climb, soft bells of peace shall
      ring its chime,
Its days shall all be holy time—O speed them!
One song shall swell from shore to shore, one hope, one faith, one
      love restore
The seamless robe that Jesus wore; God grant it.

5. *It is not impossible for me to grow by measuring my smallness against the height of Him in whom dwelleth all the fulness of the Godhead, bodily.*

Paul has a Rule for my tape measure: "For we dare not make ourselves of the number, or compare ourselves with some who commend themselves: but they measuring themselves by themselves, and comparing themselves among themselves, are not wise" (2 Corinthians 10:12).

One of the unforgettable Thanksgiving rituals down at grandmother's house was being measured against her doorjamb to see how much this small grandchild had grown since last year. And beginning with 1919 the tape measure lay side by side with Harold Monro's rebellious vine that "clomb on God's own house," but grew tired of obedience to the laws of the universe and announced to high heaven:

I will not *grow*,
I will *not* grow,
I *will* not grow,
I will not grow!

God, author of all liberty, all independence and all growth, leaned out of heaven and said placidly: *"You need not!"*

The vine could now count on this permission to stop growing. What it did not count on, however, was the boundless energy wrapped up in its own nature; and all the while it labored *not* to grow

It grew; it grew;
And all the time God knew.

Deep in South Carolina certain backcountry women made a much more marvelous testimony at a church gathering: "We ain't what we want to be; *but*—we ain't what we used to be; *and*—we ain't what we're going to be!"

Paul was always doing things "beyond measure" ("persecuting the church," Galatians 1:16; "personally pressed down," 2 Corinthians 1:8; "in stripes above measure," 2 Corinthians 11:23), was always giving of his energy in the same measureless volume, conscious of the Source "from whom cometh every good and perfect gift."

In its Invocation for Palm Sunday, the Book of Common Order of the Church of Scotland belongs also in a sewing basket: "O

Lord Jesus Christ, who on this day didst enter the rebellious city where Thou wast to die; enter into our hearts, we beseech Thee, and subdue them wholly to Thyself. And as Thy faithful disciples blessed Thy coming, and spread their garments in the way, covering it with palm branches, make us ready to lay at Thy feet all that we have and are, and to bless Thee, O Thou who comest in the name of the Lord."

After which what can a person hum in a chair by the window but the old familiar words:

> We give Thee but Thine own, whate'er the gift may be:
> All that we have is Thine alone, a trust, O Lord, from Thee.
> May we Thy bounties thus as stewards true receive,
> And gladly, as Thou blessest us, to Thee our first fruits give.

6. *It is not impossible for me to follow Thy pattern, O Lord and Master of us all.*

Mending is one thing. Difficult, but safe. But cutting out a new dress is dangerous. Everything in the sewing basket comes in handy. Tape measure to be sure Size 18 is correct. Pins to fasten the do-it-yourself pattern on the yard goods. A long breath and a prayer. Then scissors, which could be fatal if too quick here, too absent-minded there. Then more pins along the seams. And, at long last, the patient needle runs in and out, in and out, drawing its little train of thread behind it.

Neither Rome nor dresses nor characters are built in a day. And homemade ones often look just that way. Peter, who had fumbled badly himself, understood all this, for he wrote in one of his letters: "Hereunto were ye called: because Christ also suffered for us, leaving us an example that we should follow in His steps" (I Peter 2:21).

By studying this Pattern it is possible to see what lines, what sizes, what shapes my life is to take, for one thing; it is written of Him that "for our sakes He became poor, that we through His poverty might become rich." It is all too plain to be seen that when He died He left only His robe and a few friends. He had no roof over His head, but borrowed everything He used—a

manger for a cradle, a ship for His pulpit, a public Mount of
Olives and its garden as His retreat; He borrowed a tomb for His
burial, and a casual passerby to carry His cross. But the cross
was His own; the victory was His own. And if I can deny myself
daily as He did, the same victory is mine. Such stirring stewardship the world has seen only once; but the man on the street
is still on tiptoe waiting to see what the sons and daughters of
God will do.

At least one daughter sits singing the Isaac Watts hymn:

> My dear Redeemer and my Lord,
> I read my duty in Thy Word;
> But in Thy life the law appears,
> Drawn out in living characters.
>
> Be Thou my Pattern, make me bear
> More of Thy gracious image here. . . .

At the word "gracious" something clicks—for this is the ad-
vertisers' dream word: "What the Gracious Hostess Will Wear";
"Styled for Gracious Living," "Gracious Rugs to Welcome Gracious Guests." If it is not impossible for someone on Madison
Avenue to see me being and acquiring all this society glamor,
then why doubt that the Author and Finisher of our faith can
make possible someone as gracious as He—tender with the old
and ill and the very young, patient with the dull, speaking as
never man spake; practicing the Presence, here, while sewing.
Emptying the life and the purse and the dreams to give Him a
room, at last. This chair, a private chapel. This basket, a sacra-
ment of common things made gracious before another vigil, tomorrow before breakfast.

That not impossible she
who commands my love, my life, and me
                    Richard Crashawe, 1612-1649

A PORTION OF THYSELF

Therefore the poet brings his poem; the shepherd, his lamb; the farmer, corn; the miner, a gem; the sailor, coral and shells; the painter, his picture; the girl, a handkerchief of her own sewing.

Ralph Waldo Emerson, 1803-1882

They that are ensnared and entangled in the extreme penury of things needful for the body, cannot set their minds upon Thee, O Lord, as they ought to do; but when they be disappointed of the things which they so mightily desire, their hearts are cast down and quail from excess of grief. Have pity upon them, therefore, O merciful Father, and relieve their misery from Thine incredible riches, that by Thy removing of their urgent necessity, they may rise up to Thee in mind. Thou, O Lord, providest enough for all men with Thy most liberal and bountiful hand, but whereas Thy gifts are, in respect of Thy goodness and free favor, made free unto all men, we through our haughtiness and niggardship and distrust do make them private and peculiar. Correct Thou the things which our iniquity hath put out of order, let goodness supply that which our niggardliness hath plucked away. Give Thou meat to the hungry and drink to the thirsty, comfort Thou the sorrowful, cheer Thou the dismayed, strengthen Thou the weak, deliver Thou them that are prisoners, and give Thou hope and courage to them that are out of heart.

Queen Elizabeth's Prayerbook, 1559

11

WHERE THERE'S A WILL

Blessed are the dead who die in the Lord henceforth . . . for their deeds shall follow them.   REVELATION 14:13

What earthly good will it do you to know the five difficult names of Zelophehad's persistent daughters (Mahlah, Noah, Hoglah, Milcah and Tirzah), or the three difficult names of Job's three beautiful daughters (Jemima, Kezia and Keren-happuch), if you do not realize that Z's five girls contested his Will before Moses, and God Himself said that yes! certainly these daughters were well within their rights to claim their just share of their father's estate; while as for J's three girls—"the fairest in the land"—they inherited equally with their brothers in their father's will, without lifting a finger to get it.

But when you read about Mahlah, Milcah, Tirzah, Noah and Hoglah in Numbers 27:1-8 and 36:5-9, and about Keren-happuch, Kezia and Jemima in Job 42:15, the next thing to do, of course, is to go straight to your own desk and write your own Will. Leaving something sizable to the church family of the Household of God to which you belong, quite as the daughters of Zelophehad were instructed to do. It might make your Will more God-conscious if you put on your most "beautiful garments," the way Franz Josef Haydn always put on his court suit and wig when he sat down to compose; and, if he was working on some supremely important score, he also wore the ring given to him by the King of Prussia. For he was a most religious man, regarding his musical talent as a treasure lent to him from God.

71

In recognition of this stewardship each of his scores was headed "*In Nomine Domini*" and closed with the words "*Laus Deo*"— for he said of himself: "When I think of God, my heart dances within me, and my music has to dance, too!"

In your beautiful garments, therefore, what more gala way to open your Will than by singing Haydn's "Creation" music, used with the hymn "The spacious firmament on high"? For if *the heavens are telling*, that is surely your purpose also! IN THE NAME OF THE LORD you pick up your pen and write. Then pause, and begin again, thinking of the many miracles possible on earth with your money—doctors healing, preachers preaching, teachers teaching, children singing. After the list has grown, no words are right but: TO THE GLORY OF GOD. It takes a lawyer, in the end, to phrase it legally; but it takes a Redeemer to plan it regally—immortal tidings in your mortal hands.

It must have been that way with Miss Emmeline Pye when she used to sit all day long at her window watching the inhabitants of Hoo St. Werbergh walking past. At 95 she was far too frail to do much walking, herself; so she sat there with the secret satisfaction that every single person going by had been mentioned in her Last Will and Testament—and wouldn't all the school children in town be surprised to get 7 cents apiece? and all the children nearer by, 90 cents apiece, the ones whose faces were more familiar? She specified $15 for each postman and the man who brought the morning paper to her door. She had thought hard about the church choir members, for some were newer than the older faithful ones, but there was to be from $1.50 to $2.80 for each. There were larger sums, of course, such as $2,800 to the hospital, and to a faithful servant . . . and her church . . . In a way Miss Emmeline could hardly wait to die, thinking how nice it would be in town when everyone had his or her slice of her $270,000! And that is just the way it really was, with money provided to buy blankets at Christmas for all the poor, while everything left over was to be divided among professional people in need. Everyone went around smiling: "You know, we never dreamed she had such a lot of money!" But she was the one who had dreamed—saving here, skimping there; thrifty, but thrilled by all this pinching of pennies, thinking of tomorrow morning when she would be loving everybody in her tiny old English town.

Practically this same dream captured another Christian woman in Carlisle, Pennsylvania—although somewhat younger, somewhat poorer, somewhat frailer, her last seven years spent in the State Hospital. Aged 93, Miss Minnie Hennigh died just before Christmas, 1956, leaving a Will as obviously beloved as Miss Emmeline Pye's had been. Miss Hennigh and her mother had been among the first telephone operators in town, always quiet and unnoticed, although a few persons could see that Miss Minnie certainly loved missions. When she first became ill they scolded her because she was not eating enough. But she knew what she knew! Dollar by dollar she had managed to save a $40,000 estate, and she certainly had no intention of dipping into it now, at this late date, when her dream had grown nearer and dearer than ever. Just before Christmas, after her going, her pastor learned of her legacy with her whole life literally longing to carry glad tidings around the world, in no uncertain terms:

One-fifth to the United Lutheran Church for work among schools and hospitals in India and Africa.
one-fifteenth to the YWCA in Carlisle.
one-fifteenth to the Lutheran Seminary in Gettysburg.
one-fifteenth to the First Evangelical Lutheran Church, Carlisle.
the remainder in a trust fund, the income to go to her own church for its life and ministry.

What minister could fail to see a modern Magi, faithfully following a star for fifty years, in order to leave treasures of new gold, new frankincense, new myrrh?

So far this chapter has seemed to stress women. But did you not also spot that spate of brief notes to the Editor of *The Christian Century* about all those big Wills made in small towns? A retired farmer-oil worker left $36,000 to three churches in Westfield, Illinois, while in Westfield, New York, a retired business man left $60,000 to the local hospital and more than $59,000 to four local churches; and a retired industrialist in the village of Le Roy, New York, distributed $24,000 among the eight churches in his community. All of which has the right ring to it: a non-competitive interest in each congregation, impartially. Each Will saying to God and man: "Perpetually yours."

This is exactly what Christopher Columbus did in his Will, nearly five hundred years ago. He dearly prized the "Christ-Bearer" meaning of his name, and his legacy proves it: "I also order Diego, my son, to spare no pains in having on the island of Española four good professors of theology, to the end and aim of their studying and laboring to convert the inhabitants . . . in attaining which no expense should be spared. I gave to the subject six or seven years of great anxiety, explaining to the best of my ability how great service might be done to our Lord by this undertaking, in promulgating His sacred name and our holy faith among so many nations."

On a Northamptonshire tombstone two words are engraved: "DIED OPULENT." Undoubtedly the first question his neighbors asked: "How much did he leave?" was followed by: "Who got it all?" Certain it is that whatever he gave to his church while living left a large hole in the treasury after his death, if his Will forgot his own church, thus confessing to the congregation that he personally had never had any Christ-Bearer dream for the future, and no picture of something imperishably lovely because he had lived.

When Jeremy Bentham died in London a century ago he left all his large fortune to a London Hospital, with the proviso that his dried skeleton, dressed in his business suit, should be placed on a small movable platform, to be wheeled into every monthly board meeting at the head of the table, a death mask on his head, and an old hat. This has meant that for over a hundred years the secretary of the board of directors has always read in his minutes of the last meeting: *"Jeremy Bentham present but not voting."*

Not voting? yet voting by his uncomfortable Will to create this constant uncomfortable situation. But Emmeline Pye and Minnie Hennigh are present in a hundred homes and a dozen places all the way from Carlisle and Calcutta and the Camaroons, voting every moment with tenderness and compassion to be stewards of the loving-kindness of God. Mr. Bentham once wrote a pamphlet, *Auto-Icon: The Uses of the Dead to the Living*, suggesting that everybody's body should be embalmed, thus becoming his own statue—perhaps to be set up along the driveway of his estate, a tree on each side, to perpetuate his mortal motives in the minds of men. But there is a nobler way, as follows.

For Mr. Archer C. Jones, a businessman in Richmond Virginia, died suddenly on December 21, 1926, shortly before Christmas. Below, unfinished, is the last thing he wrote: a letter lending money which he could ill afford to spare, to an artist he felt could never repay it: "You have asked me to do a good deed—*to help you*—and I will. In return, I ask you to prove your gratitude by keeping alive my good deed. Pledge me *you will not let* it die. When the 'other fellow' needs help, think of this day and help him if you can: so will my good deed continue to live in yours. And if you bind *him* to help others, too, and he binds *them*, and so on, then, if they keep their pledge, neither my good deed, nor yours, nor his, nor theirs will ever die.

"Ten thousand years hereafter, perhaps, our simple deeds of kindness still will be active in the earth, passing from heart to heart of men and women who will never have heard of us but who, nevertheless, will be heartened and comforted because today I tried to help you and you, in return, pledged me truly to keep my good deed alive. Could there be any nobler immortality for any man than to live in. . . ."

Perhaps the best epitaph might be:

HE HEARD THE CALL AND HE ANSWERED IT

Has ALL a codicil?
        Emily Dickinson, 1830-1886

AN EPITAPH
for ye godly man's tomb
Here lies a piece of Christ; a star in dust; a vein of gold;
a china dish that must be used in heaven, when God
shall feast the just.

        Robert Wild, 1609-1679

Mr. Valiant-for-Truth called for his Friends and said:
"I am going to my Father's house, and though with great
difficulty I am got hither, yet now I do not repent me
of all the Trouble I have been at to arrive where I am.
My Sword I give to him that shall succeed me in my
Pilgrimage, and my Courage and Skill to Him that can
get it. My Marks and Scars I carry with me, to be a Wit-
ness for me that I have fought his Battles who will now
be my Rewarder." When the day that he must go hence
was come, many accompanied him to the River-side,
into which as he went he said: "Death, where is thy
Sting?" and as he went deeper he said: "Grave, where
is thy Victory?" So he passed over, and all the Trumpets
sounded for him on the other side.

        John Bunyan, 1628-1688

I have now disposed of all my property to my family.
There is one thing more I wish I could give them, and
that is the Christian religion. If they had that, and I
had not given them one shilling, they would have been
rich; and if they had not that, and I had given them all
the world, they would be poor.

        Patrick Henry, 1736-1799

12

FOR RICHER, FOR POORER

Both Jesus was called, and His disciples, to the marriage. . . . His mother saith unto the servants: "Whatsoever He saith unto you, do it."   JOHN 2:2, 5.

And—in Buffalo, New York—Miss Vogt was the one who did it.

Some women, of course, always weep at weddings. Weep—not wail. Tender tears—not copious crying. A mere man, watching, wonders if it is the remembrance of things past: disappointments? joys? or what? But in this case, if Miss Vogt's eyes filled with tears, how gala! For it was the wedding at Cana all over again, complete with miracle.

There is always more to any ceremony than meets the eye. And in her case the whole story began with Miss Vogt's eyes. That dreadful day in the oculist's office when he had to tell her frankly that her 20% vision was not only failing rapidly but would undoubtedly continue to fail until she became blind. Totally blind. "Unless," he added, "unless you have the one operation which might restore your vision 50%, or 60%. But I must warn you —even this operation is not always successful. Yet, if you do not have it, blindness is sure. It is up to you to decide."

This posed such a problem that she took it to her pastor: shall I? or shan't I? But how could Dr. Loew decide without Divine guidance? It was then that they both prayed; and the certainty came to her that yes! the operation! Of course, the operation!

It was absolutely successful. So much so, in fact, that she went walking on air wondering how in the world to find some way of thanking God and sharing this stewardship of sudden bliss.

While she was searching, her nephew came home from college one day and told her about a young Chinese student working for his Master's degree at the University of Buffalo. The poor fellow was blue as indigo over his fiancée in China, who had managed to escape from the Communists into Formosa. Safe! But utterly unable to get to the United States because of quota restrictions; the bridegroom in Buffalo was desolate. Instantly Miss Vogt gained even better vision: *Isn't this it?*

She went straight to her pastor again: "How can I turn heaven and earth enough to get that girl into this country?" They went together to the immigration authorities, and found that quotas were quotas; and an Oriental was an Oriental. So there was no earthly way, unless . . .

"Unless what?" asked Miss Vogt, with fire in her eyes. Both new eyes.

"Well, unless somebody or other should feel like legally adopting and sponsoring this Chinese girl; then maybe . . ."

Nothing ever seemed easier for Miss Vogt than vouching for this unknown daughter, or signing all the necessary documents, or handing over all the necessary dollars. It was a solo, a jubilate! To her pastor she must have seemed like all his stewardship sermons rolled into one text: *"The Lord loveth a cheerful giver."* And in spite of her more than sixty summers and winters it must be admitted that she lived up fully to the literal Greek meaning of the word cheerful—hilarious.

Moreover, this bliss brightened up Christmas, 1949, in Buffalo. For just when all the radios in town were sounding forth their usual "God Rest Ye, Merry Gentlemen," who but the lovely Tsiubeh should arrive from China to make one restless young Chinese gentleman decidedly merrier. And, at the New Year's Eve candlelight service in Holy Trinity Lutheran Church, Tsiubeh and Chen Hsai met at the foot of the chancel steps. Dr. Loew asked an ancient question: *"Who giveth this woman in marriage to this man?"* Miss Vogt stepped forward and said in an unusually vibrant voice: "I do!"

If all the women wept, it was vicariously—because their own Miss Vogt had provided this wonderful wedding present for her brand new daughter. The old familiar phrases suddenly took on a certain Oriental luster: "For better, for worse; for richer, for poorer; in sickness and in health; till death do us part . . . with all my worldly goods I thee endow."

And did they live happily ever afterward? You may be sure that the whole church family feels blessed because Mr. Hsai now has a good job with the New York State Department of Correction; also because he named his first child Susan Tingmay, which being translated tells its own story: "Susan-at-home-in-America."

Cana is forever!

A man's life or death may sometimes depend on a bamboo basket of rice and a bowl of soup.
                                          Mencius, 400 B.C.

Better one bite of the peach of immortality than a whole basket of apricots.   Chinese proverb

Heaven is lasting and earth enduring. The reason why they are lasting and enduring is that they do not live for themselves; therefore they live long. In the same way the Sage keeps himself behind, and he is in front; he forgets himself, and he is preserved. It is because he is not self-interested that his self-interest is established! It is upon bad fortune that good fortune leans, upon good fortune that bad fortune rests.
                          Tao Té Ching, ancient Chinese

The tree which fills the arms grew from the tiniest sprout;
the pagoda of nine stories rose from a small heap of
earth; the journey of a thousand miles began with a
single step.   Tao Té Ching, ancient Chinese

13

TIED TO HIS MOTHER'S PURSE STRINGS

Amid a severe ordeal of trouble, their overflowing joy and their
deep poverty together have poured out a flood of rich generosity;
I can testify that up to their means, aye and beyond their means,
they have given—begging me of their own accord, most urgently,
for the favor of contributing to the support of the saints. They
have done more than I expected: they gave themselves to the
Lord to begin with.   2 CORINTHIANS 8:2-5; Moffatt Translation

Apron strings are more or less obsolete. But purse strings are still
in style, just as they were that Sunday morning in Mississippi, over
a hundred years ago, when a young schoolteacher went to little
Pearl River Church and was overwhelmingly moved by a missionary sermon. So much so that when the collection basket reached
her pew she put in a five dollar bill and a note, reading: "I give
$5 and myself, Mary I. McClellan."

Five dollars was a generous gift that long ago. But as for any
young woman thinking of going out to a heathen land—unthink-
able! unheard of! The Methodist ministers wagged their heads,
wondering what on earth to do with Mary. All but Reverend
James W. Lambuth, who soon solved the unsolvable by simply

marrying Mary, and taking her along with him to China in the year 1853.

The bridegroom's background had been as dramatically handed over to the Lord as the bride's. For he was born while his father was preaching at a camp meeting in Alabama; and the moment the young preacher heard the news he said: "I dedicate this child to God as a foreign missionary, and I vow a bale of cotton to send him with!"

What more could God want?
A boy and a bale of cotton.
A girl and five dollars.

When the time came to go they faced 16,000 miles of weather and choppy seas on a small ship called *Ariel*—sailing and drifting for 135 days, with the drinking water gone bad and the bread gone moldy long before they rounded the Cape of Good Hope; moreover, it was winter, and they had to use red-hot cannon balls for warmers. Then came Shanghai. But after so much tedium it was terrifying to land during the dreadful days of the Tai-Ping Rebellion, with the city in the hands of rebels.

Most women who are going to have a first baby within two months of arrival in a strange Oriental city with a war going on, do not go out on the street and start bringing in dozens of big and little orphans—starving on the sidewalk. But young Mrs. Lambuth was still as determined as ever to give *"$5 and myself."* She housed so many orphans that soon there was no more room. She fed so many that soon there was no more food. And of course no more cash. But because there was plenty of time between meals to teach school to her brand new family, she soon found that she had no books, no slates, no pencils, no paper, no blackboards. It is even quite probable that over in Nashville her husband's Mission Board had no more patience with the steady stream of requests arriving by every ship that crossed the sea from Shanghai. There must have been men who shook their heads and said that back there when Mary wrote down *"$5 and*

myself" she really meant it, didn't she? And now she wanted them
to mean it, too. But suppose her house did seem smaller and
smaller as the orphans grew bigger and bigger, was a school their
answer?

But then drama entered the picture again. For in Nashville a
bride who had just heard about all this, suddenly began unpin-
ning all the diamonds which were holding her wedding veil in
place; and the first act of this new Mrs. McGavock was sending
these precious stones to Mrs. Lambuth. They were sold for $1,000;
and this first Chinese school built with diamonds was to become
the famous McTyeire School for Girls in the course of time; but
meanwhile, in America other Southern Methodist women felt
strangely warmed to think of one brave little woman in wartime,
with a brand new baby, working such wonders so quickly. And
if *she* thought that things should be done in China for children,
then why in the world not organize themselves into a Woman's
Methodist Foreign Missionary Society, on faith? (This too has
kept growing and growing, as the gentle reader may know.) But
what you may not know is that all this time the little Lambuth
lad was growing up, too, tied to his mother's purse strings, watching her work wonders indoors and out.

This kind of practical private wonder: the War of 1861 to 1865
cut off all Lambuth income from their home base in Nashville.
Dr. Lambuth considered taking some other job to support his
family. But no! Mary Lambuth solved all this by taking in table
boarders, so that no mission work need suffer a single second.
Even a son could see that it was still *"$5 and myself"*—this "my-
self" totally self-forgetful, totally capable of coping with every
emergency. For instance, she saw how the Chinese feared an
eclipse of the sun. Well and good! the answer she had for this
superstition was to sit down and write an astronomy, in Chinese.
She worried over Chinese women's "lily feet," bound and crippled
from childhood—this meant starting a crusade. No boy could
forget such energy; and when the family was moved to Japan
by the Mission Board, it was easy to see her still giving herself

away to the people in Osaka, where the Lambuth Bible School became a memorial to both parents. The sequel of which is that whatever small sons see, they either spurn or share. And Walter Lambuth was as startling a sharer as his mother, in the very same fashion; for not only did he become the greatest missionary bishop of China, but he touched life in every one of the major continents, equally at home in Japan, Africa, South America and Europe— generous to a fault! noble! forward-looking!

George Bernard Shaw once said that if a Cause is to grow, then instruct every woman you meet about it. She will tell her husband; contradict him with all your own arguments; and a squabble will follow. But all this time the son will be listening and set to thinking, if he is capable of thought; and so the minds of people get leavened.

In the Lambuth stewardship there was no squabbling. But a bishop was reared by the conversations overheard in his home until he too could live out Thomas Kelly's Christian dream: "WE MUST ALL BE COSMIC MOTHERS CARING FOR ALL."

Preferring to store her money in the stomachs of the needy rather than to hide it in a purse.

St. Jerome; in a letter to Principia, A.D. 400

You painted no Madonnas
On chapel walls in Rome;
But with a touch diviner
You lived one in your home.
You wrote no lofty poems
That critics counted art;
But with a nobler vision,
You lived them in your heart.

You carved no shapeless marble
To some high soul design
But with a finer sculpture
You shaped this soul of mine.
You built no great cathedrals
That centuries applaud;
But with a grace exquisite
Your life cathedraled God.
Had I the gift of Raphael
Or Michelangelo
O what a rare Madonna
My mother's life would show.
Thomas Green Fessenden, 1771-1837

. . . We're made so that we love
First when we see them painted, things we have passed
Perhaps a hundred times, nor cared to see:
And so they are better painted—better to us,
Which is the same thing. Art was given for that;
God uses us to help each other so,
Lending our minds out.
Robert Browning, 1812-1889

14

THE GOSPEL ACCORDING TO 31 WOMEN

Seest thou this woman?   LUKE 7:44

"But we know it by heart already," your group may say. "Everybody knows Luke—all those angels and shepherds and the manger and Mary and lost sheep and lost son. We grew up knowing all that!"

But did you grow up reading Luke with your five senses? *Smelling* all the fragrance in chapter after chapter? Did you grow up *tasting* meal after meal after meal? Or *hearing* all the street calls and pleas and stories? Or *touching* all those jostling mobs of people, and healing all the sick at sunset time or in synagogues on the Sabbath? And, above all, did you grow up realizing that Luke may have been a painter—did you ever really *see* the brilliant colors he lavished on his masterpieces, as vivid as Van Gogh's? Besides all this, did you know all along that Luke was writing "The Gospel according to 31 Women"? Can you name all 31 of them? Can you tell who-*smelled*-what-and-when? Who *ate*-where-and-why? Who-*touched*-whom-and-how? Who-*heard*-what-and-when? Who-*saw*-whom-and-where? For until you have read Luke with your five senses how can you develop your sixth sense which is your innermost spirit, working over these five reports from the animal kingdom, analyzing them, weighing them, judging them, discovering: "But this means me! He is writing about me—I was THERE!"

No other writer manages to present the tenderness of Jesus

85

quite so perfectly. John wrote "God so loved that He gave . . ."
But Luke shows this only-begotten Son so loving the world that
He too gave; and gave; and gave. From start to finish, therefore,
Luke is a study in the stewardship of sharing this loving-kindness
of God.

And surprisingly enough, this dramatic painter actually alter-
nates his scenes of men with those of women. As if each viewpoint
mattered equally. No writer had ever done this before. Is he describing Zacharias? Very well, Elizabeth comes next. Is Luke
telling about Mary? After which, Joseph. Later still, Simeon in
the temple, waiting for the Saviour; then in comes Anna, equally
expectant. Of all social lessons in behavior, how Emily Post
should approve of this charming courtesy. Open this gospel anywhere, go from verse to verse, and yes! the alternation offers
constant contrast. In Luke 10: that impressive stewardship model
—the Good Samaritan, tenderness personified in verses 25
through 37; then, in verse 38, the model hostess and the hot-and-
bothered hostess contrasted, a study in the stewardship of hospitality as well as of investing the sixth sense when the Guest
of guests is stopping in your house. Followed immediately by the
model prayer (11:1-4), contrasted with the not-so-model father
reluctant to get up at midnight to share bread with a neighbor in
need. This is even more subtle in contrast than it seems at first
glance: for isn't the father's grumble like Martha's mumble, preferring an apparently lazy sister's status? Next, notice chapter 12
where a rich farmer had such bumper crops that his barns were
bursting at the seams. He designs bigger and better barns; pats
himself on the back for his initiative and clever five-year-plan
until God steps in and warns him: "This night! Thy soul!" With
Jesus adding the storm signal: "*So is he that layeth up treasure
for himself, and is not rich toward God.*" In this light our Lord
then considers both ravens and lilies in words you may have
grown up knowing by heart, but still hesitate to practice. Then—
in matchless contrast with the crooked farmer—chapter 13 shows
Jesus considering the poor crooked woman and how she had

grown for eighteen years, stooped in body, but seeking the Lord's house on a Sabbath. Her cure enchanting the entire congregation.

You mentioned earlier that you have known all your life about the lost sheep and the lost coin. But did you grow up realizing that Luke is again contrasting the stewardship responsibilities our Lord expects of any man with a hundred sheep and of any woman with ten coins? A fine point—but it does add dignity to church offering envelopes and luster to teamwork on tedious committees. In fact, chapter 15 is crammed with all this, and heaven too.

Chapter 17 ends in tragedy: "Remember Lot's wife"; and chapter 18 opens with a reluctant judge who finally saves a widow as Lot's wife had never troubled to save Sodom. Notice how this same chapter then tells about certain mothers, rich in children, eager to put them into our Lord's arms; while in the next verse, a lovable young ruler, rich in treasure, will put none of it into our Lord's hands. One more striking example of masculine-feminine stewardship occurs in chapter 20: crafty chief priests are trying to catch Jesus in regard to paying tribute to Caesar (20:19-26). With everybody listening, Jesus then warns his disciples against men who go to synagogues in long fashionable robes to make even longer prayers, all the while devouring widows' houses (20:45-47). Then presto! Who walks in but the world's poorest widow to give the world's most unforgettable offering (21:1-4)!

Don't your five senses simply dance with delight every time you discover such deth-in-depth stewardship psychology? With plenty of well-to-do women spending plenty of money to provide plenty of practical things for our Lord, such as . . .

"But wait a minute! Wait a minute! This is heady stuff, totally different from what we knew before—or had we ever really read Luke, after all? And how had we better begin now?"

Five hundred years ago Thomas à Kempis suggested the only way to begin: "*Take thou the Book in thine hand as Simeon the Just took the Child Jesus into his arms to carry Him and to bless Him.*" A small separate gospel is best, the kind that the American

Bible Society sells for two and a half cents. Inside the front cover print a column of the following block letters, so that you may put the proper key letters throughout the text, opposite the proper places as you read, mark, and inwardly digest the chapters: SM for *Smell;* SE for *See;* TO for *Touch;* TA for *Taste;* HE for *Hear;* W in the margin whenever you come to one of the 31 *Women;* ? opposite each of the 94 different *questions* Jesus asked: $ wherever *money, possessions* or *gifts* are mentioned; G for *Going Places* —for this is not a static book, both Mary and our Lord are certainly agile, to say the least! S is for *Sabbaths,* a great many are mentioned, and Jesus falls into difficulties on each of them by sharing with some sick body His gift of healing. O is for *Objects:* it will be therapeutic to express out loud your private Jubilate over each of these little "schoolteachers" which Jesus Christ chose for your education—O seeds! O weeds! O thorns! O houses! O barns! O patches! O ointment! O spikenard! O lilies! O mustardseed! O leaven! O sheep! O coin! O bread! O vine! O fig! O salt! O lamp! O candle! O tree! O bird! O water! O door! Then picture Luke, the artist, painting this stewardship and *Sacrament of Small Things.*

F for *Fear,* J for *Joy,* are twins throughout this text: it always happens that when one is mentioned the other word comes along instantly. No other gospel gives this sensible reassurance to frightened persons; as if Luke, "the beloved physician," knew a *tranquilizer* worth a million Miltowns to cast fear out and bring joy in.

Because scent seems so inconsequential, you may wonder if God really needed to make things smell so deliciously. But even Paul—that stern old theologian who frowned on frivolity—called Stewardship a fragrance! And of course you are remembering that Luke traveled with Paul, and may have learned from him that scents make sense. (As well as cents! For see how Dr. Moffatt translates two of Paul's references to this vital Christian essence):

"You Philippians are well aware that in the early days of the gospel . . . no church but yourself had any financial dealings with me ... you sent money more than once for my needs. It is not the money I am anxious for; what I am anxious for is the interest that accumulates in this way to your divine credit! Your debt to me is fully paid and more than paid ... a *fragrant perfume,* the sort of sacrifice that God approves and welcomes" (Philippians 4:15-18).

"Wherever I go, thank God, He makes my life a constant pageant of triumph in Christ, diffusing the perfume of His knowledge everywhere by me. ... I live for God as the fragrance of Christ breathed alike on those who are being saved and on those who are perishing" (2 Corinthians 2:14-15).

Now notice the sense of smell which Luke writes into his gospel, beginning with the penetrating memories which Elizabeth must have had on all the latter Sabbaths in her life at every "hour of incense." She could recall that appalling moment when Zacharias stood at the altar of incense, talking to an angel on the *right-hand side* (this is Luke, the painter, seeing his subjects properly placed), daring to disbelieve that she could possibly have a baby, staying speechless the entire nine months of her pregnancy. A wife could hardly stop connecting incense and prayer with her husband's startling silences.

What could come to Mary's mind about the stable but that sharp ammonia odor of straw and cattle in a stuffy shed? A dusty setting for the Saviour of the whole world. Mary could also recall how appetizing the smell when she roasted the Passover lamb in Jerusalem that important year when Jesus was twelve: her panic over losing Him on the way home, her relief at finding Him seated among temple scholars, surrounded by ancient Scripture scrolls—did these give off the stale musty odor of old leather, to be connected ever afterward with her Son's surprising reply to her scolding: "But where should I be but here in my Father's house, learning His business?" Mothers ponder sentences like that. Nor ever forget the pungent aroma of vinegar, years later, on Calvary. What other artist paints with colors both fragrant and vocal? Consider that woman emptying her alabaster box of ointment at the Pharisee's dinner party in chapter 7: plenty there to mark SM, SE, TO, TA and HE in the margin of the text. "*Seest thou this woman?*" Jesus asks His host in rebuke—actually contrasting the man's begrudging the courtesy due to a guest with the woman's generous gesture. A threefold study in stewardship, therefore: "not grudgingly nor of necessity," "for the Lord loveth a cheerful giver" (Luke remembering Paul!) and, "it is more blessed to give than to receive."

When Luke mentions the Queen of Sheba (11:31) is he also painting in his mind's eye her thrilling train of camels bringing spices to Solomon's court? The picture in 1 Kings 10:10 could fire his imagination: "And she gave the king a hundred and twenty talents of gold, and of spices a very great store, and precious stones; there came no more abundance of spices as these which the Queen of Sheba gave to King Solomon." To which Luke adds candid camera shot of the day when Jesus says in exasperation to the people around Him: "What a miserly generation you are! Always seeking a sign; very well, I give you the Queen of Sheba herself—she would rise up in judgment over the superstitious stingy men of this generation, and condemn you all!" Aroma? Yes! Also the Divine comment on not sharing, not daring, not caring.

In Luke 15 can't you almost smell the cedar chest in which the mother of the prodigal probably stored the best robes and sandals? with perhaps a whiff or two of camphor in the folds as her properly-dressed son goes around greeting guests? Or how about certain tantalizing odors in Bethany the day that Martha hurried to and fro, carrying this or that dish from kitchen to dining room? and always those memorable "myrrh-bearing women" who recur so frequently through *The Divine Liturgy* of the Eastern Orthodox Church, for this reference to gifts brought by women is the tribute this Church places on womankind. (Going so far as to give certain women names, and even dates, to remind feminine members to remember Pilate's wife on October 27 and call her "Claudia Procula"—since who else had lifted a finger to help the Saviour in that last tragic week of His life? The same Eastern Fathers have called the Samaritan woman at the well "Photina," with March 20 as the date to recall how she gave water to the Ruler of All Nature, then herself received back the priceless water of Life.)

The final smell mentioned in this gospel is the broiled fish in chapter 24:42, when Jesus is suddenly seen standing in the same room where His disciples are wondering: "Is He really risen?" He shows His pierced hands and feet, then asks His homely, human question: "Have you any meat?" It is as they hand Him some of their fish that their giving becomes His giving, in restoring their troubled minds to peace and joy: F into J, on the margins of your text, as well as SM, SE, TA, TO, HE.

Stewardship is colorful, also. Instead of Van Gogh's yellow and orange sunflowers, Luke paints lilies more gorgeous than Solomon in all his glory. Sometimes in three strokes of his pen he does a masterpiece, such as: *"Remember Lot's wife!"* There she stands, salt-white, isolated, glistening in the sunlight—this selfish non-sharing socialite from Sodom, with the sulphur smell of its fire and brimstone still around her. If you compare Luke 17:33 with Ezekiel 16:49 you discover what indictment the artist is portraying: "Behold, this was the sin of thy sister Sodom, pride, fulness of bread, and abundance of idleness was in her and her daughters, neither did she strengthen the hand of the poor and needy." Such a salt statue stands in strange contrast to the aged Anna, gaunt from fasting, slender as a temple pillar, and probably as gray. But look again: what radiance on her face as she hears Simeon say: "Behold this child!" and then does what no other woman in the Bible has ever done, herself holding the little Son of God in her arms. No wonder it is written of her that she went around telling everybody (2:36, 38). For gray is a serene and soothing color: giving her gem to solve geriatrics.

All your life you have loved Luke's picture of the hopeful young mothers sensible enough to want their children to go through life remembering "the day Jesus took me up in His arms and blessed me." But of course the matchless side of this master-piece is that all the Cradle Roll, Primary and Junior Departments in all the churches on earth start with our Lord's rebuke to His dull-witted disciples: "Let them keep coming! My Kingdom begins with them!" You will want to write TO for *Touch* in the margin of Luke 18:15-17, as well as SE and HE for *Seeing* and *Hearing*.

In chapter 21:1-5, Luke does the outstanding stewardship portrait of all time. The curious thing about the little central figure is that she has no least idea she is "sitting" to any artist or being chosen for the Blue Ribbon, Exhibit A, Gold Medal prize by the Judge of the whole earth. For she is just a small modest soul, well aware that she is much too shabby to fit into so superb a setting. Luke shows the disciples looking around the huge temple, awestruck by row on row of lofty pillars with magnifi-cently-carved capitals, gorgeous hangings, fabulous marbles. And, right at home in this beautiful background, any number of rich personages, clothed in purple and fine linen, sweeping up im-portantly to the treasury to toss in their heavy gold coins. *Thud! Thud! Thud!* The reverberation of them echoes impressively under the high ceiling. Then in comes Cinderella. Down to her last cent, and looking it. Her gift so tiny that it tinkles as it goes skittering down the wide metal mouth into the treasury. Nobody else looks at her twice. But Jesus sees her face! Her unself-con-scious delight over this dearest dream come true at last. And of course the Master sees her secret, her expensive, extravagant secret! For He gives her the highest praise He ever spoke about anybody: "She has given more than all of them put together! For the rest of them have plenty left; but out of her penury she has put in all the livelihood she has!"

Our Lord told Mary, when she poured her precious spikenard on His feet, that wherever His gospel was preached this fragrant thing which she had just done for Him would also be told. But this is precisely the widow's wonderful reward also: for lay all the mite boxes named in her honor end to end around the earth, and even such small sums still make and maintain missions, asylums, hospitals and schools all over the globe. Marcus Aurelius once said: "The soul is dyed the color of its leisure thoughts." Daughter of Zion, put on thy beautiful garments—Luke sees them as golden, gleaming and gospel-glorious.

Such can be your stewardship study of the remaining 31 women in Luke. Not all of them are mentioned by name. The only despicable one is that miserable maid in Pilate's palace courtyard, who could find nothing better to do than to twit poor Peter—HE and SE in the margins of 22:54-62. And how about Peter's wife, who rates but a single syllable sandwiched between "Peter" and "mother" in 4:38? (Unless you agree that she may have been the inspiration of 1 Peter 3:1-6: "Some men are won by the conversation of their wives . . . whose adorning let it not be that outward adorning of plaiting the hair, and of wearing gold, or of putting on of apparel . . . but the adornment of a meek and quiet spirit, which in the sight of God is of great price.")

Included among these 31 are anonymous women often unmentioned in the text, but background necessities to round out a story. Such as the mother of the boy with five loaves and two fishes—surely she fixed his lunch basket; the mother of Jairus' daughter, told to feed her twelve-year-old girl; Mark's mother who loaned her upper room for both the Last Supper and Pentecost; how many mothers brought children to be blessed—three? How many "daughters of Jerusalem" wept for our Lord as He passed by on His way to Calvary (23:27-31)? How many "other women" stood afar off, like tragic figures etched on some Greek vase, watching the crucifixion and the arrangements at the tomb (23:55), coming with spices, early in the morning (24:1-12)? Did Zaccheus have a wife, and how would she feel when he promised Jesus half of his goods and the fourfold restoration of ill-gotten gains (19:1-10)? Was it, perhaps, the wife of Cleopas who—womanlike—saw the hands of Jesus breaking bread at her table in Emmaus and recognized the inescapable manner of His doing it (24:28-33)? Notice especially other meals deserving TA in the margin, how Jesus eats in no home without leaving it changed, and blessed. Notice, too, the fine feasts which He puts in His stories—what odor! what color! what curious guest lists!

The value of the $ sign along all the margins of Luke may disturb you and determine your expenditures. Did Dives have a wife? Then what was she thinking of to go sweeping past Lazarus at her gate—a Belle Dame Sans Merci: one of the ten-best-dressed-women-in-town, with all that purple, all that fine linen, all that sumptuous fare every day? Did Levi have a wife? How did she feel when he left his remunerative seat of custom simply to "follow"—financially insecure the rest of his life, rescuing only his pen from "the good old days"? Did she guess that he had it in him to write a Best Seller with this old pen? Did she think it socially risky to invite other tax collectors to come for dinner to meet Jesus? These are only a few of the stewardship angles in Luke, each as modern as tomorrow morning. For no doubt you put $ signs along the margins of all your days. The thing now is to be sure to let your five senses work for you; with your sixth sense appraising spiritually, analyzing intellectually, recognizing that He still sits over against the treasury.

When I sought His answer in isolation, the Voice said: "I have sunk my hearing in the deafness of mortals."
Martin Buber, 1878-

I who am blind can give one hint to those who see—one admonition to those who would make full use of the gift of sight: use your eyes as if tomorrow you would be stricken blind. And the same method can be applied to the other senses. Hear the music of voices, the song of a bird, the mighty strains of an orchestra, as if you would be stricken deaf tomorrow. Touch every object as if your

*tactile sense would fail. Smell the perfume of flowers,
taste each morsel with relish, as if tomorrow you could
neither smell nor taste again. Make the most of every
sense, glory in all the facets of beauty and pleasure which
Nature provides. But of all the senses I am sure that sight
must be the most delightful.*   Helen Keller, 1880-

*There are one-story intellects, two-story intellects, three-
story intellects with skylights. All fact collectors who have
no aim beyond their facts are one-story intellects. Two-
story men compare, reason, generalize, using the labors
of the fact collectors as well as their own. Three-story
men idealize, imagine, predict: their best illumination
comes from above through the skylight.*

Oliver Wendell Holmes, 1809-1894

1 5

WHY IS THE PLUS SIGN IN CHURCH?

*I would make up the full sum of all that Christ has to suffer in
my person on behalf of the church, His Body. . . . It is His will
that they should understand the glorious wealth which this secret
holds for the Gentiles, in the fact of Christ's presence among you
as the hope of your glory.*

COLOSSIANS 1:24,27; Moffat Translation

"Why is the plus sign in church?" a child asked her father one
day, seeing this gold symbol gleaming on the altar of a sanctuary. The most stupendous stewardship question, which all Chris-

tians must spend their lives answering—positively or negatively.

In his letter to the Colossians, Paul showed that, as for him, the + was his "I" crossed out: "I make up in my person the full sum of all that Christ suffered for the Church." To Paul it was "glorious wealth." An endless stewardship to be shared—always, anywhere, with anybody.

As for the rest of us, we are so poor at this kind of arithmetic that for all practical purposes its four usual branches are still those which Alice discovered in Wonderland: Ambition, Derision, Distraction and Uglification.

Ambition? "What were you disputing about as you walked in the way?" Jesus asked His disciples. But they held their peace; for they had disputed among themselves who should be greatest. People in the pew preferring place and position. President of. Chairman of. Moderator of. Conspicuously listed among those present. And of course seated up at the Speaker's Table. Preferably at the right of the Toastmaster. While all the time, from Peter's day to ours, the real ambition of the Christian should be *addition*: to add to the church daily those who are being saved (Acts 2:47); "to add to your faith, virtue; and to virtue, knowledge; to knowledge, temperance; to temperance, patience; to patience, godliness; to godliness, brotherly kindness; and to brotherly kindness, charity. For if these things be in you, and abound, they make you that ye shall neither be barren nor unfruitful in the knowledge of our Lord Jesus Christ" (2 Peter 1:5-8).

Derision? About this Paul wrote to the church in Corinth: "For ye are yet carnal: for whereas there is among you envying and strife and division, one of you saying: I am of Paul, another I am of Apollos. Who then is Paul, and who is Apollos, but ministers by whom ye believed, even as the Lord gave to every man?" (1 Corinthians 3:3-5). In modern church life this spirit sounds off in such a sentence as: "No, we didn't raise our budget; but thank goodness, neither did the Methodists—and you know how big and prosperous they are!"

Distraction? At this point the positive question turns negative:

"Why is the minus sign in church, too?" We go around substracting! The brother of our Lord knew the answer in his day: "Every man is tempted when he is drawn away of his own lusts and enticed." James would have understood perfectly how the man in the pew of a Sunday could stand singing bravely: *"O Jesus, I have promised to serve Thee to the end"*; but, of a Monday, on the street, use only the second stanza: *"I see the sights that dazzle, the tempting sounds I hear."*

Uglification? Advertisements are often a multiplication of uglification: if it's soap you are selling, then show two women eying another woman's laundry hanging on a clothesline, as they snicker behind raised hands: "Tattletale gray!" Such a comment so much dirtier than the half-washed wash that the publishers of Emily Post would do well to advertise a copy of *Etiquette* behind those ill-bred mouths. Or if it's automatic dishwashers you want to advertise, just pile a mile of plates in a kitchen sink and show a weary housewife staring upward in despair. Uglify to the nth degree all the tough spots in domesticity, and bear down hard. Uglify the lazy spots in daily duties and invent a gadget. Multiply! Multiply! It took our Lord to tell us the truth: "Life does not consist in the abundance of things." Blessedness and cheerfulness come with the plus sign of making up in one's own person the full sum of what Christ suffered for the church—stewards of the loving-kindness of God. Walt Whitman said it, bluntly:

> Behold! I do not give lectures or a little charity,
> When I give, I give myself.

This was what Dr. Claude Barlow did the day he deliberately swallowed the flukes, after immigration authorities refused to let him bring into the country certain bottles containing snails heavily infested with flukes. Out of Egyt. From irrigation ditches near the Nile. With half of Egypt's 19,000,000 people suffering from the dread disease these flukes produced, how should a scientist study them if port officials thought them too dangerous to bring to American laboratories? The surest way was hardest:

"I do not give lectures or a little charity, When I give, I give myself"—and his own stomach seemed the one safe hiding place. The pain was excruciating. Just as it was for Egyptians, of course. And for 400,000,000 other Africans and Asians, all of whom also used their streams as drinking fountains, laundries, baths and latrines. So Dr. Barlow was suffering now as they suffered. The only effective cure in his case was injections of tartar emetic, which left him nauseated for eight months. Just as it nauseated them for an equal time. Something better simply must be found. For even after such stiff injections and the long discomfort of the cure, one drink from an infected stream, and an Egyptian could be down with it all over again. Suppose copper sulphate in the water could kill off flukes, and yet not enough to hurt humans— how would that be? In his own body Dr. Barlow learned experimentally. Other men in the laboratories watched him with a certain awe. Ex-missionary, they said. Worried over all this in China, first. Courageous chap, all right! No wonder Egypt honors him. Et cetera. Et cetera. The trouble with work like this is that it is so daily. "Chore-work never gets done," as Robert Frost says in a poem. But a Barlow *lives* that poem; hour after hour.

As Another had done earlier in our behalf: "Surely he hath borne our griefs and carried our sorrows. Stricken. Smitten. Afflicted. Bruised for our iniquities. The chastisement of our peace was upon Him, and by His stripes we are healed."

Consider Eleanor Chestnut in this connection, also, for the strangely symbolic plus sign in her life will bear watching. She was so poor when she went to Park College that she had to be dressed from missionary barrel donations. This was cold charity, which she resented bitterly. And yet! And yet! One day she overheard her classmates talking about a most unlovely old lady totally dependent on the church, but so totally disagreeable that it was almost impossible to persuade people to support her.

That very evening Eleanor Chestnut went to Dr. McAfee to say: "I want to give you this money for that unlovely old woman. My own life has been lived so much among unlovely and unlovable people that I have learned to have great sympathy and love for them." Step Number 1 in her stewardship.

While studying medicine in Chicago, she lived in an attic, cooked her own meager meals, and practically starved. By 1894 she was in China as a medical missionary; but again without proper equipment, for she would write home to her Board in New York: "I have to perform all my operations in my bathroom." Yet this was the precise moment when she practiced enough economy to save $1,000 gold to help build the mission chapel at Lienchou. Step Number 2 in this chore-work of dailiness!

The spending of "first things first" seemed to be Dr. Chestnut's clue for decisions. Such as the case of the badly-burned beggar. No donor could be found anywhere willing to give enough skin to cover his sizable burns. After all, he was an undesirable creature, of no benefit to anybody. But one morning the nurses noticed with astonishment that overnight some donor had at last been located, for wide patches of skin were in place. Who in the world would work this wonder? It was only later that the Doctor herself was seen to be limping, when she thought herself unobserved. But one nurse would say to another: "How did she ever do it alone? Imagine being brave enough to cut away all that flesh without an anaesthetic!" If this seemed Step Number 3 to those who loved her, then all her life was a similar climbing; of a piece with the last moment of her martyrdom also.

For in the year 1900 the Boxer Rebellion threatened all the Christians in China. The day came when Eleanor Chestnut was dragged by ruffians from her hospital. But as they were hurrying her through the street toward the place of execution, she saw a small boy sitting on the curb, bleeding from a cut on his forehead, made by a stone flung by the crowd at passersby. Breaking loose from her guards, Dr. Chestnut tore off the hem of her skirt in the twinkling of an eye, and had bandaged the child's wound when the mob tore her away toward the executioner; and her life was ended. Or did it end? For to this very day, after more than fifty years, Chinese Christians tell and retell her story—how, "in her own flesh," with "glorious wealth," she "filled out the afflictions of Christ": a steward of the loving-kindness of God.

Why is the Plus Sign in church? Because it adds something Divine to something human. Because it can change anybody from a Peter asking: "Lord, we have left all to follow Thee, what then shall we have?" into a Peter writing to scattered Christians: "As every man hath received a gift, even so minister the same one to another as good stewards of the manifold grace of God." Once he had been coward enough to deny his Lord. But the Cross brought a plus into his life. "Don't be surprised at the fiery trial!" he could write to these Christians scattered by persecution. But of course they *were* surprised! No wonder he added: "Judgment must begin at the house of God." It must begin at the altar, for why else is the Plus Sign in church?

> *O Age that half believ'st thou half believ'st,*
> *Half doubt'st the substance of thine own half doubt*
> *And, half perceiving that thou half perceiv'st,*
> *Stand'st at thy temple door, heart in, head out!*
> *Lo! while thine heart's within, helping the choir,*
> *Without, thine eyes range up and down the time.*
> Sidney Lanier, 1842-1881

> *The purest among the strong, the strongest among the pure, Christ lifted with His wounded hands empires from their hinges and changed the stream of ages.*
> Jean Paul Richter, 1763-1825

16

CHECKBOOK INTO PRAYERBOOK

They shall beat their swords into ploughshares and their spears into pruninghooks.   MICAH 4:3

Nowadays nations talk in terms of Dollar Diplomacy and Point 4, in the high hope that nation shall not lift up sword against nation, that every man shall sit under his own vine and fig tree, with none to make them afraid. But all the time it is more than possible that the kinder dollar diplomacy in a Christian checkbook may pray better, dream deeper, go further, last longer.

The way Janie Barrett had dreamed of having a bathroom in her house some day. Nobody else in her Negro neighborhood had one, so she saw herself walking proudly down the street, head high, humming: "Mid pleasures and palaces though I may roam, be it ever so humble, there's no place like home." Especially one with that big bathtub, those shining spigots, and row of linen towels on a rod. Penny by penny, dollar by dollar she had been saving up for this dream, and her checkbook showed her that now there was enough to start.

But the tune hummed on Janie's street was quite different from her own, in a much more minor key, with a hint of misery:

> Sometimes I'm up, sometimes I'm down,
> Sometimes I'm almost to the ground, O yes, Lord!
> Nobody knows the trouble I see,
> Nobody knows but Jesus—

Except, of course, Janie Barrett. She could hardly help knowing about why her street hummed like that: "If only the poor things had a *sittingroom*," she would think. "But packed in boarding-houses, several to a bedroom, is no good. Folks need parlors to sit in and play in and talk in. A parlor could seem like a palace." And so her tune and their tune began to haunt her and to taunt her whenever she opened her checkbook and counted again to be sure that yes! she could start the bathroom anytime now. But something always talked back at her, about how a bathroom would benefit only herself and her husband; whereas a parlor— a big parlor, long and wide and high—would have plenty of room for little old grannies to rest their tired bones in rocking chairs, or for aged old uncles to play checkers all day around tables. So that in the end the real dream won out and Janie Barrett built her "Palace of Delight" out in her own backyard: it took up every inch of space, for it was a large and lovely room to which the neighbors themselves gave the name.

And of course it was checkbook into prayerbook. But what made a Negro woman spend her savings so unselfishly, *"baptized into the feelings of the people"* (in John Woolman's grand old Quaker phrase)? Enough of Janie Barrett's past helps to explain her act, for she herself had been sometimes up, sometimes down, sometimes almost to the ground. *Down?* as the very poor child of a very poor widow life seemed to hold no happy future. *Up?* a white woman from the North took an immediate fancy to Janie, took her into her own home, treated her exactly as she treated her own daughters, same style clothes, hats, schooling, meals; with a fairy-tale angle at every turn. *Almost to the ground?* as the children in the household grew older and neighbors started gossiping, the white woman saw with dismay that she might be ruining the black girl's whole future by overriding social customs too fast. Much as she longed to have Janie stay forever, so Janie herself had the common sense to leave luxury and choose the practical mops and brooms at Hampton Institute. No contrast could have been more complete! But one day in the school library another vista opened after reading *All Sorts and Conditions of Men*. Her whole viewpoint was altered, and she chose the most backward backwoods school in all Georgia as the place to begin.

Then came marriage, and the small beloved cottage; with the exciting checkbook holding its secret; unsuspecting neighbors always envying her simple draperies, however, the modest row of silver spoons. And then, in George Eliot's significant sentence: "the invasion of our private lives by the larger destinies of mankind." So that the palace seemed almost a natural thing to do, remembering past ups, past downs.

But George Eliot has another comment which also has Janie Barrett's name written all over it: "The world is full of hopeful analogies and handsome dubious eggs called possibilities." Such eggs proved irresistible! And the most dubious of all was the persistent question: *"Who needs happiness most?"* The answer was inescapable: Negro girls! underprivileged; undervalued; undereducated; underloved; with no hope of a beautiful background such as Janie's had been, and no earthly way of bettering themselves; unless . . .

No egg could have been more dubious. No possibility more impossible. But, singlehanded, Mrs. Barrett set herself to give up the small cottage with the large palace in the backyard, in order to move to Peake, Virginia, to start an Industrial Home School for Girls. People in Peake protested violently until Janie won them over. It took time. It took patience. And it took everything in her checkbook, of course. But her heart kept humming its own prayer: "O yes, Lord! O yes, Lord!"

It would almost seem as if once again George Eliot could sum up Janie Barrett in a sentence: *"One must be poor to know the luxury of giving."* But then Henry Wood Murdock moves into this chapter where he surely belongs, although he has plenty of money, but matches Janie in more ways than one. For he lives in a farmhouse without plumbing; without electricity; without a telephone. And yet he owns rich oil wells and rich gas wells in Oklahoma.

When people pry into why he does not buy modern improve-
ments for his house, Mr. Murdock gets a faraway look in his eye
and says softly: "Well now, it's like this. It's going to cost us all
of $50,000 to build that Home for the Aged, over in Charlotte,
and we're putting up the Children's Home, too. Then there's our
$10,000 pledge for the North Carolina College to pay off. And
we want to help build our Community Church here, of course.
So maybe we might get some modern fixings when all this is
cared for. But until then, not a useless cent spent on the Mur-
docks."

If people reply: "But why? Why when you have all those
gushers earning new money?"

Harvey Murdock has only one answer: "When God came into
my life He changed everything, and I'm simply giving everything
back to Him."

Catholics often take certain relics to Rome in the hope that the
Pope may bless them. But a far more religious requirement for
Protestants might be to kneel and literally turn each new checkbook into a Prayerbook by copying inside its front cover this 400-
year-old petition from Queen Elizabeth's Prayerbook of 1559:

They that are ensnared and entangled in the extreme penury of
things needful for the body, cannot set their minds upon Thee, O
Lord, as they ought to do; but when they be disappointed of the
things which they so mightily desire, their hearts are cast down and
quail from excess of grief. Have pity upon them, therefore, O merciful Father, and relieve their misery from Thine incredible riches, that
by Thy removing of their urgent necessity, they may rise up to Thee
in mind. Thou, O Lord, providest enough for all men with Thy most
liberal and bountiful hand, but whereas Thy gifts are, in respect of
Thy goodness and free favor, made free unto all men, we through our
naughtiness and niggardship and distrust do make them private and
peculiar. Correct Thou the things which our iniquity hath put out of
order, let Thy goodness supply that which our niggardliness hath
plucked away. Amen.

And then, on the back cover, underneath all those checks
which are soon to be written, some such personal queries as these:

God sees the stubs of this checkbook.
Did I really need to spend this particular money?
Was it a passing fancy?
How does it match up in size with my benevolence checks?
What much more miraculous, lasting thing could I have brought to
   pass in the world with this same amount?

Art thou poor, yet has thou golden slumbers?
   O sweet content!
Art thou rich, yet in thy mind perplexed?
   O punishment!
Dost thou laugh to see how fools are vexed
To add to golden numbers, golden numbers?
O sweet content! O sweet, O sweet content!
   Work apace, apace, apace, apace;
   Honest labour bears a lovely face;
Then hey nonny nonny, hey nonny nonny.

Canst drink the waters of the crispéd spring!
   O sweet content!
Swimmest thou in wealth, yet sink'st in thine own tears?
   O punishment!
Then he that patiently want's burden bears
No burden bears, but is a king, a king!
O sweet content! O sweet, O sweet content!
   Work apace, apace, apace, apace,
   Honest labour bears a lovely face;
Then hey nonny nonny, hey nonny nonny.
                              Thomas Dekker, 1570-1632

Worldliness is an immense number of allowable details
issuing in an unallowable end. This is partly from the
accumulation, and partly from the hold the details have

*on our affections. Things, which are not wrong in them-
selves, become wrong when they stand between us and
God, unspeakably wrong when they usurp God's place
in our hearts. We do not see the real malice of the separate component parts of worldliness, because we do not
really know ourselves, and are thus unable to estimate
the bad effects, or even the peculiar effects, which make
this or that illicit amusement become inexpedient in our
case, or a certain amount of it downright poison.*

Frederick Faber, *Self-Deceit,* 1859

17

MURDER IN THE CATHEDRAL EVERY SUNDAY AT 11 A.M.

. . . seeing they crucify to themselves the Son of God afresh, and
put Him to an open shame.   HEBREWS 6:6

It is a tremendous thing to stand on the same steps of the high
altar in Canterbury Cathedral where Thomas à Becket was
murdered several centuries ago. It is a tenderer thing to have the
guide confide in you: "Lady, when St. Thomas was a baby, his
mother used to weigh him in a basket on his birthdays, then fill
the basket with food and clothes and coins up to the same weight
—in order that the poor might also rejoice with her over her son!"
If your blood runs cold that so fair a child could come to so foul
an end in so sacred a spot, then say to yourself that history repeats itself: since some mother's son is still being murdered in

every church every Sunday at 11 a.m., year in and year out, from Eden until now.

For you do realize, don't you, that the first murder on record grew out of the first worship service at the first altar? Actually the book of Genesis may make your blood run even colder than T. S. Eliot's *Murder in the Cathedral*—since it sounds as modern as next Sunday morning's jealousy at offering time:

Abel was a keeper of sheep, but Cain was a tiller of the ground. And in the process of time it came to pass that Cain brought of the fruit of the ground an offering unto the Lord. And Abel, he also brought of the firstlings of his flock and of the fat thereof. And the Lord had respect unto Abel and to his offering: but unto Cain and to his offering he had not respect. And Cain was very wroth, and his countenance fell. And the Lord said unto Cain: "Why art thou wroth? and why is thy countenance fallen? If thou doest well, shalt thou not be accepted? and if thou doest not well, sin lieth at the door." . . . And Cain talked with Abel his brother: and it came to pass, when they were in the field, that Cain rose up against Abel his brother, and slew him. And the Lord said unto Cain: "Where is Abel thy brother?" And he said: "I know not; am I my brother's keeper?" And He said: "What hast thou done? the voice of thy brother's blood crieth unto me from the ground. And now thou art cursed from the earth, which had opened her mouth to receive thy brother's blood from thy hand; when thou tillest the ground, it shall not henceforth yield unto thee her strength; a fugitive and a vagabond shalt thou be in the earth." And Cain said unto the Lord: "My punishment is greater than I can bear. Behold, thou hast driven me out this day from the face of the earth; and from Thy face shall I be hid; I shall be a fugitive and a vagabond in the earth; and it shall come to pass that everyone that findeth me shall slay me." And the Lord said unto him: "Therefore whosoever slayeth Cain, vengeance shall be taken on him sevenfold." And the Lord set a mark upon Cain, lest any finding him should kill him.

Alarming? *To be plainly marked as God's own property?* Genesis 4 goes on to add that Cain went forth from the presence of the Lord to dwell in the land of Nod, east of Eden. It is no play on the words to acknowledge that the land of Nod is that semi-asleep, semi-awake state in which church members live and move and have their being Mondays through Saturdays, walking down the center aisle on Sundays, still as somnambulists. There is no other institution on earth whose membership is made up solely of sinners. A prison cribs, cabins and confines its sinners under lock and key. But the church releases each sinner back into circulation between Sundays. Presumably redeemed. Presumably washed. Rewashed. Re-rewashed. Until even the worldling expects something superlative about the Christian, or why should he say so cynically: "Now there's a sorry specimen of a saint for you"?

The test for a sorry specimen always turns out to be the thing dearest to his heart: the thing he is thinking about all day. And if his offering envelope laid on the altar every Sunday at 11 a.m. commits murder, that tells his true status, too.

Rather recently the National Cash Register Company has developed, by a secret process, a specially-sensitized paper for bank deposit slips which eliminates the carbon backing on the top slip, so that the mere pressure of the pen on this upper sheet now appears on the underneath sheet as plain as day. *As plain as day?* As plain as Sunday, also! For in the sight of God a church envelope in the collection basket is simply a deposit slip, showing to heaven above and to earth below what this so-called Christian is putting into the Kingdom of God. But suppose the Cash Register Company should invent, next, some ecclesiastically-sensitized litmus paper for church envelopes, so that while they were being dropped from the Christian's hand into a collection basket the envelopes could turn into some telltale color, with some much more appropriate Bible text truthfully replacing: "The Lord loveth a cheerful giver"?

This would be the mark of Cain, literally acknowledging the contagious state of mind and conscience transferred from fingertips to envelopes No. 1, 2, 3, 4, or 5.

1. *ADMISSION:* I admit that I am a Christmas church member and an Easter church member (liking both holly and lilies),

frankly admitting name and Bible footnote about me: "*Demas hath forsaken me, having loved this present world, and is departed unto T* . . ." (Theater? Town Hall? Tea dance? T.V.? Tasmania?) For when Abel Tasman discovered Tasmania he said, frankly: "Gold and silver are especially to be sought for, but keep the natives ignorant of the value of the same; appear as if you were not greedy for them; and if gold or silver are offered to you in any barter, you must pretend that you do not care for these metals, showing them copper, zinc and lead as if these metals were of more value to you." I, too, try to appear as if I were not greedy. (At which the offering envelope promptly turns green.)

Horace Bushnell made a penetrating list of all who might be excused from giving to missions: those who believe that it is "every man for himself" in this world. Those who believe that Jesus Christ made a mistake when He said: "Go ye into all the world and preach the gospel to every creature." Those who regret that missionaries ever came to our ancestors with this good news. Those who believe that the gospel is not the power of God and cannot save anybody. Those who want no share in the final victory. Those who believe they are not accountable to God for the money entrusted to them. Those who are prepared to accept the final sentence: "Inasmuch as ye did it not to one of these, ye did it not to me."

2. *OMISSION:* Families frequently say in funeral announcements: "Please omit flowers." But I omit offerings, too! For this isn't my funeral. And I couldn't care less that the verse on my World Relief envelope reads: "I saw under the altar the souls of them that were slain for the word of God, and for the testimony which they held; and they cried with a loud voice, saying: 'How long, O Lord, holy and true, dost thou not judge and avenge our blood on them that dwell on the earth?'" Acts 18:17 tells both my name and my mood: "Gallio cared for none of these things." (The moment I touch the offering envelope it turns blue as indigo.)

St. Vincent de Paul once made a sinner, who would not go to

communion, promise that each night for a week he would agree to kneel before the cross and kiss it three times, repeating with each kiss: "I don't care! I don't care! I don't care."

3. *INTERMISSION:* The moment has come to notice the Dives family sitting in their pew, in their usual purple and fine linen. Pleasant, prominent, prosperous; but (to borrow E. A. Robinson's phrase): *with little dollar signs in their eyes.* Sizing people up. Knowing to a T the salaries of all the other men sitting at the ends of other pews. In no way worshiping, of course; waiting, perhaps, for the intermission. For just as a coffee break is routine on weekdays, on Sundays shortly after 11 a.m. occurs that little intermission known as The Children's Sermon, which even Dives always drinks in with approval. On this particular Sunday Mrs. Dives dimpled with delight at the sight of her own grandchildren in their best bibs and tuckers, decorously filing up to receive little diplomas: "How cute!" she whispered ecstatically to her husband.

But out of the mouths of babes and sucklings came ordained strength that morning. For in their glee over surprise diplomas, each child promptly untied the ribbons and unrolled his scroll. (A Dead Sea Scroll? with a fragment from Jeremiah 22?) And although Johnny can't read on Monday in school, on Sunday in church his sound went forth through all the sanctuary and his words to the ends of the pews. Harmless as doves, deadly as serpents—read in perfect unison by everybody's grandchild:

Woe unto him that buildeth his house by unrighteousness, and his chambers by wrong; that useth his neighbor's service without wages, and giveth him not for his work; that saith: I will build me a wide house and large chambers, and cutteth him out windows; and it is ceiled with cedar, and painted with vermilion.

Shalt thou reign because thou closest thyself in cedar? did not thy father eat and drink, and do judgment and justice, and then it was well with him? He judged the cause of the poor and needy; then it was well with him; was not this to know me? saith the Lord. But thine eyes and thine heart are for thy covetousness, and for to shed innocent blood, and for oppression, and for violence, to do it. . . . I spoke unto thee in thy prosperity; but thou saidst: I will not hear. This hath been thy manner from thy youth, that thou obeyedst not my voice. The wind shall eat up all thy pastors, and thy lovers shall go into captivity: surely then shalt thou be ashamed, and confounded for all thy wickedness.

"Good gracious! What on earth does this mean?" Dives asked.

But his purple offering envelope told in full:

"Denominationally, why is your pastor's salary still a disgrace? Less than you pay your chauffeur—who did not go into debt to get a college education, nor buy books to refresh his soul and yours, nor send his children through college.

"Denominationally, how can you justify paying less than the minimum wage to janitors and cleaning women?

"Denominationally, where is the justice in employing Negro secretaries in any church office and daring to call it *'interracial goodwill,'* when actually you do it because you can pay them less than white secretaries doing comparable work?"

Thine eyes and thine heart are for thy covetousness, and for to shed innocent blood, and for oppression, and for violence, to do it. . . . O earth! earth! earth! hear the word of the Lord.

4. *PERMISSION:* It is necessary to have a permit to carry a gun; but, quite as deadly in this case, a permit to kiss a Friend: "Judas Iscariot, one of the twelve, went unto the chief priests, to betray Him unto them. And when they heard it, they were glad, and promised to give him money. And he sought how he might conveniently betray Him." No wonder that in Dante's "Inferno" the last circle of hell contains the souls of those who betrayed their masters—Dante's guide being Judas, who has "his head within, and outside plies his legs." (This envelope, of course, turns jet black—for all those other Black Fridays when my own thirty pieces of silver have also betrayed my Master.)

Over a hundred years ago a poet wrote this latest decalogue:

Thou shalt have one God only; who
Would be at the expense of two?
No graven images may be
Worshipped, except the currency:
Swear not at all; for, for thy curse
Thine enemy is none the worse:
At church on Sunday to attend
Will serve to keep the world thy friend:
Honor thy parents; that is, all
From whom advancement may befall:
Thou shalt not kill; but needst not strive
Officiously to keep alive:
Do not adultery commit;
Advantage rarely comes of it:
Thou shalt not kill; but needst not strive
When 'tis so lucrative to cheat:
Bear not false witness; let the lie
Have time on its own wings to fly:
Thou shalt not covet; but tradition
Approves all forms of competition.

Arthur Hugh Clough, 1819-1861

5. *REMISSION:* Here a Christian feels deeply grateful to the
Catholic Church for their courtesy in giving the good thief on the
cross a name—St. Dismas; for with him I too both acknowledge
and receive remission for my sins; as he said to the scornful thief:
"We received the due rewards for our deeds, but this Man has
done nothing amiss . . . Lord, remember me when Thou comest
into Thy Kingdom." Jesus instantly answering: "Today thou
shalt be with me in paradise." (The offering envelope which
began by being scarlet turns slowly white in my fingers, becoming
beautiful.)

I saw Eternity the other night
Like a great Ring of pure and endless light,
    All calm, as it was bright,
And round beneath it, Time in hours, days, years
    Driven by the spheres

Like a vast shadow moved, in which the world
  And all her train were hurled . . .
The fearful miser on a heap of rust
Sat pining all his life there, did scarce trust
  His own hands with the dust,
Yet would not place one piece above, but lives
  In fear of thieves.
Thousands there were as frantic as himself
  And hugged each one his pelf . . .
Yet some, who all this while did weep and sing,
And sing, and weep, soared up into the Ring,
  But most would use no wing.
O fools (said I) thus to prefer dark night
  Before true light,
To live in grots, and caves, and hate the day
  Because it shows the way,
The way which from this dead and dark abode
  Leads up to God.
A way where you might tread the Sun, and be
  More bright than he.
But as I did their madness so discuss
  One whispered thus:
This Ring the Bridegroom did for none provide
  But for His bride.

                              Henry Vaughn, 1622-1695

6. *COMMISSION:* This is the only offering envelope which remains the same after being touched by the donor, both beginning and ending a glorious golden color, since every offering envelope is, of course, *a Love Letter to the World,* full of the loving-kindness of God. The legend on it reads: "With great power gave the apostles witness of the resurrection of the Lord Jesus; and great grace was upon them all. Neither was there any among them that lacked . . . for distribution was made unto every man as he had need. . . . And Barnabas (which being interpreted is Son of Consolation) having land, sold it, and brought the money, and laid it at the apostles' feet."

The Sons of Barnabas are therefore both the glory and the consolation of the church on Sunday at 11 a.m. They accept their divine commission to go, to tell, to share. And in this spontaneous acceptance prove that they seek not *murder* but:

METAMORPHOSIS IN THE CHURCH EVERY SUNDAY AT 11 A.M.

In the gospel story of the transfiguration, "metamorphosis" is the Greek word used in the text when our Lord's face became luminous, His very presence dazzling.

This is the sort of changed person whom Gordon Cosby seeks in the Church of the Saviour in Washington when, on a typical Sunday at 11 a.m. (January 15, 1956) his printed order of worship included:

Let me come into the church of God to meet the Spirit of God; not to give religion an hour, but to live in the eternal; not to maintain a decorous habit, but to bow in the Holy place before the Holy One; not to judge the words of a preacher, but to draw life from the Word and Truth everlasting; not to be soothed by music, but to sing from the heart divine praises; not that mine eyes roam over architecture or congregation, but that my soul look up to the King in His beauty, and my heart plead the needs of Thy children; not that my thoughts escape out into the world, but that they be still, and know that Thou art God.

Let me go, and go again, into the house of the Lord, and be glad, and give thanks, and adore my King and my God."

THE CALL TO WORSHIP:

Minister: "Blessed be the hour, O Christ, in which Thou wast born, and the hour in which Thou didst die; blessed be the dawn of Thy rising again, an the high day of Thine ascending;

People: "O most merciful and mighty Redeemer Christ, let all times be the time of our presence with Thee, and of Thy dwelling in us."

THE PRAYER OF CONFESSION:

Minister: "Lord Jesus, let us condemn our sin in Thy company, face to face with Thy holiness . . .

Unison: "Though I bow my head and heart in shame, still let Thy hand clasp mine. Let it be Thy love which searches me, Thy sorrow which wakes my sorrow; and deepens it for knowing I have wounded my Friend, my Master, my God.

"Yea, Lord, I have crucified, and crucify Thee again, by many different sins, by often repeating each, by obeying and crowning my self.

"Forgive me, forgive me, Lord Jesus; Lord Jesus, wash me clean; Lord Jesus, make me whole; Lord Jesus, hold me fast in Thy company forever."

THE ASSURANCE OF PARDON (*to be prayed by the minister*):

"O our God, from Thee we proceed; to Thee we belong; Thee we adore. Thou art the Fountain of a thousand springs of mercy, pardon and loving-kindness; Source of light, Well of grace; Thee we adore.

"Thine is the voice of many waters now loud, now low, and lovely always; calling us to Thy work and ours; calling to faith, to hope, to resolve, to love, the greatest of these; Thee we adore.

"Fountain of joy and melody in the heart; Fountain of peace and quietness of soul, Fountain of will to do Thy will, Thee we adore.

"Spring and Fountain and River and Flood, O God most holy, from Thee we proceed, to Thee we belong, our Beginning, our Goal, our All, Thee we adore."

What think ye of Christ, friend?
When all's done and said?
Like you this Christianity or not?
It may be false, but will you wish it true?
Has it your vote to be so, if it can?
                    Robert Browning, 1812-1889

The lost days of my life until today,
　What were they, could I see them on the street
　Lie as they fell? Would they be ears of wheat
Sown once for food, but trodden into clay?
Or golden coins squandered and still to pay?
　Or drops of blood dabbling the guilty feet?
I do not see them here; but after death
　God knows the faces I shall see,

Each one a murdered self, with low last breath:
"I am thyself,—what hast thou done to me?"
"And I—and I—thyself," (lo, each one saith,)
"And thou thyself to all eternity!"
                    Dante Gabriel Rossetti, 1828-1882

Will those of you who have been putting buttons in
the collection basket, kindly put in your own buttons,
and not those from the church upholstery.
            Notice in Scotch Presbyterian Church, Scotland

18

SOME OF MY BEST FRIENDS ARE TITHERS

He that is faithful in that which is least is faithful also in much.
                                        Luke 16:10

Yes, some of my best friends are tithers. But more of them
aren't, and wouldn't be for the world. "Just an old Jewish
custom," they say, looking down their noses in a somewhat su-
perior fashion; as if, by the nineteen-fifties, all such giving was
outworn, outdated, and even a trifle outrageous, for they usually
add: "since I suppose you agree that we are all Christians, don't
you?"

Really rather rash, all things considered. Especially all Jewish
things considered. For the Jews not only brought all their tithes
into the storehouse on the Sabbath, as God had prospered them,
but there was an almost alarming list of other orders about diet
and gifts in Leviticus 23:6-22 which Dr. Moffatt translates too
clearly for complacency:

On the fifteenth day of the same month the festival of unleavened bread in honor of the Eternal begins . . . for the seven days you must make a fire-offering to the Eternal . . . you shall bring a sheaf from the first-fruits of your harvest to the priest who shall wave the sheaf to and fro before the Eternal that you may be accepted. On the day you wave the sheaf, you must offer an unblemished yearling male-lamb as a burnt-offering to the Eternal; its cereal-offering shall be a fifth of a bushel of fine flour, mixed with oil, as an offering to be burned to the Eternal for a soothing odor, the libation of wine being three pints. Till you have brought the offering for your God, you must not eat, neither bread nor grain, roasted or fresh. This is a standing rule for all time and for all the country.

From the day after the Sabbath, you shall count seven full weeks, and then you shall make a cereal-offering to the Eternal. You shall bring forward two loaves to be waved, made of a fifth of a bushel of fine flour, baked with dough, as first-fruits for the Eternal. With this bread you shall present seven unblemished yearling lambs, one young bullock, and two rams; they are to be a burnt-offering for the Eternal, with the usual cereal-offering and libation; also you shall offer a he-goat for a sin-offering, two yearling male-lambs as a recompense-offering; these the priest shall wave to and fro along with the bread of the first-fruits. This is a standing order for you and your descendents, for the whole country. When you reap your harvest you must not reap the field to the very corners, nor gather the stray ears of the harvest, but leave these for the poor folk and resident aliens: I am the Eternal your God.

This staggers today's tithers; they wonder if they have ever crossed even the first T in Tithing, or dotted the first i! Their values start shifting from that first rather virtuous sensation of having shared their required amount with God into wondering whether their tenth is a proper sum, after all. Yet how good their gladness in giving had been; almost a footnote on the Scripture: "When the burnt-offering began then the song of the Lord began also." But if the ancient Jews could rejoice over such serious sacrifices, what on earth should a nontithing Christian be giving? The answer is small but appalling: "ALL!"

It was our Lord Himself who asked this much of the rich young ruler, who "turned sorrowfully away: for he was rich." It was our Lord who praised the widow in the temple: for she was poor, "yet she has put in all that she had." Barnabas also gave all. Indeed, his generosity so impressed Ananias and Sapphira that they craved praise also and dramatically laid down their donation. "Is this all?" Peter asked them. "All!" they replied, and died of their lie, since a tidy nest egg was secretly saved up at home.

The widow's "Mite Box" is world famous. But what Woman's Society has ever distributed to its members "Sapphira's Secret Sacrificial Cheating Box"? The world church still thinks with gratitude of those women who generously supported the journeyings of Jesus and the twelve. As for Zaccheus, we have a kindred feeling with his conscience when he said to our Lord, the moment He stepped inside the front door: "The half of my goods I give to the poor, and if I have taken anything wrongfully I will restore four-fold." Europeans know an old legend: that every morning after Jesus left, Zaccheus could be seen leaving the house with a pitcher of water. This was too much for his wife's curiosity, of course; so he told her he went to water the roots of the old sycamore tree he had sat in when Jesus passed by—he wanted to make it last as long as he did. A reminder of the hour of his courageous clean-sweep? Or to revive that fleeting second when the pure in heart saw God?

The fact is that friends who are tithers are faithful about little and about much. Whereas friends who look down their noses at an old Jewish custom, might better look into their bankbooks, to see if they are indeed giving "all." William Blake found the telling words for this:

He who would do good to another must do it in Minute Particulars:
General good is the plea of the Scoundrel, hypocrite and flatterer,
For Art and Science cannot exist but in minutely organized Particulars
And not in generalizing demonstrations of the rational power.

William Colgate is a case of Minute Particulars. For as a twelve-year-old boy from a poor family, he left England in 1795 to make some sort of a future for himself in America. While walking along a towpath from Baltimore to New York a canal boat captain asked what he was good at, and young William said: "Well, about all I know is making tallow candles and soft soap" —as if this wasn't much. But the captain got right down to Minute Particulars: "Figure it out thisaway—won't somebody get to be top soapmaker in New York? Well then, why shouldn't this fellow be you? Only thing is, you better give your heart to Christ, right off. Then take Him into partnership with you, too, and give Him the ten cents out of every dollar you make. See to it that you make an honest pound. So let's get down on our knees and tell God what you've decided on and get Him into the business."

With such Minute Particulars in mind, young Colgate reached New York. He joined a Baptist church. He joined a soap firm, also. Before long he rose to be manager. Within a few years he started his own soap manufacturing business. But always the particularly honest soap; the particularly honest pound. And always the particular tenth of every dollar for God's work entered in a particular ledger labeled: "Account with the Lord." As his enterprises grew increasingly large, he also increased his one-tenth to two-tenths to five-tenths. When he found that he no longer needed any of this income for himself, he set up certain Minute Particulars of a plan to put all his profits into Christian philanthropies while he lived, with the same Particulars in his will.

Many a tither and nontither probably is saying at this point: "What a coincidence—I used Colgate soap this very morning! I wish more American businessmen were like him!"

That wish is coming true in Mexico, this moment—for it would be provincial to think that Minute Particulars in the *U.S.A.* are not equally *American* in Mexico, since we do not compose the whole continent, nor all the Christian laymen. For Señor Fernando Rodriguez has been a name in Mexico City ever since the day in 1940 when he dedicated his new six-story furniture store in a manner nobody in town had ever seen before, for who had ever consecrated his business to God, publicly? On a platform gorgeous with flags and flowers? With all his store employees and their families on the front seats? And hundreds of fascinated citizens saying "Oh!" in Spanish? For the service began by Señor Rodriguez's announcement: "The minister of my church will open this ceremony with prayer."

This Presbyterian layman then told his life story, from the day he started so poor, aged fifteen, to this particular moment of prosperity, dedicating his *"Muebleria Nueva"* to God: "For years ago I made Him my partner, and to God I owe the growth of my business."

For one thing, he explained how he began by setting "fixed prices" on his pieces of furniture, instead of the old Spanish custom of bargaining back and forth over every purchase. People said he would surely fail. But today he does a three million dollar business. He pays much better salaries than the average in similar stores. At a Christmas party all the employees receive an extra month's pay as a gift. Add to all these Minute Particulars the rare one that in a Catholic city he is greatly honored, that half of his five dozen employees are also active Protestants, and that the Boss himself was their evangelist. His Bible classes are popular. For more than thirty years he has been an elder in the largest Presbyterian church in Mexico City, and for twenty years he has been superintendent of the Sunday School. More recently his denomination elected him Moderator of the General Assembly of the Presbyterian Church of Mexico. During his term of office he achieved another dream of his life in making his denomination nationally self-supporting, with no need for donations from across the border.

As a tither who took God into partnership so long ago he could say frankly that Christian giving cannot stop with the tenth, which belongs to the Lord, anyhow; but if a man does not want to be an unprofitable servant he must go far beyond the tithe.

This he himself does. Nobody knew how far beyond this generous giver had gone until a close friend discovered that the amount was never less than $3,500 a month.

But rich as he is, this Mexican merchant would feel at home in the Church of South India where all converts are required to accept the same Minute Particulars which have governed his own use of his purse, his Bible, his behavior. These seven "Standards" in India are:

1. Attend all services of worship;
2. Daily private worship;
3. Attend a class of doctrine;
4. Must learn to read the Bible for himself;
5. Must tithe;
6. Must eat a meal with someone of another caste, and thus lose caste with one's own, and prove he is a Christian;
7. Must win someone else to be a Christian.

Such is the stern stuff of stewardship, the sharing of all of life in Minute Particulars. There may be other churches in our country requiring standards as high, but the Church of the Saviour in Washington, D.C. stands as witness that it can be done, that in the very testing there can be triumph.

As William James said: "If one-tenth of the things we say we believe as Christians are true, then we ought to be ten times as excited as we are!" Every visitor in Gordon Cosby's church senses this something special: for his 52 members obviously live in some tenth-degree excitement of mingled discipline and delight. Lest they forget, each Sunday bulletin reprints on its back page:

MEMBERSHIP COMMITMENT OF THE CHURCH OF THE SAVIOUR

I come today to join a local expression of the Church, which is the body of those on whom the call of God rests to witness to the grace and truth of God.

I recognize that the function of the Church is to glorify God in adoration and sacrificial service, and to be God's missionary to the world, bearing witness to God's redeeming grace in Jesus Christ.

I believe as did Peter that Jesus is the Christ, the Son of the living God.

I unreservedly and with abandon commit my life and destiny to Christ, promising to give Him a practical priority in all the affairs of life. I will seek first the Kingdom of God and his Righteousness.

I commit myself, regardless of the expenditures of time, energy, and money to becoming an informed, mature Christian.

I believe that God is the total owner of my life and resources. I give God the throne in relation to the material aspect of my life. God is the owner. I am the ower. Because God is a lavish giver I too shall be lavish and cheerful in my regular gifts.

I will seek to be Christian in all relations with my fellowman, with other nations, groups, classes, and races.

I will seek to bring every phase of my life under the Lordship of Christ.

When I move from this place I will join some other expression of the Christian Church.

All Israelites are mutually accountable to one another. In a boat at sea, one of the men began to bore a hole in the bottom of the boat. On being remonstrated with, he answered: "I am only boring under my own seat." "Yes," said his fellow passengers, "but when the sea rushes in we shall all be drowned with you." So it is with Israel. Its weal or its woe is in the hands of every individual Israelite.

from *The Talmud*

To the eye of a miser a guinea is far more beautiful than the sun and a bag worn with the use of money has more beautiful proportions than a vine filled with grapes. As a man is, so he sees.

When the sun rises, do you not see a round disk of fire something like a gold piece? O no, no, I see an innumerable company of the Heavenly host crying Holy,

Holy, Holy is the Lord God Almighty. I do not question
my bodily eye any more than I would question a window.
I look through it and not with it.

William Blake, 1757-1827

19

PENNYWISE AND OTHERWISE

For who hath despised the day of small things? For they shall
rejoice, and shall see the plummet in the hands of Zerubbabel,
with those seven; they are the eyes of the Lord which run to and
fro through the whole earth.   ZECHARIAH 4:10

Nothing could be smaller than two mites. So that it must still
seem astonishing to the Widow to be greeted gaily and daily on
the golden streets of heaven by all sorts and conditions of men:
"So you're the little woman who started this big Mite Box
Movement? It may surprise you to know that I can't remember a
time when my own wife didn't have such a box sitting right out
on her bureau, and every once in a while I would hear a clink,
and there she would be dropping in a penny or two, and I would
always say: 'Now what's *that* one for?' and she would say: 'Oh,
for gratitude, and for grace and gumption'; and sometimes I
guess she gave from sheer relief that something bothersome
had been banished overnight. But I kept telling her: 'Honey, if
you ask me, that's blooming little to give Almighty God! You
wouldn't dare tip anybody else that little and not get it thrown
right back in your face! Let me remind you that the original
Mite Box Widow gave all that she had—every last red cent; true

or false?' And my wife used to say, sort of saucylike: 'Yes, but I'm not a widow!' So now that she really is one, I notice that whenever she drops in a nickel or two, she sort of stops, sadly, and chases it up with a dime or two, like I always thought she ought to, or even a whole buck—if the Mission Board had only made that slot big enough! I have a peeve about those people down there at headquarters—that slot of theirs won't even take a fifty-cent piece; now, I ask you, is that good psychology, to keep expecting only petty cash? Anyhow, madam, I just thought I'd look you up and tell you that you sure have made friends and influenced people, like Dale Carnegie said. You wouldn't know him from Adam, of course, but his whole tune was that small things matter plenty, such as remembering the other party's name the next time you meet on the street. Which reminds me— would you mind telling me yours? For the Bible doesn't always give a fellow all he wants to know about his favorites, and you've been sort of a Pin-Up Girl down in our house all these years!"

It is also to be hoped that such a saved soul could find much in common with St. Teresa of Avila. For she used to go walking barefoot across Spain seeking to save the churchwomen of her day from their own too-easy Christian living. Pledged to poverty and obedience, plagued all her life by opposition and open hostility from prosperous churchmen who preferred wealthy ecclesiastical establishments, still Teresa serenely went around founding more and more houses where women could live and learn disciplined Christlikeness. When money was scarce for going on to the next place she simply said: "Teresa and three cents can do nothing. But God and Teresa and three cents can do anything!"

Generations later, another earth-moving woman duplicated Teresa's saintly simplicity. For there was that dark day when Martha Berry dared to ask Henry Ford for a million dollars for her school and he gave her a dime. But what was ten cents good for, when she herself had already given up her own home in Georgia to take in every possible mountaineer boy and girl, until now there was no more room and not nearly enough equipment?

But—a dime is a dime. At least enough to buy a bag of peanuts. She set her schoolboys to planting them. The crop was prolific; and she had every nut planted, also. The next crop was large enough to divide—part to plant, part to sell in bags down at the nearby country crossroads. She made a scrupulous annual accounting of all such sales across the years until at last she could write Henry Ford, triumphantly: "Remember that dime you gave me? Well, Sir, I invested it in peanuts and now it has finally earned enough to buy a piano for our music students! How's that for dividends?"

It was so dramatic a way to spend both sides of a dime that Mr. Ford invited her to Detroit, fed her his favorite soybean dinner, and gave her the belated million dollars then and there; followed by other millions through the years.

This same indomitable spirit of a gentlewoman-with-a-dream took Martha Berry into the White House, to win the confidence and help of Theodore Roosevelt, and into Andrew Carnegie's Pullman car for breakfast, followed by a handsome contribution for her famous "book-larnin'" institution, until now the Berry Schools cover the largest campus in the world, with more than one hundred buildings. Built by the students themselves, across the past fifty years, as part of their training.

At this point in low income but large outgo, consider also Sue Weddell—a living footnote on the wise old saying: "Handsome is as handsome does." For although she has always been lovely to look at you will probably agree that, with her legacy, Miss Weddell answered the question: "Mirror, mirror, on the wall, who is fairest of them all?"

Oh! what a wonderful morning when that long legal envelope arrived in the mail stating that fifteen years after the death of her uncle, Joseph K. Weaver, a residue of his estate had been discovered, and would therefore be distributed among his thirty-five inheritors, including herself. Including also her two sisters and her five brothers.

Instantly these scattered heirs started expensive and excited long-distance telephone calls to one another, from places as far apart as Chicago, New York, Springfield and Washington, D.C.; with everybody daydreaming deliciously over trips they could now afford, mortgages they could pay off, houses they could paint, two cars in the garage, et cetera. After which they held their breath in suspense as they sat watching for the postman to bring the next important envelope from "dear Uncle Joe."

What a letdown, therefore, when the envelopes came and each check amounted to exactly 43 cents! Wires were busy again as brothers called brothers and sisters called sisters. Then, as far as it went, the heirs squandered their substance in riotous living; all except Sister Sue. She found herself suddenly remembering Uncle Joe with deepened tenderness: how he had put her through college, how she had spent Christmases and Easters at his house; somehow it seemed impossible to squander such a sacred sum as this tiny legacy. For she was a Secretary of the Foreign Missions Conference of North America, and knew that sometimes small sums can go a long way on this earth, working wonders.

And in no time at all these wonders began. For Sue Weddell mailed her legacy to Edna Beekman in China. "What can this do in your mission?" she asked. It could do plenty! For the rates of exchange were such at the moment that her 43 cents instantly became $8.16, enough to buy cod liver oil for sick Chinese babies, enough to supply lunches for three months for little Glory, the daughter of the Chinese cook at the Girl's School in Kulangsu, across the bay from Amoy. While all this was happening overseas, the legacy began growing by leaps and bounds in America. For Miss Weddell was on a speaking trip across Michigan and Wisconsin. In Grand Rapids she happened to tell a few women at a small luncheon party about the miracle of little Glory. By Kalamazoo, the chairman of the public meeting was asking: "Won't you please tell us your legacy story?" Back in New York, at another large meeting, Mrs. Romig announced: "I see Sue Weddell in the back of the church. Will she please come forward and tell us . . ."

That did it!

The next thing anyone knew the Y.W.C.A. of the City of New York chose this project for their Christmas offering. Then the Reformed Church in America chose it for their national "Children's Offerings." All this money was channeled through The Church Committee for China Relief, amounting in the end to many thousands of dollars: for "Little Glory" became a symbol that attracted people; and it seemed something special, too, to discover that in Chinese the name "Susan" was "Su Cheng," meaning "Deep Wisdom."

In 1946, when Miss Weddell had been sent as an observer to the formation of the United Nations in San Francisco, she was invited to a tea party, where Bill Henry interviewed her and wrote up her story in "Bill Henry's Column" in the *Los Angeles Times*. He told how the other heirs had squandered their legacies, adding: *"Not so, Sister Sue—she was a missionary! If you are interested, Sue's address is 156 Fifth Avenue, New York City."*

Moreover, if the Gentle Reader will consult his banker, he can discover that any forty-three cents represents a larger-than-usual annual interest on a $10 investment. And any canny shopper can save ten cents a day by buying less and dreaming more of his $36.50 at work for the greater glory of God on earth.

The poor man is not he who is without a cent, but he who is without a dream.

Harry Kemp, 1883-

Be not penny-wise; riches have wings, and sometimes they fly away of themselves, sometimes they must be set flying to bring in more. A great estate left to an heir is as a lure to all the birds of prey; defer not charities till death; for, certainly if a man weighs it rightly, he that doth so is rather liberal of another man's than his own.

Sir Francis Bacon, 1561-1626

Some have too much yet still do crave;
I little have, and seek no more.
They are but poor though much they have,
And I am rich with little more;
They poor, I rich; they beg, I give;
They lack, I leave; they pine, I live.

Sir Edward Dyer, 1550-1607

Give me not pallid ease;
Give me races to run,
Mountains to climb,
Burdens to lift.
Give me not nations to rule;
Give me people to love,
Worlds to serve
And God to know.

C. Ward Crampton (from calendar of Park Avenue
Christian Church, New York City)

20

A POOR MAN'S GUIDE AROUND
THE WORLD FOR $79.95

And it came to pass afterward, that He went throughout every
city and village, preaching and showing the glad tidings of the
Kingdom of God: and the twelve were with Him. And certain
women, which had been healed of evil spirits and infirmities,

Mary called Magdalene, out of whom went seven devils, and
Joanna, the wife of Chusa, Herod's steward, and Susanna and
many others, who ministered to Him of their substance.

LUKE 8:1-3

Some church members, of course, are merely neo-orthodox. But
ever since the movie *Around the World in 80 Days,* an astonishing number of Christians have also become Neophileasfogg and
Neonelliebly. Travel agencies have been swamped with all these
would-be travelers. Such guided tours are usually much more
carefully screened than that mentioned in Luke's gospel, above.
Imagine deliberately letting a trip be underwritten from day to
day and from place to place by twelve poor men and certain sick
women, only recently recovered from seven devils and the like.
Although this was a shining success, there is a much more modern
way of going around the world without nearly so much bother or
expenditure.

For too many globetrotters take their vacations the hard way.
They spend huge sums of money. They stand in line to buy tickets.
They buy clothes to suit a variety of climates. They pack and
unpack and repack everything every few days the rest of the
trip. Off they go, doomed to be uncomfortable until their return
—cramped into smaller quarters than home would provide, choosing food from menus with alarming prices listed beside every
item. *And feet?* Who ever figured on such constant tramping
around strange towns taking in such swift successions of strange
sights? Forever lingering behind to snap the picture ahead, forever hurrying to catch up with quicker tourists. All to be able
to show these sights to stay-at-home friends some evening, back
home, saying nonchalantly: "Well, there we are—beside the
Mediterranean!"

And sure enough, there they are, with a few tame waves as
backdrop, even a sail or two in the offing as more convincing local
color. The best part of this picture may be the chorus of friends

sighing enviously: "Some people certainly have all the luck!"

But Anatole France had another idea entirely: "What is traveling? Changing your place? By no means! Traveling is changing your ideas and enlarging your horizons."

Suppose that this could be done for as little as $79.95, with any poor Neophileasfogg or Neonelliebly able to stay right at home without benefit of boats, buses, baggage, tickets, trains, tips, hotels, motels, or laundry-done-and-returned-the-same-day? With a thousand tempting extra detours which no tourist ever yet stayed behind long enough to enjoy? For as the Chinese proverb suggests: "Traveling is a perfect nuisance, you tear your clothes and there is no one to mend them." But by this simple plan, clothes are to be laid down—just as on Palm Sunday—in order that Jesus Christ may have another triumphal entry into another new town, with everybody shouting: "Who is this who comes in the name of the Lord?" Imagine twelve jobless men and a few ex-invalid women financing this beautiful tour for $79.95, guaranteed to last one year, and warranted renewable if the tourist so requests. Could Thomas Cook and Son offer more for less? Ask Mr. Foster! And watch their clerks fainting in coils.

Other people may flock in droves to Italy, come spring. To collect Roman ruins, Florentine palaces, Uffizi pictures, Pompeian volcanoes, an Alp or two. But any Neonelliebly knows that live people are more immortal. And that several hundred orphans in Casa Materna can become anything on earth which the tourist helps them to become. The way a California sergeant during the war years discovered how many of these orphans had no shoes; that same afternoon he drove up to Casa Materna with a truck full of footballs, boxing gloves and baseball mitts: "Make shoes of them!" he called. And so leather shoes with wooden soles were possible. Another time a Lutheran chaplain from Wisconsin found the food supply shockingly low; he came back with a jeep full of bread and beefsteak. The Quakers sent also; Switzerland sent money over the Alps; Church World Service sent relief funds; and dozens of American Neophileasfoggs invited the Casa

Materna choir to come and sing in their home churches, where the wonderful story got told and retold. About Riccardo Santi's birthday, back in 1905. How Pastor Santi took a walk down a Naples street, and there sat Angelo and Rosetta on the curb, shivering, scared, and selling matches.

That did it! Forever after he would say: "I never ask myself if a child is suffering—I become that child!" And so, of course, he took Rosetta and Angelo home. His wife, Ersilia, was worried: how could there possibly be enough for two more on the pastor's small salary, with their own two children? Yet soon the good Pastor Santi brought home another orphan; then another; another. This kept on endlessly. Occasionally someone in his equally poor congregation would bring a bed, a chair, a dish or two. But it was always a struggle, especially with several hundred orphans. After World War I the Methodists bought the Santis a large house on the Bay of Naples. Enough *room*, at last. But still all those hungry children. It is comforting to know that $1 will provide food for one child for several days. Both Neonelliebly and Neophileasfogg feel firmly: "But out of our $79.95 we intend to stay longer, thank you. How much will $20 do?" Splendidly enough—complete food, shelter, clothing and education for more than two months! An irresistible idea, of course; this *bona fide* child walking around Naples, properly fed, living at 35 Corso Garibaldi, Portici, for sixty-two days, completely cared for. Thomas Cook and Son have nothing as delectable as a detour. (Checks, of course, are payable to Casa Materna Aid Society, at the above address.) Which simply means that on the very first leg of the journey: *Faith Raises a Family!*

But a stopover in France can prove equally provocative and picturesque. The slogan that fifty million Frenchman can't be wrong, *is* wrong, when more than thirty million of them are unconnected with any church. Working people and peasants in particular seem peculiarly isolated from Christian influences; and it is to reach these indifferent people that the McAll Mission has a simple hall, called a *Fraternité,* in twelve different industrial centers throughout France. Each such hall has a playground, a chapel, a health clinic with a nurse-evangelist, and a preacher. In America such a *Fraternité* would be called a "store-front church." A simple sign on the door may say: "TO WORKINGMEN—Some friends desire to speak to you of the love of Jesus Christ." Another fascinating aspect of McAll work is *La Bonne Nouvelle,* a chapel boat which plies the rivers, canals and back-country waterways of France. The captain-evangelist has living quarters on board, there is also a chapel; organ; etched glass windows showing pictures from the gospels. The boat anchors near some factory or industrial area. The organ starts playing. A congregation starts coming. Any Phileas, neo or not, who has ever hankered for his own private yacht, now has this enchanting chance to go sailing through a part of France which other tourists never get time to see, winning friends and influencing people whom other travelers never meet. What a candid candid snapshot: "Me and my yacht." The entire expense of an evening meeting with refreshments for a youth or adult group, would be $5; or, $10 will give the sick both medicine and services of a nurse-evangelist for a week. (American McAll Association, 23 East 26th Street, New York 10, N.Y.) Thirty dollars, gone? No! thirty dollars invested. With dependable dividends, for: *Faith Floats a Boat!*

It would be easy to linger longer in Europe; but suppose Phileas and Nellie have always had a yen for the Orient. Then they ought not to lose a minute in meeting the average farmer of Asia and the Middle East. He lives in a mud hut and plows one to three acres of land with a crooked stick. Most of the time he is hungry. Sickness is his constant companion. Tuberculosis, malaria and other diseases are as much a part of his life as the air he breathes. Without nourishing food, he tires easily. And his spirit grows heavy with discouragement. When he is harvesting his thin crop of rice or millet with an ancient sickle his feet drag, so that often he must work fifteen hours a day. Some years, when he is too weak to swing the sickle, the crop rots in the field. Phileas and Nellie will understand why his life expectancy is less than thirty years.

Where this poor fellow lives there are no schools and no doctors. He has never learned to read, nor to write his own name. Everybody takes advantage of his ignorance—the landlord takes two-thirds of his crop as rental, the moneylender charges exorbitant rates of interest. He is therefore always hopelessly in debt, and his yearly income hardly ever comes to more than $50. Multiply his plight by two-thirds of the people on earth who are also hungry, sick, despairing. The anxious Christian asks the burning question: "What on earth can I do?"

But with $49.95 left from unspent passage money, there is a fabulous and literally Biblical thing to be done: *Faith Feeds the Five Thousand!* For there is a "share-our-surplus" food bargain —for less than a penny a pound any Christian can send food from our vast national surplus for free distribution overseas, a gift from the people of the United States to the undernourished of the world. This distribution of foodstuffs is on such an efficient basis that $1 given through churches sends more than 100 pounds of food to hungry men, women and children! Since there is no cost for the surplus food, the necessary costs are then for distribution and administration.

Nothing could delight a world traveler more than this life-giving food to strengthen faith and friendship. Church World Service has wisely figured out what various sums of money will do—$10 will give rations of rice to more than 700 hungry persons for a week; $1 will give cheese to more than 200 protein-deficient persons in Asia daily for more than a week. Which would mean that $25 could do this for 5000 persons, not feeding them just once, as in the Bible—but with twelve baskets full to go on feeding them the next six days, also! This is almost too good to be true; but it is true. Neither Phileas nor Nellie should eat another mouthful until they too have worked this marvelous miracle. (The address is: Church World Service, Inc., 215 Fourth Avenue, New York 3, N.Y.) And every Neonelliebly should send for their free leaflet, . . . *And Ye Clothed Me,* with practical suggestions in regard to clothing, blankets, bedding, yard goods, et cetera.

There seems to lodge in almost every Neophileasfogg a foggy

sort of hope that some day, somehow, he too can go Big Game Hunting in Africa with the best of them. Well, the mists have rolled in splendor, at long last; the most terrific Hunt is on, down there; most spectacular specimens to hang on his wall— straight from Kenya and the recently ferocious Mau Mau tribe.

Under the sensible slogan H.E.A.R.: "Help East Africa Read," a campaign for books and primers has just been launched by the Committee of World Literacy and Christian Literature (156 Fifth Avenue, New York 10, N.Y.). A team of experts were sent to Tanganyika and Kenya to prepare primers and charts in eight languages spoken by about four million people. A whole series of simple readers were written for newly-literate village folk, under such titles as 1. *Reading for Joy Series:* Ilamba-Turu Legends, Tanganyika Folk Tales and Animal Tales, Song of Rejoicing; 2. *Village Improvement Series:* The People Learn to Read, The People Learn New Ways, Towards the Future; 3. *The Women's Readers:* My Home and My Children, The Women Learn New Things, The Women Help One Another, The Women Learn about Child Care; 4. *The Good News Series:* God Our Father, The Story of Jesus, The Question Book (a simple catechism).

A gift of $25 will pay for printing one hundred primers and books. Picture what a Hunt that will be—chasing down new words, new worlds, new ideas. Since there will not be enough left from the $79.95 passage money to buy a full hundred books, at least the $20 check can go partway toward waking up a whole village, with the most spellbinding trophies on earth: *Faith Hunts Big Game in Africa!* In case Nellie Bly has her doubts about this, let her send a three-cent stamp to the above-mentioned Lit.-Lit. organization for their exciting leaflet called *If*, with its actual picture chart and opening lesson showing how other illiterates learn to read.

With only $4.95 now left—where to go? what to see? whom to bless? School? Hospital? College? Since the first graduates have just received their diplomas in Tokyo from the International

Christian University, why not let both the Neos become "Foster-Alumni," and invest their small sums in some Japanese student's new diploma? For the University is a dream come true; it belongs to every Christian on earth. But how calamitous if funds failed— therefore: *Faith Presents a Diploma!* (The Japan International Christian University Foundation, Inc., 44 East 23rd Street, New York 10, N.Y.)

Every project renewable, reproducible each recurring year by armchair voyagers, to whom St. Augustine would give a warning:

Dost thou not see that God knowest all that is in the heavens and all that is in the earth? Three persons speak not privately together, but He is their fourth; nor five, but He is their sixth; nor fewer nor more, but wherever they be He is with them. Then on the day of resurrection He will tell them of their deeds; for God knoweth all things.

$

A CHARM FOR TRAVELERS

Here I ame and fourthe I mouste,
& in Iesus Criste is all my truste.
No wicked thing doe mee no dare,
Nother here nor elles whare.
The father with mee; the sonne with mee;
The holly gosste & the trienete,
Bee by-twyxte my gostely Enime & mee,
In the name of the father & the sonne &
*   the holly gosste. Amen.*
                    from an early English manuscript

Send me to the hearts without a home,
To the lives without a love,
To the crowd without a compass,

To the ranks without a refuge.
Send me to the children whom none have blessed,
To the famished whom none have fed,
To the sick whom none have visited,
To the demoniacs whom none have claimed,
To the fallen whom none have lifted,
To the lepers whom none have touched,
To the bereaved whom none have comforted,
Then shall I have the birthright of the first born;
Then shall I have the blessing of the mighty God of
    Jacob.

George Matheson, 1842-1906

They change their climate, not their disposition, who run
beyond the sea.

Horace, 65-8 B.C.

21

1040, AND ALL THAT

Withhold not good from them to whom it is due, when it is in
the power of thine hand to do it. Say not unto thy neighbor: "Go,
and come again, and tomorrow I will give"; when thou hast it
with thee. Devise not evil against thy neighbor, seeing he dwelleth
securely by thee.   PROVERBS 3:28-29

It is second nature for professors of history to know dates. And
deadlines, too, for that matter. So that for such a sophisticate to
sit down at bedtime on April 14 to start coping with his Income

Tax Return was surely the eleventh hour of a born procrastinator.

Half asleep, he glanced up at the clock—*10:40 p.m.*

Still half asleep, he glanced down at the Revenue Return on his desk—*Form 1040.*

Registering this neat coincidence, he remembered hearing from a member of the Layman's Movement for a Christian World that there were 1040 references to WORK in the Bible. The night being still young, it was second nature for a professor to verify this; so he reached for his Concordance, and began thumbing through the Scriptures: "everyone whose heart stirred him up brought the Lord's offering to the *work* of the tabernacle of the congregation"; "the stuff was sufficient for the *work* of the Lord"; "so the *work*men wrought, and the *work* was perfected by them, and they set the house of God in its state, and strengthened it"; "I am doing a great *work,* so that I cannot come down; why should the *work* cease?" "They worship the *work* of their own hands"; "Now if any man build upon this foundation gold, silver, precious stones, wood, hay, stubble, every man's *work* shall be made manifest . . . of what sort it is"; "make you perfect in every good *work*"; "study to show thyself unto God, a *work*man that needeth not to be ashamed"; "*work* out thy own salvation with fear and trembling"; "for I have not found thy *works* perfect."

"Almost alarming to plow through all ten-forty of these hints!" the Professor admitted, as he closed the Bible and settled down to the work in hand: filling in the blank spaces after NAME, HOME ADDRESS, YOUR SOCIAL SECURITY AND OCCUPATION, EXEMPTIONS, INCOME, ITEMIZED DEDUCTIONS.

It was at this spot that he found himself groaning: "Oh, my dear Deductibles, where are you?" For although he searched frantically through his checkbook it began to look as if he had not given even 10% to the work of the Lord; and here was the Government expecting him to give 20% of line 11, page 1, and up to 30%, if for church. Of course, there was the merciful "Miscellaneous" to account for a few stray dollars—the loose collection on the World Day of Prayer, $2 for Christmas Tuberculosis seals;

but even so, had he not been withholding more than was meet?

"Indeed you have!" Clio agreed crossly, sitting down opposite him.

"Good gracious! Who are you?" he asked in alarm.

"Poor fellow! Probably the last person you want to face in this fix—I'm the Muse of History! *Clio,* short for *Collector,* by simply changing E for 'Excellent' (which you seem not to have worked for!) into I for 'Imemyself'! You have indeed been withholding more than is meet. For there's an endless line of stewardship splendor traceable through English History which you have never shared with a single student. As Collector of Internal Revenue I had high hopes of you that first day when the faculty flung you into Freshman History. 'Listen, young ladies, and you should hear the wonderful statement of Henry Wadsworth Longfellow,' you began friskly enough, reading from the poet this excerpt: *'The history of the past is a mere puppet show. A little man comes out and blows a little trumpet, and goes in again. You look for something new, and lo! another little man comes out and blows another trumpet, and goes in again—and it is all over.'* 'Tell me—true? or false?' 'False!' they all trumpeted properly. So then you tried a spot of Shakespeare:

> *Tomorrow, and tomorrow, and tomorrow*
> *Creeps in this petty pace from day to day*
> *To the last syllable of recorded time;*
> *And all our yesterdays have lighted fools*
> *The way to dusty death. Out, out, brief candle!*
> *Life's but a walking shadow, a poor player*
> *That struts and frets his hour upon the stage*
> *And then is heard no more: it is a tale*
> *Told by an idiot, full of sound and fury,*
> *Signifying nothing.*

'Again I ask—true? or false?' 'False!' shouted all your own sweet young idiots, thinking of you just exactly as you hoped: 'what a jolly old codger!' So then, of course, your clue was to jolly up history. Take yesterday—whatever made you cut Alfred the Great down to puppet size by telling the Baby-Sitters in your class that lo! they had become Big Business in America, to the tune of an incredible billion per year, and you handed them King Alfred as patron saint. Hadn't a peasant woman asked him to sit and watch her oven while she did other work? Hadn't he sat, manlike, watching the oven, while the cakes burned inside? What more could Baby-Sitters want? But would his stewardship of time and travel and treasure have meant nothing? How about the year when ferocious Vikings from Denmark were fighting his Saxons in England, and Alfred felt that it was his dangerous duty to go into Denmark to convert King Guthrum? For this he did! Why withhold from students the fact that forever after his own people called him '*Englishman's shepherd! Englishman's comfort! Englishman's darling!*' What made you withhold some of his rare proverbs which Englishmen collected after his death in 901? Would no Baby-Sitter have thought of her own earnings while you read aloud:

> *Thus quoth Alfred:*
> *Without wisdom wealth is worthless,*
> *For though a man had seventy acres,*
> *And he had sown it all with red gold,*
> *And the gold grew as grass does on earth,*
> *For all his wealth he were never worthier*
> *But if he had made a friend of the stranger.*
> *For what is gold but a stone*
> *Unless a wise man owns it?*

'Surely it would have been sensible to add that when King Alfred collected the old Saxon laws for his people, he put the Ten Commandments first, as the basic law of the land. And why did you ever withhold Alfred's astonishing act in sending Sighelm, one of his own Christian monks, to India with money enough to start mission work there? Professor, I conclude this brief tirade by singing to you part of the hymn I heard you singing in chapel today:

> *So let our lips and lives express*
> *the holy Gospel we profess.*

The Professor began holding his head and groaning: "I must be having a nightmare!"

"Stuff and nonsense! This is simply such stuff as dreams of fair women are made on! To proceed, therefore. Think back over what you withheld from your class today about King Canute. To be sure you were a jolly enough old codger sitting there in your chair, calling it a throne, pretending to plant it down on the sea-shore at Southampton, just as the tide was turning one day in the year ten-sixteen. Pretty dramatic of course, to hold up your hand like a traffic cop and shout to the entire Atlantic Ocean: 'Stop!' Every student felt how sopping wet you were getting as the sea came swishing and swirling up around your ankles, then up to your knees, and at last to your waist; whereupon you swung around to the blackboard as you called to your courtiers on dry land: 'I tire of your flattering me and calling me divine, when see! I cannot stop so much as one wave of this small portion of water!' Neat work, professor! But why should you have snapped off the stewardship of *inheritance,* by never connecting Canute's Christian humility with Alfred's conversion of his grandfather Guthrum in Denmark, years earlier? And why—in this morning's lecture— did you present the saintly Edward the Confessor with no smallest mention of his beautiful benevolences throughout his gentle reign? And how could you forget the fabulous fact that he built Westminster Abbey out of his *tithe?* Professor, *tithe* might have been a timely matter for Baby-Sitters to think about seriously on April 14, while struggling with their own Dear De-ductibles: *20% of line 11 on page 1.* You could have led up to it easily enough, for it was pretty neat the way you held up a small book called *1066, And All That* as you said: 'Young ladies, it is none too safe to spoof at history, as this volume does. For tomor-row you will reach a date in history you might dub *1040, And All That;* and you will see that history is really an unusually long Income Tax Return.' So far, so good! And I thought it was highly imaginative of an old codger like you to hand over 214 feet of white shelf paper, 20 inches wide, to the art students in your class, together with red, green, blue and yellow crayons asking them to turn it into the Bayeux Tapestry, with series of scenes from the life of Harold to the invasion of England by William the Conqueror, in 1066. You fired these young ladies by saying that Queen Matilda worked her 214-foot tapestry in these four colors of wool, representing her own husband and his companions and their Conquest. But why leave out Westminster Abbey, which still covers several feet of this huge embroidery? The fact is, Professor, haven't you been leaving out the church every day, on purpose?"

"No! No!" the Professor protested.

"All right, we'll see tomorrow. For *ten-forty* and *ten-sixty-six* is as nothing compared to the year *twelve-fifteen!* For with Magna Carta, in the meadows of Runymede, taxes were to be collected by legal means, not by force, and a council of churchmen stood by as King John signed it. It seems to me your Baby-Sitters might fairly say to you what the men of England said that day to their king: *'We who are no better than you are, say to you who are no better than we are, that if you who are no better than we are will work with us who are no better than you are, then we will follow you. But if not—NOT!'* "

Fall behind me, States!
A man before all—myself, typical, before all.
Give me the pay I have served for,
Give me to sing the songs of the great Idea, take all the
    rest,
I have loved the earth, sun, animals, I have despised
    riches,
I have given alms to everyone that asked, stood up for
    the stupid and crazy, devoted my income and labor
    to others,
Hated tyrants, argued not concerning God, had patience
    and indulgence toward the people, taken off my hat
    to nothing known or unknown,

*Gone freely with powerful uneducated persons and with
   the young, and with the mothers of families,*
*Read these leaves to myself in the open air, tried them
   by trees, stars, rivers,*
*Dismissed whatever insulted my own soul or defied my
   body,*
*Claimed nothing to myself which I have not carefully
   claimed for others on the same terms. . . .*
*I am willing to wait to be understood by the growth of
   the taste of myself,*
Rejecting none, permitting all. . . .
Years of the modern! years of the unperformed!
*Your horizon rises. I see it parting away for more august
   dramas.*

Walt Whitman, 1819-1892

*It is when the hour of conflict is over that history comes
to a right understanding of the strife, and is ready to
exclaim: "Lo! God is here, and we knew it not."*

George Bancroft, 1800-1891

22

DEATH AND TAXES: A CANTICLE FOR
AN INNOCENT CHURCHGOER

And now concerning the collection, brethren.

1 CORINTHIANS 16:1

Year after year, century after century, churches have been
skipping over their two most obvious stewardship seasons. Paul
is almost the only preacher to connect collections with Easter

resurrection sermons, or taxes with Christmas. In the fifteenth chapter of his first letter to the church in Corinth he wrote that death had lost its sting in the resurrection, adding in his next pen stroke: "And now concerning the collection, brethren." As if their budget and the resurrection were one theme about one subject: "For if any man is in Christ Jesus, he is a new creature" —with a new purse in his transfigured Easter clothes, and a totally transformed attitude toward the old-new contents of his new-old baptized purse. Also, how discerning of him to tell the Galatians: "When an heir is a child he is under tutors and governors . . . but when the fullness of time was come, God sent forth His Son, made of a woman, made under the law . . . to redeem those who were heirs, so that they could cry Abba Father (our dear, dear Father!) and not turn back to weak and beggarly bondage."

The fullness of time was the very moment when a decree went forth from Caesar Augustus that all the world should be taxed, including that one woman whose time had come to bear the Saviour of the world. Therefore, with both Easter and Christmas so naturally gift-wrapped by inheritances and collections, there ought to be some natural way of recalling all this natural joy and goodwill to the attention of church members.

But how? When even the choir may be singing: "Nothing changes here." And even the midweek meeting arranges its chairs as pews—all pointed toward the preacher. Whereas by turning all the chairs on the left side of the room to face all the chairs on the right side of the room, with a row of collection baskets sitting along the middle aisle, a sudden sense of suspense may come over the innocent churchgoer: "What on earth does this change mean?"

It means that all the men of the congregation are to sit on the left-side chairs facing the women on the right-side chairs. Such a meeting should be held as close as possible to Easter and April 15, so that the full impact of Easter and taxes, collections and Christmas can challenge the pocketbooks of these innocent churchgoers through an unusual arrangement of antiphonal

readings and singings, mimeographed, ready to place in everybody's hands on arrival; and to become quotable afterward, when
carried home. A few men singers and women singers on both
front rows can carry off the hymn-leading more easily.

The chairman begins by saying: "Heirs and heiresses of this
church, welcome! We are met to consider the collection baskets
which you see down our middle aisle, as well as to think about
death and taxes so uppermost in our minds at this season of the
year." After which the chairman repeats the opening paragraphs
of this chapter; adding: "A few years ago an amusing *Lament
for April 15* was sung by a chorus of men's voices at the famous
Berkshire Musical Festival, held under the Boston Symphony
Orchestra at Tanglewood, in Lenox, Massachusetts. The polite
audience was reduced to hopeless laughter by this unexpected
madrigal, which our men's voices will now repeat for your
enjoyment."

From here on the antiphonal responses all appear on the mimeographed service in everybody's hands, and proceeds unan-
nounced, alternating between the men's side and the women's
side. If it seems desirable to have this *Lament for April 15* (by
Avery Claflin) sung, rather than read in unison, a recording may
be ordered from Composers Recordings, Inc., 250 West 57th
Street, New York 19, N.Y., for $4.98, postage 23 cents.

Men (reading in unison): Hear the *Lament for April 15:*

Who must file. Every citizen of the United States—
Whether an adult or minor, who had six hundred dollars
Parenthesis . . . twelve hundred dollars if sixty-five years of
    age or over. Close parenthesis.
Or more gross income in nineteen-fifty-five, must file.
Most of your tax is withheld from your wages every payday,
Or paid on declarations of estimated tax every quarter.
Parenthesis. See page fourteen relative to the declaration of
    estimated tax.
However, the law requires you to file an annual return
To determine whether you owe more or should get a refund.

You are entitled to one exemption for each dependent who
meets all the following requirements:
One; received less than six hundred dollars,
And, two; received more than one-half of his support from you,
Parenthesis, or from husband or wife if this is a joint return.
Close Parenthesis.
And, four, was either a citizen or resident of the United States,
The Republic of Panama, Canada, Mexico, or the Canal Zone.
And, five Parenthesis, a, close parenthesis,
Was related to you in one of the following ways:
Mother, Father, Grandmother, Grandfather, Brother, Sister,
Grandson and Granddaughter, Step-brother, Step-sister, Step-
mother, Step-father, and Mother-in-law.
You can deduct your Mother-in-law, Father-in-law, Brother-in-law,
Sister-in-law, Son and Daughter-in-law—
But—in the case of children who are residents of the Republic
Of the Philippines—
And who were born to, or were legally adopted by servicemen
in the Philippine Islands
Before July five, nineteen-forty-six, consult your
Internal Revenue Office.
After hearing these instructions, you should be able to prepare
Your own return
Unless you have complicated problems.

Women (in unison): Christmas also began with taxes; for a decree
went forth from Caesar Augustus that all the world should
be taxed. But there was no Lament that dark night when
the hopes and fears of all the years met in the little town
of Bethlehem. (Women singing; tune: "St. Louis"):

For Christ is born of Mary, and gathered all above,
While mortals sleep, the angels keep their watch of wondering love.
O morning stars, together proclaim the holy birth;
And praises sing to God our King, and peace to men on earth.

Men: We can match your carol with a new version of another
carol from a recent Christmas card, published in London by
Raphael Tuck and Sons, Limited. The picture shows a

small boy in striped pajamas and long red bathrobe, lustily shouting with his mouth wide open in a gigantic letter O, as he adds the extra word "ON" to the familiar words (Men singing; tune: "Adeste Fideles"):

> O come ON, all ye faithful, joyful and triumphant,
> O come ye, O come ye to Bethlehem!
> Come and behold Him, born the King of Angels!
> O come, let us adore Him, (3 *times*) Christ, the Lord.

Women: Financially speaking, have you men of the church ever figured out what the first Christian tax collector wrote in his book about finances?

Men: Extravagantly speaking, Matthew begins his gospel by telling how wise the Wise Men were to bring their treasures of gold and frankincense and myrrh. (Singing; tune: "Kings of Orient"):

> We three kings of Orient are, bearing gifts we traverse afar,
> Field and fountain, moor and mountain, following yonder star.
> O star of wonder, star of night, star with royal beauty bright,
> Westward leading, still proceeding, guide us to thy perfect light.

Women: Economically speaking, we women of the church are glad the Wise Men brought treasures instead of toys, gold instead of baby garments, spices instead of more swaddling clothes! For is it not possible that these gifts supported the Holy Family down in Egypt, where there may have been prejudice against employing a refugee carpenter just as in our day?

Men: Stingily speaking, how true! For not every old Scrooge has a Dickens to make him learn through a Ghost in his *Christmas Carol:* "Dreadful apparition, why do you trouble me?" cried Scrooge. "I am here tonight to warn you that you have yet a chance and hope of escaping my fate," replied the Ghost. "I wear the chain I forged in life. I made it link by link, yard by yard . . . It is required of every man that the spirit within him should walk abroad among his fellowmen, and travel far and wide; and if that spirit goes not forth in life, it is condemned to do so after death. It is doomed to wander through the world—Oh, woe is me!—and witness what it cannot share; but might have shared on earth and turned to happiness . . . Business! Mankind is my business; charity, mercy, forbearance, and benevolence, were all my business. The dealings of my trade were but a drop of water in the comprehensive ocean of my business!"

Women: Charitably speaking, Matthew also says that if you bring your gift to the altar, and there remember that somebody has something against you, then leave your gift at the altar, and go, be reconciled to your brother. It adds an enormous new dimension to our church collection baskets!

Men: Creditably speaking, Matthew quotes Jesus as saying: don't do your alms to be seen of men, in order to get public credit on a donor's list in the newspaper! St. Francis Xavier sang this in his hymn (men singing; tune: "St. Anne"):

My God, I love Thee not because I hope for heaven thereby,
Nor yet for fear that loving not, I might forever die.

Women: Prodigally speaking, one day Francis Havergal was packing some of her old clothes in a mission barrel, and was shocked to see how very shabby they were. For she was remembering the place in Matthew's gospel where Jesus had said that if anybody asks for your coat, let him have your cloak also. And she also remembered a hymn she had just written: "Take my life and let it be consecrated, Lord to Thee!" Ashamed of herself, she sent off her entire jewel box to be sold with its contents for mission work abroad, in order to live up to her own verses (women singing; tune: "Hendon"):

Take my silver and my gold, not a mite would I withhold,
Take my love, my Lord, I pour, at Thy feet its treasure store.

Men: Opulantly speaking, Matthew quotes Jesus as saying: don't spend your time laying up treasure on earth, but treasure in heaven—which alone *lasts*. When Philip Guedella was writing the life of the Duke of Wellington he went through the duke's receipted bills; after which he wrote: "Find out how a man spends his money, and then you will know what kind of man he is!"

Women: Bountifully speaking, Matthew quotes Jesus as saying: don't call me "Lord! Lord!" unless you are the sort of Lady Bountiful who does the will of God. Thackeray has a character in one of his novels of whom he says: "What dignity it gives an old lady—that balance at the bankers! How tenderly we look at her faults, if she is a relative; what a kind, good-natured old creature we find her."

Men: Selfishly speaking, the tax collector tells how the rich young ruler turned sadly away when Jesus told him to sell what he had, and give it to the poor—for he had great possessions. As Herbert Spencer wrote: "A golden age cannot be made of leaden instincts."

Women: Compassionately speaking, no wonder Louise Imogene Guiney could write: "O close my hand upon Beatitude— not on her toys!" For in another place she said: "My passion all my life has been *non*-collecting! There was once a golden age because golden hearts beat in it. If it comes again, it will scarcely be through scientific progress."

Men: Parsimoniously speaking, Tennyson makes his Northern Farmer say:

Doesn't thou hear my horses' legs as they canters away?
Property! Property! Property! that's what I hears them say.
But I knowed a Quaker fellow who often has told me this:
"Don't thou marry for money, but go where money is."

Yet it was Tennyson who offset this story of avarice by his hymn (men singing; tune: "Waltham"):

1. Ring out old shapes of foul disease; ring out the narrowing lust of gold;
   Ring out the thousand wars of old, ring in the thousand years of peace.

2. Ring in the valiant man and free the larger heart, the kindlier
hand;
Ring out the darkness of the land, ring in the Christ that is to be.

Women: Fragrantly speaking, the tax collector writes of the
woman in Bethany who poured out on Jesus her precious
box of oinment. When the disciples grumbled at the waste,
the Lord promised that wherever His gospel would be
preached in the world, her fragrant gift would also be mentioned. (women singing; tune: "Love's Offering"):

Master, no offering costly and sweet
May we, like Magdalene, lay at Thy feet;
Yet may love's incense rise, sweeter than sacrifice,
Dear Lord, to Thee, dear Lord, to Thee.

Men: Profitably speaking, the tax collector tells us how Peter
reminded Jesus: "We have left all to follow Thee, what then
shall we have?" Yet in our own day, the scientist, Louis
Agassiz, could say: "I cannot afford to waste my time making
money!" And the financier, Otto Kahn, could say: "I must
atone for my money!"

Women: Voluntarily speaking, like the women mentioned in
Matthew's gospel who ministered to Jesus as He journeyed
in Galilee, Jean Kenyon MacKenzie invested all her life so-
journing in Africa, where she prayed: "May it never be said
of us who are Thy stewards that, having come to an open
door we closed it, having come to a lighted candle we
quenched it, having heard the voice of the neighbor begging
bread we made denial, speaking of our own ease and the
children who are with us in the house. Rather may Thy
great gifts to us, both of means and of opportunity, work in
us Thy will, and may we become, for Jesus' sake, Thy perfectly faithful stewards. Amen."

Men: Deceitfully speaking, the tax collector quotes Jesus in
regard to the deceitfulness of riches, and the cares and tares
of this world which choke off the word of God until it becomes unfruitful. We men of the church are therefore proud

of Aloysius "Patty" Mozier, a second engineer on a freighter of the American President Lines! For he is a modern sea-going Johnny Appleseed, whose ship stops at ports in far corners of this globe. "Patty" drew all his cash from the bank—$1,500—bought vegetable seeds; and, during one year, left more than one hundred thousand seed packages in the ports of Korea, India, the Philippines, the Near East and Africa, to feed the hungry! (Men singing, tune: "Festal Song"):

Rise up, O men of God! Have done with lesser things;
Give heart and mind and soul and strength to serve the King of kings.

Women: Fashionably speaking, we women of the church are ashamed of the wife and daughter of Herod—the only women in Matthew's gospel who let the social sins of drunkenness and adultery destroy that flaming prophet of God, John the Baptist. We remember an old legend about the day the Lord reproved the devil for tempting a young girl; and Satan said crossly: "Then why was she walking around on my territory?" (women singing; tune: "Angel's Story"):

1. O Jesus, I have promised to serve Thee to the end,
   Be Thou forever near me, my Master and my Friend:
   I shall not fear the battle if Thou art by my side,
   Nor wander from the pathway if Thou wilt be my Guide.
2. O let me feel Thee near me, the world is ever near,
   I see the sights that dazzle, the tempting sounds I hear;
   My foes are ever near me, around me and within.
   But, Jesus, draw Thou nearer, and shield my soul from sin.

Men: Commercially speaking, the tax collector tells us how Judas went to the chief priests and bargained bluntly with them: What will you give me if I deliver Jesus to you? And they promised him thirty pieces of silver. But he was better than he knew! For when he realized his dastardly deed, he went back to cast the thirty coins on the temple floor, crying: I have sinned! I have sinned! And went out, and hung himself.

Women: Sacrificially speaking, what a contrast were the brave women whose love overcame obstacles—whether sorrow at sunset, or darkness before dawn the next morning, or the great sealed stone at the sepulchre. They were determined to bring their spices, their final offering for their Friend.

Men: Courageously speaking, Easter has no more valiant character than Joseph of Arimathaea, for Matthew tells us that he dared ask Pilate to let him have the body of Jesus to place in his new tomb—thus publicly acknowledging that he was the Lord's disciple.

Women: Biographically speaking, we have seen that Christmas and Easter are both one day, with a tax collector showing us how wrapped up both dates were in treasures and gifts, in sharing and in caring—a stewardship of the loving-kindness of God.

Men: Spiritually speaking, St. Augustine was writing our modern problem back in the year 400—"How many come and say: 'The Government has taken away all my property, and I shall die poverty-stricken!' But how few come and say: 'Christ has taken away my property so that I need never die at all!'" In our own country, Ralph Waldo Emerson once gave us the vision we need in regard to offerings and collections: "Who would decline a sacrifice if once his soul had been accosted, his virtue recognized and he was assured that a Watcher, a Holy One, followed him ever with long affectionate glances of inexhaustible love?"

Closing Hymn (both men and women singing; tune: *"Lasst Uns Erfreuen"*):

> Ye Watchers and ye Holy Ones,
> Bright seraphs, cherubim and thrones,
> Raise the glad strain, Alleluia!
> Cry out, dominions, princedoms, powers,
> Virtues, archangels, angels' choirs,
> Alleluia, Alleluia, Alleluia, Alleluia, Alleluia! *Amen.*

Benediction (read in unison): Therefore with angels and arch-angels, and with all the company of heaven, we laud and magnify Thy glorious name; evermore praising Thee, and saying: Holy, Holy, Holy, Lord God of hosts, heaven and earth are full of Thy glory: glory be to Thee, O Lord most high. Amen.

OUR LIFE IS BUT A LITTLE HOLDING,
LENT TO DO A MIGHTY LABOR

Epitaph on the tombstone of
George Meredith, 1828-1909

My business is not to remain myself, but to make the absolute best of what God made.

Robert Browning, 1812-1889

A vain man's motto is: Win gold and wear it.
A generous man's: Win gold and share it.
A miser's: Win gold and hoard it.
A prodigal's: Win gold and spend it.
A broker's: Win gold and lend it.
A gambler's: Win gold and lose it.
A Christian's: Win gold and use it.

Author unknown

Who are these that go about the streets of the city and upon the paths of the world? The Word of God is in their mouths, the bread in their hands they share, they bind up the wounded, and they comfort them that mourn. Who are these?

These are the stewards of the loving-kindness of God, and day laborers in His Kingdom.

They are the harvesters of children, the saviours of the sick, and the consolers of the desperate, friends of the prisoner and the family of the poor.

They are of every race and every tongue, and they are indestructibly one.

They are the pioneers of Peace, and the fellows of Christ in action.

Jean Kenyon MacKenzie, 1928

23

THE KING WAS IN HIS COUNTINGHOUSE

Sell that ye have and give alms; provide yourselves bags that wax not old, a treasure in the heavens that faileth not, where no thief approacheth, neither moth corrupteth. For where your treasure is, there will your heart be also. LUKE 12:33-34

Whenever the budget of a church begins sounding as shapeless and uncorseted as some bulging old moneybag tied in the middle, then it is high time to be more creative about it. This could be accomplished with considerable merriment and warm interpretation by three brisk scenes—simple to set up, yet unforgettable. Four actors will be needed: a King, a Queen, a Maid, a Voice. The Voice comes from the rear of the room, behind the audience; announcing:

Scene 1: The King Was in His Countinghouse, Counting out His Money.

This needs only a table set up on the extreme left side of the stage; piled high with dozens of unusually large grocery bags, stuffed full of crumpled newspapers; each bag tied at the top and bearing a mammoth dollar sign painted to face the audience, also such key expenditures printed on different bags, as: COAL, ELECTRICITY, SALARIES, WATER, PRINTING, REPAIRS, BENEVOLENCES, and any other items conspicuous in the local budget. Stacks of coins also are piled at the corners of the table, and torn church envelopes are tossed on the floor at intervals by the Treasurer, who sits behind this mountain of bags. Nothing but his gold crown looms over them; he is heard crooning the actual church statistics: "Current Expenses, $25,000; Coal, $—; Salaries, $—; etc." After the word "Benevolences" and the amount, he should say: "Too little, too late! Too little, too late!" And then repeat Luke 12:33-34. He remains in his "countinghouse," the clink of coins heard throughout the program, with an occasional church envelope landing on the floor.

The Voice then announces:

Scene 2: The Queen Was in the Parlor, Eating Bread and Honey.

On the extreme right side of the stage the Queen sits behind another table, dressed in a purple dress, gold crown; eating bread and honey. This is the responsive reading portion of the service, and the Audience has received mimeographed sheets; as follows:

Queen: Something keeps telling me that all this is probably the worst diet on earth for me—all this starch! all this sweet! It isn't enough to be Queen-for-a-day, when I would give anything to have ability enough to last a lifetime; but how? or where? can anybody tell me?

Audience: Covet earnestly the best gifts: and yet show I unto you a more excellent way. Though I speak with the tongues of men and of angels—

Queen: I need His ability in my quotability;

Audience: And have not love, I am become as sounding brass and a tinkling cymbal,

Queen: I need His ability in my lovability;

Audience: And though I have the gift of prophecy, and understand all mysteries and knowledge,

Queen: I need His ability in my knowledgeability;

Audience: And though I have all faith, so that I could remove mountains, and have not love, I am nothing,

Queen: I need His ability in my movability.

Audience: And though I bestow all my goods to feed the poor, and though I give my body to be burned, and have not love, it profiteth me nothing,

Queen: I need His ability in my expendability.

Audience: Love suffereth long and is kind,

Queen: I need His ability in my vulnerability;

Audience: Love envieth not,

Queen: I need His ability in my enviability;

Audience: Love vaunteth not itself, is not puffed up,

Queen: I need His ability in my stability.

Audience: Doth not behave itself unseemly, seeketh not her own, is not easily provoked,

Queen: I need His ability in my imperturbability;

Audience: Rejoiceth not in iniquity, but rejoiceth in the truth;

Queen: I need His ability in my imperishability;

Audience: Beareth all things, hopeth all things, endureth all things,

Queen: I need His ability in my endurability;

Audience: Love never faileth: but whether there be prophecies they shall fail; whether there be tongues they shall cease; whether there be knowledge, it shall vanish away,

Queen: I need His ability in my inexhaustibility.

Audience: For we know in part, and we prophesy in part,

Queen: I need His ability in my interchangeability.

Audience: But when that which is perfect is come, then that which is in part shall be done away with.

Queen: I need His ability in my perfectibility.

Audience: When I was a child, I spake as a child, I understood

as a child, I thought as a child, but now when I have become
a man, I put away childish things,
Queen: I need His ability in my pliability.
Audience: For now we see through a glass, darkly,
Queen: I need His ability in my inscrutability,
Audience: But then face to face; now I know in part; but then
shall I know even as also I am known,
Queen: I need His ability in my discoverability.
Audience: And now abideth faith—
Queen: Availability!
Audience: Hope—
Queen: Demonstrability!
Audience: Love, and the greatest of these is love.
Queen: Amiability! Inseparability! Imponderability! Uncontesta-
bility! Immeasurability! Delectability!
Audience: You in whose veins runs the fire of loving,
For people, for plants, for little animals,
For rocks and earth, stars and the elements,
You have a secret Voice, always singing.
It is never still. It runs with your haste
And idles in your silence. It is everywhere.
O you, for whom this passionate Voice sings

And will not be silent, think now of those
For whom no voice sounds. Of those who toil
Without the singing voice,
And live in a world which has not yet come through
Into your world.
Oh, can you not hear that the song your Voice is singing
Is the song which is to bring that world of theirs
Into the light which must light all men?
Why else do you imagine that this Voice is singing?
Why else do you imagine that the fire of love
Runs in your veins?   Zona Gale

Queen: I never cut my neighbors throat;
My neighbor's gold I never stole;
I never spoiled his house and land;

But God have mercy on my soul!
For I am haunted night and day
By all the deeds I have not done;
O unattempted loveliness!
O costly valor never won!

                              Marguerite Wilkinson

Hymn (sung softly, as a prayer): 'Where Cross the Crowded
Ways of Life." The Voice then announces:

Scene 3: The Maid Was in the Garden Hanging Out the Clothes.

The Maid wears a black dress, white apron, white cap; enters
by a side door carrying an enormous laundry basket, piled high
with costumes of all the various nationalities included in the
church's missionary budget. Before the meeting opens several
clotheslines have been firmly stretched from left to right across
the room, above the height of the Maid's head.

It is not possible to foresee what this particular church supports, at this writing; but the procedure may be on this order:
the Treasurer stands up, unties the string of the large moneybag
marked "Benevolences," beckons to the Queen to help him: "Your
majesty, as president of our Women's Society, it becomes your
duty to see that the Maid gets enough proper clothes washed for
our missionary family." One by one the Queen then removes
numbered slips of paper, bearing notes to direct the Maid about
what to hang on the line. The directions (more or less as follows):
"Our denomination supports a total of——missionaries in the
United States and around the world, of whom——are men and
——women." The Maid immediately starts pinning on the clothesline men and women's hose. Try having a solo sung while she
continues this slow work; perhaps "How Beautiful upon the
Mountains the Feet of Them That Bring Glad Tidings."

The Queen mentions the names of all missionaries supported
by the church; their stockings are pinned up separately; and, if
there are children in any of these families, small hose and bootees
should be used also. Immigrant aprons, American Indian blankets,
Japanese kimonos, Alaskan fur coats, etcetera for work at home;

Filipino large-sleeved gowns, Chinese coats, etcetera for work in the Orient. In each case, the story of the field is told by the Queen as the Maid is working with her clothespins. If the amount of money allotted to each field is mentioned clearly, there may be a sickening sensation of "too little, too late," as the Treasurer suggested earlier.

From time to time the Maid turns to the audience as she hangs up some garment and herself comments tellingly. For example, about a child's small kimono: "I was touched to find this little Japanese verse pinned to this sleeve:

'See the kimonos
Dry in the sun.
O little sleeves
Of the child that died.' "

Or about some picturesque yard goods from Africa: "Until I heard this story of a young African woman, I had not thought before how much my laundry work is like baptism! The missionary was testing the young convert; 'What is baptism?' he asked. 'Well, it's like our law suits,' she said. 'If someone accuses me, the case goes to the judges. If they paint my left arm with chalk, that shows everybody that I am guilty. But if they paint my right arm white, that shows that I am innocent. So baptism is just like they painted my right arm white, to show that the church judges my life worthy in the Lord for baptism."

Or this Arctic version of the Lord's Prayer, to go with the fur coat on the line: "Our God Father who is this time in His village, holy is that name. Your Kingdom come. Please our Father, you do for this place the same like in your village. Seal meat this day you give us. Our many things we owe people and village, we give the people. Send people many things good like that peoples is good the same. And from many bad days save every people. So be it."

Or: "One of the great scientists has figured out that if all the atomic energy in a single drop of water could be released and controlled it would be sufficient to supply 200 horsepower for a year! And he said there was enough energy in even a small card —a *pledge card*, probably!—to drive a ferry boat across the Hudson River for a year. And what do you make of this—if the molecules in one pint of water were placed end to end, they would form a chain that would encircle the earth over two hundred million times! If that isn't missions in action—all that energy from one small pint! Who would have thought it possible? No wonder the book of Deuteronomy practically says to me: 'Blessed by thy laundry basket, if . . .' *If what?* If I listen to the voice of the Lord, and make a pledge, of course."

When all the clothes are hung and enough life stories told to make the budget come alive, then "We've a Story to Tell to the Nations" would seem like a suitable climax. And in case anybody present has a good enough memory to complain: "But where's the *blackbird* that belongs in this picture?" then a really enterprising Treasurer may pass pledge cards, then and there.

TRUE GREATNESS
(being an essay by a little schoolgirl)

Once there was a woman that had done a big washing and hung it on a line. The line broke and let it all down in the mud, but she didn't say a word, only did it all over again, and this time she spread it on the grass where it couldn't fall. But that night a dog with dirty feet ran over it. When she saw what was done she sat down and did not cry a bit. All she said was: "Ain't it queer that he didn't miss nothing?" That was true greatness, but it is only people who have done washing that know it.

from the bulletin of St. George's Episcopal Church, New York City

THERE WAS *a River flowing wide and long*
  called Jordan.
There was a Prophet baptizing to repentance and belief
  called John.
There was a people living high and loose
  called Lost.
There was the Savior praying forgiveness and release
  called Jesus.
There was a Man doubting
  called Me.

  The River found itself cleansing.
  The Prophet found himself preaching.
  The People found themselves listening.
  The Savior found Himself giving.
  I found myself seeking.

There is a Spirit prompting justice and fidelity
  called Holy.
There is a land desiring honor and integrity
  called Free.
There is a people wanting righteousness and peace
  called Christian.
There is the Savior teaching faithfulness and love
  called Christ.
There is a Man hoping
  called Me.

  The Spirit finds Himself leading.
  The Country finds itself fulfilling.
  The People find themselves praying.
  The Savior finds Himself proclaiming.
  I find myself believing.

John Fremont Merrill, 1949

24

YOU MUST HAVE SOMETHING
THAT NEEDS WASHING

Even as Christ also loved the church and gave Himself for it,
that He might sanctify and cleanse it with the washing of water
by the word, that He might present it to Himself a glorious
church, not having spot or wrinkle, or any such thing; but
that it should be holy and without blemish.   EPHESIANS 5:25-27

Since hotels dare to do it for profit on their bedroom dressers,
how much more haunting if churches dared to do it in their pews,
also for profit, of course. Hotels prop their cards beside the
Gideon Bibles with a finger pointing straight at your shirt sug-
gestively: YOU MUST HAVE SOMETHING THAT NEEDS WASHING! No
excuse, then, to be like one of the characters about whom Shakespeare specified "the sin of not noticing," when there is a mirror
directly behind both card and Bible, with the sign also promising
two other important items: RETURNED CLEAN THE SAME DAY, IF
DELIVERED BEFORE 9 A.M.! CLEAN CLOTHES PACK BETTER!

The church has never been able to work that promptly, even
between Sundays. For although conversion can certainly be de-
fined as washed habits, practically everybody empties his pockets
before the laundering process, especially all his valuables and his
purse—objects most in need of cleansing! It is for this reason that
it would be properly disturbing if churches could have laundry
cards put in the pews with their pledgecards, to sit beside those
lonely little half-pencils which wait so patiently behind grillwork
windows—for all the world like tellers in a bank, waiting for depositors. It could be headed:

161

LAUNDRY LIST

1. Between two astonishing Sundays God created. And said of His handiwork: "It is good."

2. Between two astonishing Sundays hands like yours have done all the Christian washing, scrubbing and cleaning which has been done on earth this past week in the name of Jesus Christ: what have you yourself been washing? (please fill in dotted line . . . .)

3. Between two astonishing Sundays hands like yours have provided fresh clothes for soiled ones (please specify what you yourself have provided . . . .).

4. Do you feel that you have passed from the Bread Basket Stage of feeding your own hunger in church, through the Tin Cup Stage of begging other handouts, into the Laundry Basket Stage of helping Jesus Christ to make His world spotless? (please check which stage you are in . . . .).

5. Do you agree that the pure in heart shall see God? If so, can you see Him in Case 707 (It is the Lord!)? . . . Can you see Him in every homeless orphan needing protection? (Every child is the Christ-Child)? . . . Can you see Him in every starved stranger with a hungry heart? (It is the five thousand! And you have five loaves and two small fishes; but what are these among so many?) . . . How recently have you washed your spending habits and your giving habits into cleaner fresher giving habits? (It is the Stranger: "Ye did it unto me!") . . . .

Between two astonishing Sundays hands like yours have run a Chinese laundry, raised eight children alone, managed somehow to make both ends meet, and found that there was still deep common sense in the ancient words of Confucius: "When you go forth from your door, behave to all you meet as though you were meeting some distinguished guest. When employing the people, be as though you were taking part in some religious ceremony. For what you would not wish done to yourself, do not unto others. . . . For when the Great Way is followed, all under heaven will work the common good. There will be a dislike for the accumulation of goods, a refusal to store up for self, none will be for himself. For self-aggrandizement will not be known, and robbing and thieving will cease. When this time comes it will not be necessary to close the outside gates. Then will be Universal Brotherhood."

When Toy Len Goon came to America as a bride thirty-five years ago, Mr. Goon almost led her to think she was entering such a Brotherhood. Although she noticed that he did lock the laundry door! "It is to protect the customer's shirts," he explained, "after all, Confucius lived in 500 B.C."

"B.C.?" inquired Mrs. Goon, who had not been to school.

"Before Christ," Mr. Goon explained.

"*Christ?*" repeated Toy Len Goon, puzzled.

"You will hear in church about Him. Keep your eyes open, too."

So she handled her husband's laundry baskets between all astonishing Sundays; then, in the Baptist Church, she handled the Collection Basket. Smaller. But full of cash.

"Will he take some *out?*" she wondered. But no! Mr. Goon put some *in.* She marveled at her husband every Sunday; so poor, and all the new babies coming—five boys so hungry, three girls needing clothes—but always cash for God, too. It pleased her and troubled her. And especially it troubled her when Mr. Goon lost a leg in the First World War, never recovered strength, and left her with the endless Laundry Baskets, eight children, and, those endless Collection Baskets on Sundays. Should God still come first for a widow? It was astonishing to discover between Sundays that yes! nine-tenths would go just as far as ten-tenths would go, provided the widow were thrifty. Her thrift was as New England as anything the Maine town of Portland practiced: "Eat it up! Make it do! Do without!"

Between Sundays every child worked. The tiniest emptied pockets of rings and valuables. The next larger size swept the floor. And so on through suds and shirts to deliveries, everybody living up faithfully to the original sign Mr. Goon had put outside his laundry door: "*Shirts, Socks and Underwear All Expertly Hand Ironed.*"

Nobody was allowed to be unbusinesslike under such endless

hand labor. But Mrs. Goon was wonderful about play, too: "If there is harmony in the family, there is food in the larder and peace in the country," an old Chinese proverb had told her; and it proved true in Maine as well. Her children played in ball games and school orchestras; somehow Mrs. Goon pinched here and there for cash to send Caroll through Johns Hopkins eventually, Edward through the Massachusetts Institute of Technology, Albert through the Law School at Boston University, Arthur through Maine University. Yet everybody in Portland learned that if something was to be done: "Ask the Goons!" And her church knew this family's dependability.

The end result of such remarkable responsibility is shown in two pictures propped on my desk at this writing, both pictures clipped from New York City newspapers dated May 5, 1952, each showing the hands of Mrs. Toy Len Goon in quite different gestures. The 4 x 7 cut in *The New York Times* is headed: AMERICAN MOTHER OF THE YEAR, showing Mrs. Goon in an apron, her hands sorting bundles on the shelves of her laundry; each bundle expertly oblong and neat, with Chinese identification labels. She told the reporter that she could not dream of leaving yet, she still had three more pairs of pants to iron, in spite of such a surprising national fuss. The heading in the *New York Herald Tribune,* under the 9 x 5 cut: CHINATOWN HONORS AMERICAN MOTHER OF 1952. Mrs. Goon is shown in a seventeen-car motorcade, standing, wearing a wide-brimmed hat, her right hand in long white glove held high in a salute, her left arm full of American Beauty roses. All sorts of gay Chinese banners are waving overhead as her car rides through Mott, Doyers, Pell, Mulberry and Worth Streets and the Bowery; the sidewalks crowded with spectators. She stayed in the same suite at the Waldorf-Astoria where Queen Juliana had been entertained. Similar parades were held in Boston and in Washington, where the Wellington Koos gave a reception for Mrs. Goon at the Chinese Embassy, presenting her with a large silver tray.

When all sorts of people asked all sorts of questions about how on earth she had ever managed to do so much for so many with so little her answers were sheer common sense: "I never let my children spend money freely." But it was perfectly plain that in her laundry, between two astonishing Sundays, she had done more than wash and iron shirts, she had been the sort of steward to present one totally clean Christian family to the Lord of the church. No spot. No blemish. All hand labor. Business as usual. Or, business as unusual. A haunting hint to hecklers who complain that Christianity has been in the world for twenty centuries, "and look at the church!" To which Mrs. Goon's entire life seems to say: "Honorable friends, water has been in the world a good deal longer than that, and look at your hands!" YOU MUST HAVE SOMETHING THAT NEEDS WASHING.

WHAT DO YOU DO ON MONDAYS?

Blessed be our Sister Water, serviceable, precious and very clean.   Francis of Assisi, 1181-1226

Every man must purify the springs of history in his own breast.   Giuseppe Mazzini, 1805-1872

We squint, each one through his own keyhole, and dream broad heaven is but the patch we see.
                                        Chinese proverb

All human affairs are my affairs.   Chinese proverb

Truth is like a wild goose flying down from Mongolia to India. And every country over which it flies, it has a different name; but it is still the same goose.
                                        Mencius, 372-289 B.C.

25

RIGHT IN THE MIDDLE OF HER FOREHEAD

Instead of well-set hair, baldness.   Isaiah 3:24

Everybody knows about the girl with the curl right in the middle of her forehead: so very very good; or, when bad, so horrid. This, then, is the horrid record of her later badness as a lady, when her constant concern over her well-set crowning glory takes more of her entire budget than her entire concern over the glory of God, well-set on the face of the whole earth. Nationally she has grown into Big Business, to the tune of over $500,000,000 a year, double the benevolence budgets of all the churches in the nation.

The hairdresser might well unlock his Beauty Parlor door in the morning with a special Psalm of Praise, thanking God for all His benefits in numbering each of the lady's 120,000 hairs and making them grow at the rate of half an inch a month. Delightful briskness. Of which he can and does take advantage by keeping short hair fashionable—since what lady can conveniently trim her own hair evenly in back? Thus bringing her to his door at frequent intervals.

If he has his Psalm, then she should have something more divine than *Vogue* and *Vanity Fair* to thumb through while waiting under the dryer. Why not consider its covered isolation as a Tent of Meeting? a Private Chapel? a Chair of Recollection in which to hear the music of the spheres? a Pew, to keep in tune with the Infinite? letting the hum become:

HYMN WHILE UNDER A HAIR-DRYER

WHILE Thee I seek, protecting Power,
Be my vain wishes stilled;
And may this consecrated hour
With better hopes be filled.

Thy love the powers of thought bestowed;
To Thee my thoughts would soar:
Thy mercy o'er my life has flowed;
That mercy I adore.

In each event of life, how clear
Thy ruling hand I see;
Each blessing to my soul more dear
Because conferred by Thee.

Helen M. Williams, 1786

*I wait for the Lord, my soul doth wait, and in His word do I hope.
My soul waiteth for the Lord more than they that watch for the
morning: I say, more than they that wait for the morning.*

Psalm 130:6

HAIR-DO'S AND DON'TS:

(DO): Fear not, therefore, for there is nothing covered that
shall not be revealed; nor hid, that shall not be known. What
I tell you in darkness, that speak ye in light; and what ye hear
in the ear, that preach ye among the housetops. The very hairs of
your head are all numbered. Fear ye not, therefore, ye are of
more value than many sparrows. Whosoever shall confess me
before men, him will I confess before my Father who is in heaven.
But whosoever shall deny me before men, him will I also deny
before my father in heaven. (Matthew 10:26-33.)

(DON'T): Likewise, ye wives . . . whose adorning let it not be
that outward adorning of plaiting the hair, and of wearing gold,
or of putting on of apparel;

(DO): but let it be the hidden man of the heart, in that which is not corruptible, even the ornament of a meek and quiet spirit, which in the sight of God is of great price. For after this manner in the old time the holy women also, who trusted in God, adorned themselves . . . that their own husbands also, may, even without the word, be won by the conversation of their wives. (1 Peter 3:1, 3-5.)

Give beauty back, beauty, beauty, beauty, back to God, beauty's
     self and beauty's giver.
See; not a hair is, not an eyelash, not the least lash lost; every hair
Is, hair of the head, numbered.
Nay, what we had lighthanded left in surly the mere mould
Will have waked and have waxed and have walked with the wind
     what while we slept,
This side, that side hurling a heavyheaded hundredfold
What while we, while we slumbered.
O then, weary then why should we tread? O why are we so
     haggard at the heart, so care-coiled, care-killed, so fagged,
     so fashed, so cogged, so cumbered,
When the thing we freely forfeit is kept with fonder a care,
Fonder a care kept than we could have kept it, kept
Far with fonder a care (and we, we should have lost it) finer,
     fonder
A care kept.—Where kept? Do but tell us where kept, where.—
Yonder.—What high as that! We follow, now we follow.—
     Yonder, yes yonder, yonder,
Yonder.

Gerard Manley Hopkins, 1882

THE ONLY PERMANENT THAT LASTS FOREVER

Sitting there under the humming roof of this little Private Chapel, let her acknowledge that Shakespeare described her perfectly in one sentence: *"The wealthy curled darlings of our nation!"* In fact all of Isaiah 3 is also the portrait of a modern woman walking down the street. Any street! And at almost any time since Julia Ward Howe wrote in 1861: *"When I see the elaborate study and ingenuity displayed by women in the pursuit of trifles, I feel no doubt of their capacity for the most herculean undertakings."*

Some such herculean labor of love as was shown on the day when all the Jewish women gladly gave up their metal looking-glasses in order that Moses might melt them into beautiful basins for use in Jehovah's new temple, where priests might wash their hands at times of worship. (Exodus 38.) Or perhaps some such herculean gift as all the Japanese women gave when the huge Higashi Hongwanji Temple in Kyoto was being rebuilt, and news went forth that ropes of superlative strength would be needed for hoisting the gigantic pillars and the heavy rooftree timbers into place. No sooner had a Buddhist suggested that human hair made the most unbreakable rope, than 30,000 Buddhist women in one province alone cut off their crowning glory for Lord Buddha's greater glory. Today a tourist looks at the two hundred and twenty-one feet of this immense rope, thicker than a man's wrist, and realizes how many hundreds of thousands of other women also sacrificed their personal beauty to make their religious dream come true, which now all the world may see.

Did Mary of Bethany guess, when she emptied her alabaster box of ointment, "very precious," and wiped the foot of our Lord with her hair that this was a permanent, to last forever? And yet He Himself promised: *"Wherever on earth my gospel is preached, this that she has done unto me shall also be told."*

How perfect to pour out something precious and find it imperishable! Bethany was a little town the day Jesus paid this tribute to Mary. And in the year 1800, New York with only 30,000 people, was little, also; but of them all Pierre Toussaint was by far the most unforgettable character in town—although he was a slave, arriving with a wealthy French family when they escaped from Haiti because war had broken out on that island.

Monsieur Jean Bérard was so sure that their exile would only be brief, that he brought enough money to support his household in its usual lavish fashion for a single year. But when fighting grew worse in Haiti, he ventured down to the island to see what more of his wealth he could rescue; but unfortunately died on the trip.

The gay young Madame Bérard was left in New York, both disconsolate and with no funds whatever. It was at this time of trouble that Pierre Toussaint became her tower of strength. For Monsieur Bérard had already apprenticed his slave to a fashionable hairdresser. Therefore out of his earnings Pierre began going to market, secretly buying food for all the usual meals to which his mistress had become accustomed in more luxurious days. Because she was now so sad, he would also buy rare tropical fruits and pastries, hoping to win back her appetite. As time went on, Pierre would urge her to invite friends to her home, although he himself provided the beautiful refreshments—with nobody guessing that all this hospitality was his.

Every morning at six Pierre went to kneel in St. Peter's Church, to seek a blessing on his day. Then down the street to keep his mounting list of appointments to dress the hair of wealthy clients. It was the period when hair was worn in high elaborate pompadours. But his skill was more than merely scissors and comb and pomade. For he was becoming almost a father confessor to these restless society ladies; his quiet courteous way of hearing confidences, his instinctive sympathy and his total lack of gossip combined to make him seem like everybody's friend. A woman sat facing her mirror, pouring out her anguish, seeing above her the reflection of Pierre's black face—gentle and grave, quietly understanding.

For twenty years this curious role as chief breadwinner continued, with Pierre giving nearly all his earnings to the support of a mistress who could pay nothing back. The very day of her death, however, she had her lawyer write papers freeing Pierre from slavery. During all his twenty years in New York, the only money he had withheld from Madame Bérard had been saved to buy the freedom of his own sister and of a young fifteen-year-old girl. Years later, with Madame Bérard gone, he then married this girl, grown older. They began taking Negro orphan boys into their home, training them in useful trades, then finding them jobs. There is no way of counting how many helpless homeless persons were supported under Pierre's roof, nor how many troubled souls he visited daily and nursed during times when terrible plagues swept town—with streets roped off, and nobody but the police and Pierre permitted to enter.

Meanwhile every fashionable New York lady wanted Pierre Toussaint to dress her hair; so that his reputation spread all over town, people equally enthusiastic over his skill with a coiffure and over his skill as a steward. A client said, half laughing: "You are the richest man I know, Pierre, why on earth don't you stop working?"

"But, Madame, then I should not have enough for others!"

A man in the famous Schuyler family said of Pierre Toussaint: "I have known Christians who were not gentlemen, and gentlemen who were not Christians, but only one man I know is both—and that man is black."

Two thousand letters which Mr. Toussaint left in the hands of the Schuylers were presented to the New York Public Library, and are now filed in their manuscript room. Perfect Americana! More perfect Christiana! For the letters prove that there was no end of the people who depended on him for aid, no end to his daily errands of mercy during sixty-eight years in New York: *all errands on foot*—since a Negro was forbidden by law to enter any public conveyance.

He was by far the best-known parishioner at St. Peter's Church, everybody revering him as friend and saint. On the day of his funeral, his non-Catholic friend, Mrs. George Schuyler, was touched to see that no prince or nobleman could have had a higher Mass, nor more solemn music, incense, candles. Nobody mentioned his color. Or his station in life. He was simply the most beloved gentleman of little old New York: steward of the loving-kindness of God from 1766 to 1853.

While the hum of the dryer still sounds in her ears, and before

leaving her Private Chapel, a lady might try humming John
Wesley's hymn to the rhythm of the vibration overhead:

Teach me, my God and King, in all things Thee to see;
And what I do in anything, to do it as for Thee!

All may of Thee partake: Nothing so small can be,
But draws, when acted for Thy sake, greatness and worth from Thee.

Done to obey Thy laws, e'en servile labors shine:
Hallowed is toil, if this the cause, the meanest work divine.

> *Rise, woman, rise*
> *To thy peculiar and best attitudes*
> *Of doing good and of enduring ill,*
> *Of comforting for ill, and teaching good,*
> *And reconciling all that ill and good*
> *Unto the patience of a constant hope—*
> *Rise, with thy daughters! If sin come by thee,*
> *And, by sin, death, the ransom—righteousness,*
> *The heavenly life and compensative rest*
> *Shall come by means of thee. If woe by thee*
> *Had issued to the world, thou shalt go forth*
> *An angel of the woe thou didst achieve.*
> *Be satisfied;*
> *Something thou hast to bear through womanhood—*
> *Peculiar suffering answering to the sin;*
> *Some pang paid down for each new human life;*
> *Some weariness in guarding such a life—*
> *Some coldness from the guarded.*
> Elizabeth Barrett Browning, 1806-1861

> *Dear, dead women, with such hair, too!*
> Robert Browning, 1812-1889

"I quite agree with you," said the Duchess; "and the..
moral of that is—'Be what you would seem to be'—or,
if you'd like to put it more simply—'Never imagine
yourself not to be otherwise than what it might appear to
others that what you were or might have been was not
otherwise than what you had been would have ap-
peared to them to be otherwise.'"

Lewis Carroll, *Alice in Wonderland,* 1865

2 6

NEVER UNDERESTIMATE THE POWER OF

Gentlemen, how can women not be mighty when they act like
that?   1 ESDRAS 4:32;   Goodspeed Translation

Bankers look over lists of depositors and discover that women
now own 70 per cent of the wealth of this country. Preachers
look over the pews and discover that women make up three-
fourths of their congregations. Merchants look over charge accounts and discover that women do 90 per cent of the purchasing
done in their stores. The *New York Times* looks over the widows
of this nation and writes an article, wondering: Who are all
these wealthy old ladies living out their lives in luxurious hotels
while their husbands lie in early graves from overwork in earning large fortunes? Women look over themselves and wonder:
Are we worth it?

Bankers think so. Watch them move their banks out from the
center of town to residential neighborhoods, just to be nearer by,
or even out to Suburbia, decorating all these new walls with a
riot of delicious colors to catch my lady's eye.

Preachers think so. They look down from their pulpits on Sundays into earnest feminine faces, and on Mondays see earnest feminine hands doing earnest feminine work.

Merchants think so. They see themselves annually redecorating all the household interiors in town with new furnishings and new draperies; and of course every season changing the clothes, the hats and even the figures of every woman with a charge account; always encouraging lists of The Ten Best-Dressed Women in America.

But the earnest woman still looks in her mirror and asks earnestly: *Am I worth it?*

If she has a book, she looks at her world through its pages and discovers that people in India still lie down hungry every night, and that 90 per cent of the women there still cannot read or write. She reads about refugees in Europe still waiting for resettlement somewhere on earth, long years after war's end. She reads about slums in her city and recalls how much more energetic and practical Theodore Roosevelt had been, going straight to Jacob Augustus Riis's office the next morning to leave a note saying: "Have just finished your book, *How The Other Half Lives,* and have come down to help."

Leisure? Cash? Intelligence? But restless. And far too careless.

She opens her Bible at Isaiah 32 and finds her candid camera snapshot:

Rise up, ye women that are at ease; hear my voice, ye careless daughters; give ear unto my speech. Many days and years shall ye be troubled, ye careless women: for the vintage shall fail, the gathering shall not come. Tremble, ye women that are at ease; be troubled, ye careless ones: strip you, and make you bare, and gird sackcloth upon your loins. They shall lament for the teats, for the pleasant fields, for the fruitful vine. Upon the land of my people shall come up thorns and briers, yea, upon all the houses of joy in the joyous city: because the palaces shall be forsaken; the multitude of the city shall be left; the forts and towers shall be done forever, a joy of wild asses, a pasture of flocks; until the Spirit be poured out upon them from on high . . . then judgment shall dwell in the wilderness, and righteousness shall be peace; and the effect of righteousness quietness and assurance forever. And my people shall dwell in a peaceable habitation, and in quiet resting-places.

Never underestimate the power of even a careless woman to want this bliss, or of a thoughtful woman to read further on in Isaiah 59 why it has not come true on earth: "Behold, the Lord's hand is not shortened, that it cannot save; neither His ear heavy, that it cannot hear; but your iniquities have separated between you and your God."

The Christian woman knows enough to turn to a New Testament picture gallery for pen portraits of persons who actually accomplished marvels for God before they died. Hebrews 11 is full of such names. Except that the writer breaks off in a hurry: "What more shall I say? For time would fail me to tell of those who by faith subdued kingdoms, obtained promises, stopped the mouths of lions, escaped the edge of the sword, waxed valiant in fight, turned to flight the armies of aliens." And undoubtedly used up all their hard-earned savings? Never underestimate the power of a churchwoman to take time off to bring this Honor Roll up to date; for in doing so she will be both asking and answering: *"Am I worth it?"*

By faith Marie Durand, Huguenot, endured thirty years of imprisonment in the Bastille for her Protestant beliefs, and scratched daily on the walls of her solitary cell the single word: "RESIST."

By faith Madeleine Barot, three hundred years later, could follow in her steps, working in the French resistance movement, secretly collecting into CIMADE young French Christians eager to befriend Jewish refugees in Nazi concentration camps, dangerously helping them to escape over the Alps into freedom in Switzerland.

By faith Anne Hutchinson found courage to continue interpreting the Reverend Cotton Mather's two-hour sermons to women in the Colony, for which she was excommunicated from church and "banished from out our Massachusetts Jurisprudence forever as a woman not fit for our Society." Her husband could have stayed behind, but said to the court, bluntly: "I am more dearlie tyed to my wife than to your church, and I doe thinke her a Sainte and a Servante of God." (Never underestimate the power of a New York woman driver to recall all this when observing the speed limit along the Hutchinson Parkway!)

By faith Sojourner Truth, born a slave, unable to read or write, saw her husband beaten nearly to death and her children sold into slavery; yet went up and down our country in her white cap and apron, speaking for God's truth, into the homes of the great and the humble—making friends and influencing people to accept emancipation.

By faith Hannah Tubman, another slave who never learned to sign her name (yet that name now in the *Encyclopedia Britannica*), was called the Moses of her people during the Civil War, when she led over 300 Negroes up from slavery into freedom; saying of herself: "On my underground railroad I nebber run my train off de track, an' nebber lost a passenger!" (The citizens of Auburn, New York, so proud of her that on their courthouse wall they have printed a long citation to Hannah Tubman, ending with these words.)

By faith Harriet Beecher Stowe had been watching slavery with prayer, but without lifting a finger to help until her sister wrote her: "If I could use a pen as you can, Hattie, I would write something that would make this whole nation feel what an accursed thing slavery is!" *Uncle Tom's Cabin* sold 5,000 copies the first day; 10,000 in ten days; 300,000 the first year. Three paper mills tried vainly to supply the needed paper; three printing presses ran twenty-four hours a day; and she put $10,000 into her bank within four months; although, womanlike, she began by dreaming wistfully: "I hope it will earn enough so I can buy a silk dress!" She became by far the most famous woman in the world at that time, with her book being translated into Armenian, Bohemian, Danish, Dutch, Finnish, French, German, Greek, Hungarian, Russian, Servian, Spanish, Swedish.

By faith Helen Hunt Jackson wrote *Ramona*, ashamed that senators and congressmen in Washington had broken 392 treaties with American Indians, passing unjust laws to dispossess them of their rightful inheritance, pushing them further and further west into the most undesirable territory.

By faith Melinda Rankin heard that mission work was needed among the Mexicans near the Texas border, wrote articles to secure volunteers; and, when none appeared, said: "God willing, I will go myself!" Adding: "The word discouragement is not in the dictionary of God."

By faith Narcissa Whitman was the first white woman to cross the Rocky Mountains when her husband Marcus Whitman was sent west to the Nez Percé Indians in Oregon. On foot or in a covered wagon she made this enormous journey; and when her own child was drowned while playing too near a riverbank, Mrs. Whitman eased her sorrow by adopting eleven of the motherless orphans of the fated Donner Expedition.

By faith Ann Hasseltine Judson sailed to Burma with Adoniram Judson, saw him imprisoned by a cruel jailor, had ingenuity enough to hide her husband's recent translation of the Bible inside an old pillow where it was rescued, years later.

By faith Elizabeth Cady Stanton, Lucretia Mott and Susan B. Anthony worked fifty years that women might not only have the vote but the right to their own bank accounts and checkbooks.

By faith Carrie Chapman Catt looked at the careless women voters of her day: "If any of you are bored, go out on the street and do one good deed ten times."

By faith Frances Willard looked at the liquor business increasing sevenfold from 1860 to 1880, and in that same period increased her own life sevenfold also, founding the Woman's Christian Temperance Union, visiting all forty-eight states in this country— heckled on platforms, hit by rotten fruit on sidewalks, but saying of herself: "I am but one, but I am one; I can't do much, but I can do something; what I can do, I ought to do; and what I ought to do, by the grace of God I will do." Men in government in

Washington thought enough of such valor to give up a whole day in her honor when she became the first woman to appear in their Hall of Fame, her immortal words written on the pedestal of her statue.

By faith Jane Addams as a child of six, from a pioneer town in Illinois, saw her first slum, and made her vow: "When I am a grown lady I am going to live in a big house near poor people so that they can visit me." If an institution is indeed the lengthened shadow of a person, then Hull House began covering Chicago by faith from that day. Years later, at her funeral, Maude Royden called Jane Addams *Mother Earth:* so all-maternal and all-inclusive had been her hospitality, so deep the vision of this Nobel prize winner that men did not underestimate the power of such a woman.

By faith Grace Dodge invested her millions in the National Young Women's Christian Association, and said to the members: "Usefulness is the rent we pay for room on earth."

By faith Henrietta Szold, in poor health and over seventy years old, went to Palestine in wartime to invest all her strength and all her money in maintaining new villages for Jewish youths who had been rescued from European concentration camps and ghettos.

By faith Michi Kawaii dared to refuse the obligatory "shrine worship" enforced during war years in Japan, but was wise enough to offset this constant disobedience to a government edict by starting an agricultural department in her school, so that her students could graduate prized for this necessary new knowledge in a hungry nation.

By faith Helen Kim had to move her college from bombed Seoul to makeshift huts and lean-tos in Pusan, but lost no students; at the end of the war, with startling success, she rebuilt Ehwa University campus into the largest women's college in the world, with over 4,000 Korean students and over a hundred buildings.

By faith the nurses in the Martha-Mary Hospital endured the heavy air raids over Nuremberg several times each night during the war years—although this meant moving all their patients down into a bomb-proof cellar at the sound of the first warning siren; then up again at the all-clear signal, since the air in the cellar was dangerously breathless for patients. Were there three or four raids a night? Very well! Three or four of these ceaseless carryings-down of cots, with three or four tedious carryings-up again. But—not a single patient died by bombing, although the hospital itself was destroyed overhead three times! Each time these deaconess-nurses would tirelessly chip old plaster from the dislodged bricks so that they could be built back again into new walls. All this with courage in both hands, explained by a sentence now inscribed on their refectory wall: *"We do not know what is coming, but we know Who is coming—and it is Christ."* ("They looked unto Him and were radiant, and their faces were not afraid.")

By faith a little Scotch woman could say of herself: "I'm a wee, wee wifie, no very bookit, but I grip on well, nonetheless." In fact Mary Slessor gripped on so well that she lived safely among savages in Africa for thirty-nine adventurous years. Going off alone into the jungle, she built herself a two-room hut of bamboo, daubed it with red clay, made a fireplace, a dresser and a sofa all of clay as a protection against termites, took in a number of little black girls for her family, lived in mortal danger all her days in the midst of primitive people as their judge and teacher, yet wrote back to Scotland: "In a home like mine, a woman can find infinite happiness and satisfaction. It is an exhilaration of constant joy. I cannot imagine anything to surpass it on earth."

Unguarded, Mary Slessor walked through jungles where leopards swarmed about her. "I did not used to believe the story of Daniel in the lion's den," she said, "until I had to take some of these awful marches, and then I knew it was true. Many times I walked along praying: 'O God of Daniel, shut their mouths,' and He did. My life is one daily hourly record of answered prayer. For physical health, for mental overstrain, for guidance marvelously given, for errors and dangers averted, for enmity to the Gospel subdued, for food provided at the exact hour needed, for everything that goes to make up life and my poor service, I can testify with a full and often wonder-stricken awe that God answers prayer."

No wonder that the chieftain of her tribe could say to an outside official who scoffed at the idea of such a small woman judging and changing such a troublesome tribe: "But in estimating the power of this woman, sir, don't forget to estimate the power of this woman's God!"

"And these all, having obtained a good report through faith, received not the promise: God having provided some better thing for us, that they without us should not be made perfect."

And I?
Is there some desert or some pathless sea
Where Thou, good God of angels, wilt send me?
Some oak for me to rend; some sod,
   Some rock for me to break,
   Some handful of His corn to take
   And scatter far afield
   Till it, in turn, shall yield
     Its hundredfold
     Of grains of gold
   To feed the waiting children of my God?
Show me the desert, Father, or the sea.
Is it Thine enterprise? Great God, send me.
And though this body lie where ocean rolls,
Count me among all Faithful Souls.
               Edward Everett Hale, 1822-1909

Every man has two angels, one on his right shoulder, and another on his left shoulder. When he does anything good, the angel on his right shoulder writes it down in his Book and seals it, because what is done is done forever. When he has done evil, the angel on his left shoulder writes it down; he waits till midnight; if before that the man bows down his head and cries: "O God, I have sinned, forgive me."; the angel rubs it out with a sponge; if not, at midnight he seals it up in the Book. And the angel on the man's right shoulder weeps.

from a Turkish Legend

Wherefore seeing we also are compassed about with so great a cloud of witnesses, let us lay aside every weight, and the sin which doth so easily beset us, and let us run with patience the race which is set before us, looking unto Jesus the author and finisher of our faith.

Hebrews 12:1-2

2 7

THE PLUMBER AND THE PILLAR
AND THE PREACHER

Study to show thyself approved unto God, a workman that needed not to be ashamed.   2 Timothy 2:15

The Pillar was permanent in the church. An ample woman, prominent, well-to-do, and inclined to boss in benign fashion whenever benignity served; but exerting more pressure whenever her pediment needed propping. As seemed necessary not too long after the new Preacher moved to town.

Since there was no parsonage, he bought a house on a pleasant side street. With only one bathroom. But finding an idle clothes-press between bedrooms, the Preacher employed a Plumber to turn it into a bathroom. Now the Plumber was the Pillar's son. And thereby hangs this tale.

For the Plumber had been both swift and careless. So that the new bathroom became a big embarrassment. Persons sitting in the parlor underneath always leaped in alarm and looked up apprehensively whenever waterworks overhead were turned on, expecting a major Johnstown flood to deluge the premises at any moment. The Preacher complained to the Plumber, and the Plumber tinkered briefly; but to no purpose. So that the family had to hang a storm warning on the bathroom door: *"Company Below. Don't Use!"*

So far this story seems simply domestic. But the Preacher was eloquent, with sermons strong enough to move mountains, and they moved the Plumber enough one Sunday so that he turned up on Monday in the Preacher's office to say: "I have come to join the church!"

"Splendid!" said the Preacher, shaking hands. "Do sit down, my dear fellow, and tell me, what led you to this decision; is it sudden?"

"Not at all," the Plumber smiled, "you know my mother, Dominie! Well, she's always been at me and at me to take this step ever since I first opened my establishment; but lately, when business has been falling off, she keeps reminding me of all the good church folks I am missing out on. Only last week she says to one in her earnest way: 'You know, Tom, they've *all* got bath-rooms!'"

The Preacher drew a long breath: "But my dear Mr. Beebee, if that is your only reason for joining the church, are you sure you are ready? For we think of this as the Church of the Carpenter. You may remember how He said of Himself: 'My yoke is easy, my burden is light.' This must have meant that none of the oxen ever had chafed necks from poorly-turned joinings. But the fact is that all over this town you have earned a name for the same sort of careless plumbing installed in my house. Forgive me for reminding you that a Christian is someone to whom God entrusts all his fellow men! All their houses and purses and plumbing; in this case, all your clients and influence on the plumber's assistants working under you. We all serve on God's staff—they, and you, and I! He is our only Employer, as I see it. Are you sure you are ready to join the Church of this Master Workman?"

The Plumber rose up dumbfounded the moment it dawned on him that he was receiving the thumbs-down treatment. He turned on his heel, slammed the office door behind him and stamped straight to the Pillar, shouting: "That blankety-blank Preacher of yours!"

She listened in frozen silence. Then took to the telephone, telling all the lesser pillars what insults her poor son had endured. A chorus of commiseration came from trustees, deacons, officers and the Ladies' Aid. So that in no time at all little battles of the Pillar, the Plumber and the Preacher were being fought out all over town. Certain pews phoning other pews with high merriment on the part of those who had also patronized the Plumber, were suffering their own considerable embarrassments, and were therefore proud of their Preacher's prophetic stand.

Meanwhile the Preacher's wife made her own quiet Quaker comment: "This is only a tempest in a teapot, and thee has been like Mr. Valiant-for-Truth, risking all for God at a clap! But now thee can make it thy dish of tea by loving him into the Kingdom. Doesn't thee think that maybe the apostle Paul would have done this by *mail?*"

The Preacher took pen in hand at once, to begin the first of many warmhearted letters to his angry Plumber: "Dear Mr. Beebee, Let me tell you, good friend, that I have been thanking God that you came here yesterday morning at 10 wanting to join our church. For more than anything else on earth this is my own desire for you also—so much so that every morning at 10 please think of me here in the study remembering you with the greatest friendliness before God, until this dream comes true. Do you recall the day you came to repair a leak and stopped by my study door to admire my books? You said you wished a plumber's life left more time for thinking things through, but that your job used only your hands. *'Like that,'* you said, and pointed to a picture on the wall showing Michelangelo's Creator reaching out His finger to put the spark of life into Adam's outstretched fingertip. My dear Beebee, I remind you of that remark now because when God finished His work He could look around on all that He had made, and say: *'It is good!'* And when Michelangelo was at his own work he too could write: 'Nothing makes the soul so pure, so religious as the endeavor to create something perfect. Perfection is a matter of trifles; but perfection is no trifle.' I am copying this off for you because of something you also said that day by the door, you said you wished you had time to dip into my books and jot down some of the same stuff that I put into my sermons. I am taking the liberty, therefore, of sending you this loose-leaf leather notebook with your name on the outside, and these first pages to go inside, with some of the *'stuff'* which I have jotted down. Other mornings at 10 I shall be dipping up more stuff, and sending it along, with prayer and affection."

The next morning's offering on the $3\frac{1}{2}$ x $6\frac{1}{2}$ page read: "Dear Beebee, Although we know now that Albert Einstein thought through what Relativity meant, did you know that he also thought through what a *Plumber's* relationship might mean, as he saw it? I dipped this up from one of his letters and jot it down for you: 'If I would be a young man again and had to decide how to make my living, I would not try to become a scientist or scholar or teacher. I would rather choose to be a plumber or a peddler, in the hope to find that modest degree of independence still available under present circumstances.'

"This reminded me of an epitaph I copied down years ago in England on coming across a carved stone in the Cloister pavement in Westminister Abbey: 'HERE LYES THE BODY OF PHILIP CLARK, PLUMBER OF THIS COLLEGIATE CHURCH, 1707, IN THE 43RD

YEAR OF HIS REIGN.' I keep wondering what memorable thing a plumber could do for Westminster Abbey to rate an epitaph among England's great."

The next day's page followed this up: "Dear Beebee, This morning at 10 I went into our sanctuary to sit in your mother's pew, in order to feel more aware of your family's relationships with our church—their long years of devotion and contributions of labor and of money. I had with me a copy of Charles Rann Kennedy's *Servant in the House*; you may recall that it has to do with trouble in the drain pipes as well as with practicing the presence of God! I am enclosing herewith my copy of the passage which has made your long line of inheritance from childhood with this pew both mystical and practical: 'When you enter it you hear a sound. Listen long enough, and you will learn that it is made up of the beating of human hearts, of the nameless music of men's souls—that is, if you have ears. If you have eyes, you will presently see the church itself. The pillars of it go up like the brawny trunks of heroes; the sweet human flesh of men and women is molded about its bulwarks, strong, impregnable; the faces of little children laugh out from every cornerstone; the terrible spans and arches of it are the joined hands of comrades; and up in the heights and spaces there are inscribed the numberless musings of all the dreamers of the world. It is yet building-building and built upon. Sometimes the work goes forward in deep darkness; sometimes in blinding light; now beneath the burden of unutterable anguish; now to the tune of great laughter and heroic shoutings like the cry of thunder. Sometimes, in the silence of nighttime, one may hear the tiny hammerings of the comrades at work up in the dome—the comrades that have climbed ahead.' So I have been sitting here, good friend, rejoicing in the remarkable reputations of your father and your grandfather as pillars of this church."

"Dear Beebee, Since writing you yesterday about prayer in *church*, a few lines from Phillips Brooks keep coming to mind as a follow-up: 'In each man's life there is some spot comparable to the temple of Jerusalem, a central sanctuary where he can sense God's presence and find help and inspiration.' This is Ezekiel 11:16 in modern speech: 'I will be to them a little sanctuary in all the places where they shall come'; it is also in Ecclesiasticus 38:34: 'They will maintain the fabric of the world; and in the handiwork of their craft is their prayer.' Remembering Philip Clark's epitaph in Westminster Abbey, it seems as if plumbing was a prayer, too."

"Dear Beebee, I am preaching on John 17 next Sunday where Jesus says: 'Father, I pray that they may all be one,' and I want to share with you, this morning at 10, Arthur Gossip's comment on this: 'Hush! the Lord Christ is praying for you! And what is it He asks of us? That we be given such a spirit of unity and brotherliness and Christlikeness that people coming upon us, will look at us, and look again, and then from us to Jesus Christ, seeking the explanation of us there.' This is strong stuff for preachers and plumbers and pillars, eh?"

"Dear Beebee, Next Sunday comes our annual budget sermon, stressing the financial fact that in God's sight the earning of a livelihood is as much a stewardship practice as the spending of this money is. See what I dipped up out of Shakespeare:

> 'Good name in man or woman, dear my lord,
> Is the immediate jewel of their souls:
> Who steals my purse steals trash; 'tis something; nothing;
> 'Twas mine, 'tis his, and has been slave to thousands;
> But he that filches from me my good name
> Robs me of that which not enriches him,
> And makes me poor indeed.'"

"Dear Beebee, Thank you for the note in this morning's mail saying that you value the stuff I am sending and the time I must spend in digging it up. But my dear fellow, that's the job God sets me to. The Catholics call it *the cure of souls.* Just as your job is the cure of valves! There is nobody in this town as important to me right now as you yourself. For as we go around town, you and I, in and out of the houses of 'customers' all day, we both have the same mighty motto in Mark 12:33: 'To love one's neighbor as oneself is much more than whole burnt offerings and sacrifices.' Way back in 1595 Sir Francis Drake put it in a prayer I repeat each morning: 'O Lord God, when Thou givest to Thy servants to endeavor any great matter, grant us also to know that it is not the beginning, but the continuing of the same until it is thoroughly finished, which yieldeth true glory; through Him that for the finishing of Thy work laid down His life. Amen.' "

"Dear Friend, Yesterday I sent you this preacher's morning prayer; now let me share a favorite evening prayer from Bishop Cosin's pen, dated in the 1600's, but too modern for comfort: 'Forgive me my sins, O Lord, forgive me the sins of my youth and the sins of mine age, the sins of my soul, and the sins of my body, my secret and my whispering sins, my presumptuous and my crying sins, the sins that I have done to please myself, and the sins that I have done to please others. Forgive me those sins which I know, and those sins which I know not; forgive them, O Lord, forgive them all, of thy great goodness. Amen.' "

"Dear Beebee, See what I dug up just now from Julian Huxley: 'The ledger of the Almighty is strictly kept, and every one of us has his operations paid over to him at the end of every minute of his existence.' Plus this verse from an unknown pen:

> 'Who does God's work will get His pay.
> God hurries not, nor makes delay.
> Who works for Him will get his pay,
> Some certain hour, some certain day.
> He does not pay as others pay
> In gold or land or raiment gay,
> In goods that perish or decay.

But God's high wisdom knows a way,
And this is sure, let come what may,
Who does God's work will get God's pay.' "

"Dear Beebee, Here is a treasure from Goethe: 'Whatever we come on that is great, beautiful, significant cannot be re-collected. It must from the first be evolved from within us, be made and become a part of us, developing into a new and better self, and so, continually created in us, live and operate as part of us. There is no Past that we can bring back to us by longing for it, there is only an eternally new NOW that builds and creates out of the Past something new and something better.' "

"Dear Beebee, I have always noticed that you hum as you work and enjoyed it immensely. Did you ever hear this from William James: 'To some of us the thought of God is like a sort of quiet music playing in the back of the mind'? A hymn in our Hymnal begins with the words: 'Sometimes a light surprises the Christian as he sings, It is the Lord who rises with healing in His wings.' Have you ever figured out *why* you hum? and *what* you hum? Whether from satisfaction over your particular job or just a sense of general well-being, completely detached from the significance of the job itself? Is the latter enough? That empty space in your round of duties is a God-shaped space. The very squares on your calendar look up at you, just as Luke wrote centuries ago: *'They all were waiting for Him.'* Every deed from dawn to dark is a rendezvous with the Redeemer of the whole earth. His business, your business."

"Well, Beebee, in case you feel I peg the ideal too high, here's a word from Deuteronomy 30 which is down your street: 'For this charge which I am enjoining on you today is not beyond your reach; it is not up in heaven that you should say: Who will go up for us and bring it down to us and let us hear it, that we may do it? Nor is it over the sea that you should say: Who will go over the sea for us and bring it to us and let us hear it, that we may do it? No! the word is very near you, it is on your lips and in your minds to be obeyed. See! I have set before you this day life and good and death and evil; in that I charge you this day to love the Lord thy God.'"

Day after day, month after month the Preacher dug up his stuff for the 3½ x 6½ pages. Night after night the Plumber came home to find an envelope waiting. Bedtime after bedtime he would add the new page to the leather notebook engraved in gold: "THOMAS BEEBEE: PLUMBER OF THIS PARISH."

It took a great many envelopes. But one morning at 10 the Plumber arrived at the Preacher's door with a smile that entered even before he himself got in: "Dominie," said Thomas Beebee, "there isn't a bathroom in this town that I've ever had a blooming thing to do with that doesn't work perfectly, *as of now!* I'm earning an honest penny, at long last; so would you think it quite O.K. to let me join the church of this parish mighty quick? I feel like maybe I couldn't wait another minute!"

Joy in the presence of the angels of God over one sinner, repenting. And on earth, peace and goodwill among the plumbing.

PATER NOSTER

Our Father, our all-wielding is,
God let us never His mirthesniss.
　　Lord, hallowed be Thy name.
In Heaven and earth Thy will
Be done and that is skill
　　Or else we been to blame.
Our each day's bread give us today
That we may trustily, when we shall away
　　To come to Thy Kingdom.
God keep us to our last ending,
Let never the fiend with false fending
　　Cumber us in no shame. So be it.

The Lay-Folks' Mass Book, 1450

No Business Serious seemed but one; No Work
But one was found; and that did in me lurk.
  D'ye ask me What? It was with Cleerer Eys
To see all Creatures full of Deities;
Especially Ones self: And to Admire
The Satisfaction of all True Desire:
Twas to be Pleasd with all that God hath done;
Twas to Enjoy even All *beneath the Sun:*
Twas with a Steddy and immediat Sence
To feel and measure all the Excellence
Of Things: Twas to inherit Endless Treasure,
And to be fild with Everlasting Pleasure.
Thomas Traherne, 1634-1704; from "Dumnesse"

A Christian is a Christian even in the dark.
Dwight L. Moody

28

THE GIFT IS FOREVER

Thanks be unto God for His unspeakable gift.
2 CORINTHIANS 9:15

The moment the Christmas "Thank You" letter came from Africa, two quite different things happened at once. The entire church was simply staggered into asking with awed voices: "But what on earth did we send which produced this electrifying result?" And everybody looked with delight at the little lady who bought the gift, as if here was Genius for you! With a capital G!

Whereas she, poor woman, went around wringing her hands

and almost wailing into any willing ear: "Don't you dare con-
gratulate me! I deserve to be shot! I really do! It was too dreadfully dumb of me. Too totally, terribly dumb. Perhaps if there
had been even one snowflake falling that day, or one Salvation
Army Santa Claus ringing his bell at the street corner, perhaps
then I could have worked up a proper Christmas mood. But July
is really too early to do Christmas shopping! Oh, I deserve to be
dropped from the membership! Or put on a probation list for the
next twelve months!".

Preachers are patient persons. So hers said calmly: "Why not
tell me from A to Z why you feel so low while the rest of us walk
around on tiptoe in a sort of ecstasy at what our church has done?
For nothing clicks! We don't even know from the letter exactly
what you sent. Was it really only a box of candy?"

"That's just it! I didn't know a thing about this woman in
Africa. I didn't know we supported her. For I'm new on the
Friendship Committee. So our chairman phoned me, long distance, from Maine, and asked me please to go straight downtown
and get something mailed at once to our missionary in Africa,
since it ought to have gone in April; but she had forgotten. She
said I needn't spend much. And she said the mailing address was
long and queer and involved, did I have a pencil handy? After
which she told me I was an absolute lamb, and thanks a million.

"So I didn't have a thing to go by! I tried to conjure up this
unknown person of whom I had never heard one syllable before.
By and by I conjured up a porch with wide overhanging eaves;
thatched, you know. And then I saw a rattan rocker, side view.
After which it wasn't any trick at all to conjure up a sort of dim
and wistful lady, on the order of Whistler's mother, staring off
into space. Brooding over how far she was from the Old First
Church back home. Like all the dear old maiden aunts in history.
So that was when hard candy popped into my mind! Wouldn't
it sweeten her forlornness to sit there rocking and rocking and
rocking; and sucking and sucking and sucking? One box might
make Christmas last forever, that way!

"Oh, I deserve to be shot! When the poor darling is really so young and such a bundle of energy, and was living in such vivid anticipation of all those specific trinkets listed for us, which nobody seems to have remembered at all. And now everybody keeps congratulating me: 'Hello, heroine!' Whereas she is the only one to talk about. So ingenious and forgiving and adjustable and brimful of life. When I heard you read her alarming letter right in the middle of your Sunday morning sermon, I nearly jumped out of my skin! Imagine my thinking 69 cents could create Christmas for a whole mission compound . . . I deserve to be shot at sunrise!"

Pastors are born with a sixth sense. This one instantly reached into his pocket and drew out a letter: "Why wait till morning? Let's get it over with, right now, at sunset! I'll shoot you painlessly, with a slow rereading of this long frank letter, since you are the one and only member of my church responsible for this momentous miracle. So sit back and relax. And since you are so good at conjuring, then conjure up your Bible with a twenty-ninth chapter being tacked on to the Acts of the Apostles: written by two lady apostles (under God) who are adding to the church daily such as are being saved. Your trouble is, now that you are suddenly famous among us, you wish to goodness you had been more glamorous about it! Somehow a 69-cent miracle doesn't flatter your ego! But God delights in tiny items—mustard seeds sprouting up into giant trees, leaven bulging up into a big loaf. Now listen!" And he opened the letter from Africa:

Dear Fellow Members of the Old First Church:

Even although I wrote you soon after Christmas to thank you for your corporate gift, politeness is hardly enough now that time keeps adding a strange sheen to the sudden surprise. How slow and stupid I have been in recognizing what you and the Holy Spirit have been doing for us! Just as I was dreadfully dull, when the present first came, to see what glory it could bring.

As women will, I had been dreaming lesser dreams, all rooted back in that silly list of trinkets I asked for in my last letter, in the early spring. Perhaps I should explain my days a little more fully, for it must have seemed a stupid list—pencil stubs, scraps of paper, half-used spools of colored thread, flower seeds, et cetera. Not even as flashy as Woolworths.

But let me tell you that ever since the principal of our Girls' School went on furlough, her job has fallen into my lap, too. So early every morning I dash over there and inspect the dormitory. Did they have grace at meals? Good! Are they more clever at sewing a straight seam? Wonderful!

So then I turned one of my doorposts into a regular totem pole of ideas for the Girls' School: *Memo*—would it cheer up the needlecraft children if I made each of them a personal sewing kit out of the gingham remnants I asked the Old First Church to send? Inside, a spool apiece, a thimble apiece, ten pins stuck in a yellow cardboard star, five needles stuck in colored cork. *Query:* could I entice these infants into hemming diapers for the maternity ward? How can I ever get the underloved more loved around this compound?

You can see that none of this is very profound; but I had let my dim wits dwell on such plans that eventually I used them as bait for the girls: "If you get it right, maybe at Christmas . . ." All very bad pedagogy; but it worked like a charm. Their output doubled! Their neatness grew fantastic!

And toward November the hints were heartbreaking: "Mamma, when the box comes from your white tribe, you won't forget that I . . ." et cetera. And then the inevitable next question: "Mamma, *has* the box come?" "No, not yet." "Mamma, should we start praying for a big wind to push the boat, maybe?" "No, no!" "But Mamma, what will you *do* if none of those fine things come?"

So here were forty black girls with forty stiff questions. Sixty black boys grumbling over gardening. It is, they tell me, women's work. So I planned on a big Christmas envelope for each boy. Another *Memo* on the doorjamb dedicated to the Youth Hostel, reminded me to cut out every advertisement of every farmer I could find, to paste on these big envelopes . . . with flower seeds inside; and later, could my boys be persuaded to take their flowers over to our hospital patients? Creating this small extra loving-kindness? Well, drop a few hints.

So, one by one, the boys, too, would come shouting: "Mamma, the post is in!" Then, as I sorted it and found no box somebody would always ask: "Mamma, would you have to forgive the robbers down the river who stole your Christmas box? Mamma, would God expect you to go *that far*?" So we mixed ethics and hope and agriculture until the day in December when the box did come, some saint somewhere along the line having actually nudged the porters into hurrying. So here it was: your box!

Not very big. But everyone shook it delicately. "Mamma, it rattles! Is that good?" So in my recklessness, not having X-ray eyes, I explained everything: "Spools and pencils and pins and seeds always rattle." They shivered with suspense. "Mamma, you go and open it, and see what the tribe of God has sent you. Forgive us, but could you hurry just a little?"

For that is how much Christmas and boxes matter. So I hurried more than a little. Need I confess to you that at first you turned me into a footnote on every despairing Psalm which David ever wrote? And I too laid my complaint before the Lord! For your box of hard candy had turned gummy and sticky at the edges; red from the peppermint drops had run into the brown stripes from the hoarhound drops, with dashes of green from the wintergreen pieces. And it was only too obvious that there were not nearly enough pieces to go around among my tribe.

It is proper to confess all this now, because it loomed so large at the time that I could barely hear what God was trying to tell me. Probably it is right to let you know how your missionary got educated. For it was exactly as if a Voice were saying: "Daughter, what have you in your hand?"

So I held up your box: "See! This miserable mess, melting right before my eyes, after that long, damp trip and this horrid humid weather. You certainly don't pamper lonely women with a whole station on their hands!"

Imagine getting that low! Imagine reminding God all over again that there wasn't even a candy apiece for my people! *So many people,* God, perhaps two hundred.

This is where He is most sensible with single-track minds like mine. He reminded me that once the Saviour had had even less to feed five thousand!

"But this disgusting stuff is melting right before my eyes!"

Let it melt some more. A lot more. Daughter, where are your wits?

"Melt, Lord? But why?" So then the lovely divine idea was born: melting meant multiplying! With perhaps a little drop of water . . . Oh, David, David! Did God bring you out of all your woes in this same creeping inch-by-inch, foot-by-foot fashion? And the Psalmist honestly told me that yes, God had! Which is why joy comes in the morning. Only our joy in Africa was utter jubilance: the bouncing extravagant kind that permanently pleated our smiles and captured our sentences.

This way: First, on Christmas Eve, I melted the contents of your box, stingy with the water, but enough to fill my little silver bowl. It looked absolutely beautiful: pinkish, greenish, thickish, lying there in lovely little whirls and swirls. I sent out word on our drum (we are primitive here) for everybody to bring a large green leaf to receive the present from Mamma's tribe of white men over the sea. We grow our leaves in outsizes over here, so everybody brought the biggest, widest one he could find. So then God and David and I passed out your marvelous gift.

Three deacons stood on each side of me, with verses from Psalms 34 and 126 to recite. We did it all in action, so that the drama was thrilling to watch—it was ritual, yet it was fun; it was good theology, yet it was unforgettable; it was rhythm, yet it spoke to our hearts. It meant that something was always being said to seven of the tribe as they filed past, and with utterly charming gracefulness men and women and children flung themselves into the motions.

When the first deacon said: *"O magnify the Lord with me, and*

let us exalt his name together!" then the deacon held high that
person's leaf as far as their arms would reach. But the second
deacon asked this same person to look beyond the leaf to God
himself as he said: *"They looked unto him and were radiant, and
their faces were not afraid!"* The third deacon walked arm in arm
with this person in a complete circle: *"The angel of the Lord
encampeth round about them that fear him, and delivereth them."*

And now this mystified person had reached your gift. He knew
that it was something special and spiritual. He lowered his leaf:
"Mamma, may I have some, please?" And as I shared a precious
drop in the center of that leaf, I quoted from David: *"O taste and
see that the Lord is good: blessed is the man that trusteth in Him."*
So he bent his head to taste and see! Even although I repeated this
over two hundred times on Christmas, it was thrilling to have
each person look up earnestly and nod emphatically: "Yes,
Mamma, that is a true word from your tribe; you must thank them
for remembering me!" Immediately the fourth deacon took over
this person and touched the lips symbolically: *"Keep thy tongue
from evil, and thy lips from speaking guile."* Then the fifth deacon
added exuberance to our rhythm when his verse said: *"Then
was our mouth filled with laughter, and our tongue with singing:
then said they among the heathen. . . . The Lord hath done great
things for us; whereof we are glad!"* And of course, the sixth deacon sang with our pilgrim the great Christmas hymn: *"O come all
ye faithful . . . come let us adore him, Christ the Lord."*

How can I ever tell you of this slow, reverent, yet lively pro-
cessional—all that lovely lifting, looking, turning, tasting, laughing? The echo of it has never stopped. A difficult woman said to
me about one of our Christians: "I can't quarrel with her any
more, Mamma. Now she just sits with me and comforts me." And
I am the poor goose who thought visible flower seeds and tangible
flowers could create a Christian climate! But you knew better, beloved friends. For on every hand I still see the invisible touching
our spirits.

Yesterday I called on an old chieftain. Seeing a withered leaf in a jar I said: "Brother, what is this?" And his answer told the whole story: "Mamma, that is the Christmas leaf, and at the full of the moon I always take it out and lick it, and remember how lovely Christmas was!"

As if it would last forever; due to your giving us this taste of God's goodness. On behalf of everybody in my town. I thank you.

Come, Thou long-expected Jesus, born to set Thy people free; from our fears and sins release us; let us find our rest in Thee. Israel's Strength and Consolation, Hope of all the earth Thou art, Dear Desire of every nation, Joy of every Longing heart.   Charles Wesley, 1744

Rejoice, O heavens and earth. Truly! Truly! . . . Be as sure of it as you are that God lives: at the least good deed, the least bit of good will, or the least of good desires, all the saints in heaven and on earth rejoice, and together with the angels, their joy in this world cannot be compared to it. The more exalted a saint is, the greater his joy; but the joy of them all put together amounts to as little as a bean when compared to the joy of God over good deeds. For truly, God plays and laughs in good deeds. . . . Thus He says: "Rejoice, O heavens, for the Lord hath comforted His people."
                    Meister Eckhart, 1260-1328

29

TWO FOR THE PRICE OF ONE

Therefore in their land they shall possess the double: everlasting joy shall be unto them. For I the Lord love judgment, I hate robbery for burnt offering: and I will direct their word in truth, and I will make an everlasting covenant with them.

ISAIAH 61:7-8

Serendipity is the word for Isaiah. You go searching for some rich lost sentence of his, and suddenly you have found a dozen other richer ones which you had forgotten you had ever lost. With nothing more charming than Isaiah's astonishing habit of doubling his phrases for emphasis: two for the price of one! A disturbing habit through the New Testament also: "*Martha, Martha!* thou art cumbered over many things, but one thing is needful." "*Simon, Simon!* I have prayed for thee that Satan may not sift thee." "*Jerusalem, Jerusalem!* how often I would have gathered you in my arms—and ye would not." "*Saul, Saul!* why persecutest thou me? It is hard for thee to kick against the pricks." "*Verily, verily!* I say unto thee." "*Truly, truly!*"

Isaiah well knew all such cumberings with, such prayings for and siftings by, such gatherings up, and such kickings against. He puts these into dozens of doubled phrases until it seems like his favorite fad, a case of serendipity for any steward searching for one lost coin and suddenly finding two. Pencil in hand, therefore, he hurries through the entire prophecy, underlining every paired phrase; in the end immensely richer than he dreamed he could be. In love, too, with all this poetic cadence and balance, this forcefulness and rhythm of repetition. A subtle study of an aristocrat; another way of seeing Isaiah as Sargent painted him in his "Frieze of Prophets": in royal blue, hands held high in adoration, everlasting joy upon his forehead as if seeing the Lord high and lifted up, hearing that angelic chorus: "Holy! Holy! Holy!" Yet—politically, the land in chaos, King Uzziah having died. Doing the best things in the worst times; fully as thrilling as entering the apse of Westminster Abbey and suddenly coming upon a recent altar with a window behind it, with the light shining through the blue seal of the Royal Air Force Pilots, and this perfect phrase from Shakespeare's *Henry V,* where the king says to his soldiers riding to Agincourt: "WE FEW, WE HAPPY FEW, WE BAND OF BROTHERS."

Isaiah also manages to sound as modern as this morning: "Their land is full of silver and gold, neither is there any end of their treasures; their land is also full of horses, neither is there any end of their chariots; their land is also full of idols; they worship the work of their own hands, that their own fingers have made: and the mean man boweth down, and the great man humbleth himself: therefore, forgive them not."

Modern as this sounds, Edward K. Ziegler has rephrased it from a familiar psalm: "Science is my Shepherd, I shall not want; He maketh me to lie down on foam-rubber mattresses; He leadeth me beside six-lane highways. He rejuvenateth my thyroid glands; He leadeth me in the paths of psychoanalysis for peace of mind's sake. Yea, though I walk through the valley of the shadow of the iron curtain, I will fear no communist; for Thou art with me; Thy radar screen and Thy hydrogen bomb, they comfort me. Thou preparest a banquet before me in the presence of the world's billion hungry people. Thou anointest my head with home permanents, my beer-glass foameth over. Surely prosperity and pleasure shall follow me all the days of my life; and I will dwell in Shangri-la forever."

No steward can read this without profound uneasiness, as a mood of the moment. Therefore he starts finding Isaiah's twin touches, to see what light they cast on complacency: "Woe to them that join *house to house, field to field*" (5:8), "that call *evil good, good evil*; that put *darkness for light, light for darkness*; that put *bitter for sweet, sweet for bitter*" (5:20), which paints a bleak picture of today's absentee landlords letting plantations turn into dustbowls ("the hay withered away, the grass faileth, there is no green thing" [16:6]); and whole city blocks turned into slums ("howl, O gate; cry, O city [15:31]). Because of an immense Ford factory in England, the chief librarian in Dagenham began investigating the history of this area, and found that one of the earliest purchasers of the site was a member of Parliament named John Ward. Mr. Ward bought the land when it was flooded, and therefore cheap; his next move—to have a bill passed in Parliament to have the land drained at public expense. After his death this very specific prayer was found among his deeds: "O Lord, Thou knowest that I have certain estates in the city of London, and likewise that I have recently purchased an estate in fee simple in the County of Essex. I beseech Thee to preserve the two counties of Middlesex and Essex from fire and earthquake; and as I have a mortgage in Hertfordshire, I beg of Thee likewise to have an eye of compassion on that County; for the rest of the counties, Thou mayst deal with them as Thou art pleased." The chief librarian then noted that Mr. Ward died in a debtor's prison.

"*Gird yourselves, and ye shall be broken in pieces, gird yourselves, and ye shall be broken in pieces*; say ye not: '*a confederacy . . . a confederacy*,' neither fear ye their fear, nor be afraid" (8:9, 12)—as if a big enough corporation meant security, or peace, or goodwill. For thirty-five years the story has been going the rounds of America of how the seven highest financial leaders in the world met in Chicago in the year 1923—the president of the largest independent steel company, the president of the largest utility company, the greatest wheat speculator, the president of the New York Stock Exchange, a member of the President's cabinet, the greatest "bear" on Wall Street, the president of the great Bank of International Settlement, and the head of the world's largest monopoly.

How secure and important they must have seemed! But within twenty-five years, Charles Schwab died poverty-stricken; Richard Whitney had served a term in Sing Sing; Albert Fall was released from prison to die at home; Leon Fraser, Jesse Livermore and Ivar Kreuger committed suicide when their gross misuse of public funds was discovered. Centuries earlier, in the debauchery of the dying Roman Empire, Seneca wrote: "There will be no new sins committed. We have committed them all." Benjamin Franklin put his finger on the sin: "He that is of the opinion Money will do every Thing may well be suspected of doing every Thing for Money." To which Isaiah would surely have answered: "*The treacherous dealer dealeth treacherously,* and the *spoiler spoileth*" (21:2).

Within a few sentences Isaiah will be adding: "Babylon *is fallen, is fallen*" (21:9). Vast panoramas of recent destruction sweep into the steward's mind: Tokyo, Hiroshima, Nagasaki, Berlin, London, Coventry, Warsaw, Budapest: "*city against city, kingdom against kingdom*" (19:2).

At this point a glorious repetition recalls a Christmas hymn: "*Watchman, what of the night? Watchman, what of the night?*" (21:11). The watchman's answer is very beautiful: "The morning cometh, and also the night; if ye will *inquire, inquire* ye. . . . The inhabitants of the land of Tema brought water to him that was thirsty, they went out with bread to meet the fugitives" (21:12, 14). Among those who have "inquired—inquired," Caryll Houselander has brought back from Germany one of the choice stories. For there was a certain German woman who was mourning the loss of her only son, killed in the last war. The neighbors were greatly surprised to see that not only had she adopted another son, but one who was also absolutely different in appearance. Where her own son had had blue eyes and golden hair, this one had brown eyes and curly black hair, where her own boy had been exceedingly fair-skinned this one was exceedingly dark-skinned: "How can you love this Negro equally when he is so totally opposite?" the neighbors inquired. The old mother said, patiently: "But there is only one child—the Christ Child!" So the morning really does come; and the night also.

Isaiah's next doubling also has a familiar sound; a man with a key is to be a father to the exiles in Jerusalem: "He *shall open and none shall shut*; and he *shall shut and none shall open*" (22:22). In this connection any steward of any nationality would do well to rejoice that the superb story of all "Orphaned Missions" began with a Scottish steward who heard that German missionary funds were frozen inside Germany because of the War, and so this generous soul sent a sizable sum to Edinburgh House with the request that it be sent on to continue such interrupted work abroad; and from that day to War's end other equally imaginative givers carried on this orphaned work, so that nothing was ever closed down from lack of funds.

Nietzsche once said: "I will believe redemption when Christians are more redeemed!" He should have known of this generous giver from Scotland. Instead of which he may have known Shakespeare's actors: "They neither have the accent of Christian nor the gait of Christian, pagan nor man . . . they imitate humanity so abominably." Isaiah has a remarkably modern doubling for this: "But I said, *My leanness, my leanness,* Woe unto me! *The treacherous dealers have dealt treacherously,* yea *the treacherous dealers have dealt very treacherously*" (24:16). This phrase seems to be one Isaiah finds descriptive enough to use again, reminding of the prayer the Lord answered: "But, He sent leanness into my soul." Lyman Abbott wrote such a lean prayer: "Our brethren who are upon the earth, hallowed be our name; our kingdom come, our will be done on earth, for there is no heaven. We must get our daily bread. We neither forgive nor are forgiven, for nature knows no forgiveness. We fear not temptation, we deliver ourselves from evil. And ours is the kingdom, and ours the power, for there is no glory and no forever. Amen."

No wonder every other bed in our hospitals is occupied by a mental patient. No wonder the whole town takes Miltown to tranquilize itself. Isaiah has even described the bed: "For the bed is shorter than a man can stretch himself on it: and the covering narrower than he can wrap himself in it" (28:20); but the Lord shall rise "that *He may do His work, His strange work*; and bring to pass *His act, His strange act*" (29:21); "for *precept* must be *upon precept, precept upon precept*; *line upon line, line upon line*; here *a little,* there *a little*" (28:10). For all the world like some boy kept after school to write a hundred times on the blackboard some sentence which may then stick with him the rest of his life, turning him into a Christian steward: "a hiding place from the wind, a covert from the tempest, a great rock in a weary land" (32:2). Isaiah seems to have chosen this sentence for the blackboard: "The vile person shall be no more called liberal, nor the churl said to be bountiful. . . . The instruments of the churl are evil: he deviseth wicked devices to destroy the poor; but the *liberal* deviseth *liberal things*; and by *liberal* things shall he stand" (32:5, 8).

It might prove more $ugge$tive if each letter "s" were copied a$ a dollar $ign—$en$ing the $obering $tory of $hebna, the trea$urer with hi$ con$picuou$ $epulchre, yet violently to$$ed by God like a ba$eball, off-field, a $hame to all the $pectator$ (22:15-19). Al$o the $tory of riche$ carried on the $houlder$ of a$$e$, trea$ure$ on the hump$ of camel$, when their actual "$trength i$ to $it $till" (30:6-7). This should remind a steward of the sensible Dame Edith Sitwell, in England, listing as her favorite hobby "the love of silence." To be alone with God and the Book. To read and reread of the fearfulness that surprises sinners, whereas he that "speaketh uprightly, that despiseth the gain of oppressions, that shaketh his hands from the holding of bribes, that shutteth his eyes from seeing evil . . . shall see the King in His beauty; they shall behold the land that is very far off" (34:14-24).

Isaiah paints devastating pictures of the ten best-dressed women of his day. Isaiah 3:16-26 sounds like a Christian Dior display. Isaiah 32:9-20 is a study in carelessness among charge-account women. Isaiah 47 is one long lament against the fine lady who says: "*I shall be a lady forever,* so that thou didst not lay these things to heart," given over to pleasure, dwelling carelessly, saying in her heart: "I am, and none else beside me," "let now the astrologers, the stargazers, the monthly prognosticators stand up, and save thee from those things that shall come upon thee." It is strong medicine!

But it leads to straight common sense: "He awakeneth me *morning by morning*, he awakeneth mine ear to hear as the learned" (50:4-9). Then three times over the stimulating: "*Awake, awake!*" (51:9, 17; 52:1) and "put on thy beautiful garments"; "see *eye to eye*," "*depart ye, depart ye*," "*come ye, come ye*," "*my thoughts* are not *your thoughts*, nor *my ways, your ways*" (52:8, 11; 55:1, 8).

John Bunyan describes a Madam Bubble in Vanity Fair with a striking resemblance to Isaiah's careless women. Mr. Honest asks if she is not "a tall comely dame? Doth she not wear a great purse by her side; and is not her hand often in it, fingering her money, as if that were her heart's delight?" "She is a great gossipper; she is always at one pilgrim's heels or another; she always laugheth poor pilgrims to scorn; but highly commends the rich. If there be one cunning to get money in a place, she will speak well of him from house to house. . . . She hath her times and open places of cheating. . . . She will cast out of her purse gold like dust, in some places, to some persons. She will promise to some crowns and kingdoms, if they will but take her advice; yet many hath she brought to the halter, and ten thousand times more to hell."

The choice is any woman's! To be another Dinah—going out to see the daughters of the land, but meeting a Prince Charming and bringing on a bitter battle. To be another Delilah—cutting away the strength of a strong man. To be another Jezebel—threatening a prophet. To be another Herodias—getting even with John the Baptist. Or, to be another woman whose price is above rubies, who cares for the poor and for her own household, her dignity and her duty "known in the gates."

That was a good day in 1647 when George Fox wrote in his *Journal*: "I met with a sort of people that held women have no souls, adding, in light manner, no more than a goose. But I reproved them, and told them that was not right; for Mary said: 'My soul doth magnify the Lord, and my spirit doth rejoice in God my Saviour.' "

It remains, therefore, only to note Isaiah's last down payments of two for the price of one: *"cast ye up, cast ye up"* (57:14); *"peace, peace"* (57:19), *"fast, fast, fast, fast"* (58:4-7), *"go through, go through,* prepare ye, *cast up, cast up* the highway" (62:10), and *"behold me, behold me . . . I create, I create"* (65:1,-18).

That was a creative moment when Luther's Bibles swept into Silesia and a medical student named Johann Scheffler read with delight, saw deeply, renamed himself Angelus Silesius, and from 1661 to 1675 wrote verses which still can stab a steward wider awake:

> I am a blessed Thing if I
> Can but un-thing myself, forego
> All my community with things,
> My cognizance of things unknow.

> Man never will possess
> Perfect beatitude,
> Until what single is
> Swallows up all otherhood.

And so a steward learns to rise out of his old torn-to-tattershood by un-thinging himself from ownhood into otherhood then Godhood—paid double every inch of the way: "to give them beauty for ashes, the oil of joy for mourning, the garment of praise for the spirit of heaviness" (61:3)

> *Whate'er thou lovest, man,*
> *That too become thou must,*
> *God, if thou lovest God,*
> *Dust, if thou lovest dust.*
> Angelus Silesius, 1675

So what is there to frown or smile at?
What is left for us, save, in growth
Of soul, to rise up, far past both,
From the gift looking to the giver,
And from the cistern to the river,
And from the finite to infinity,
And from man's dust to God's divinity?
Take all in a word: the truth in God's breast
Lies trace for trace upon ours impressed;
Though He is so bright and we so dim,
We are made in His image to witness Him.

Robert Browning, 1812-1889

I can hardly think there was ever any scared into Heaven;
they go the fairest way to Heaven that would serve God
without a Hell; other Mercenaries that crouch into Him
in fear of Hell, though they term themselves the servants,
are, indeed, the slaves of the Almighty.

Sir Thomas Browne, 1605-1682

3 0

DRAWING ON THE BANK OF THE SAINTS

Do you not know that the saints shall judge the world?

1 CORINTHIANS 6:2

The truth is that it is much too convenient for a Protestant to put
the saints into a Catholic category, as if making a clean sweep of
all these debonair and witty creatures—poverty-stricken, every

one of them, yet so outgiving that they make our purses wince, so penetrating in their observations that they embarrass us.

But saints belong to us. We have inherited every one of them from all Christendom; and the more we read, the more we keep copying down their crisp and quotable quotes. Especially about money! The wonder of it is that every finance and stewardship chairman or secretary has not long ago adopted a patron saint: for the sheer pleasure of being encouraged on blue days or energized when in the red. Of course St. Paul is different: his "Cheerful Giver" lands on almost all church offering envelopes, with an occasional bold robbing Peter to pay Paul, by printing: "As every man has received the gift, even so minister the same one to another, as good stewards of the manifold grace of God."

But God did not stop writing after His Book had gone to press; and if all the things which Jesus said and did through His saints' ideas about giving could be printed in a twenty-ninth chapter of Acts, a preacher would have texts enough for stewardship sermons the rest of his life—with William James' warm endorsement: "The saints, with their extravagance of human tenderness, are the great torch-bearers, the tip of the wedge, the clearers of the darkness. . . . The world is not yet with them, so they often seem in the midst of the world's affairs to be preposterous. Yet they are the impregnators of the world, and vivifiers and animators of the goodness which, but for them, would lie forever dormant. It is not possible to be quite as mean as we naturally are, when they have passed before us. One fire kindles another; and without that over-trust in human worth which they show, the rest of us would lie in spiritual stagnation."

Coventry Patmore had insight also: "A saint is a person who does almost everything any other decent person does, only somewhat better and with a totally different motive."

Their giving is never because the community chest is collecting this month, or because the denomination has a drive and their names must head the lists of donors. Theirs is a lifelong discipline. An absolute sharing. An abandonment. A joy. There is no better way to prove this in the late nineteen-fifties than to read what they said in the earlier days of Christianity. Even the brief benedictions which follow bring this great cloud of witnesses closer: are they often conscience-stricken for our sakes? Even the humble Curé d' Ars said: "Do only what you can offer to God"—echoing our Lord's own words: "I do always those things that please God."

St. John Chrysostom (347-407) told his congregation in Constantinople: "Every man is the sculptor and the painter of his own life"; "nothing is more fallacious than wealth. Today it is for thee, tomorrow it is against thee. It arms the eyes of the envious everywhere. It is a hostile comrade, a domestic enemy." And how about this superb city mission stewardship sermon preached in Antioch by that golden-mouthed orator: "Recall that money is like water. It goes bad if it does not run. Don't think that you have done enough because you beat down your body with fasting. I don't object to your fasting, but helping others is more important. And don't ask for lovely things if they are made by blood. Recall: a ship has to be fitted and rowers enlisted, a man for the prow and helmsman. A sail is spread and an ocean covered. Wife and children are left behind. The merchant entrusts himself to the waves and goes to the lands of the barbarians and undergoes innumerable dangers. And for what? In order that you may have colored threads to weave into your slippers! Better use your money for the poor. How many are there in Antioch? I should say fifty thousand. And how many Christians? I shall say one hundred thousand and the rest Jews and pagans. Now if the Christians were to bring in goods, and share them like the Apostles, couldn't we take care of the poor?"

No wonder he could write the prayer still used every Sunday somewhere in Christendom: "Almighty God, unto whom all hearts are open, all desires known, and from whom no secrets are hid, cleanse the thoughts of our hearts by the inspiration of Thy Holy Spirit, that we may perfectly love Thee, and worthily magnify Thy Holy Name; through Jesus Christ our Lord. Amen."

From a brilliant but profligate youth devoted to the wildest pleasures in Africa and Italy, note what St. Augustine (354-430) came to believe about money after he had given everything back to God, and—although Bishop of Hippo—preferred living in a simple cell: "All abundance which is not my God to me is neediness." "Without God, we cannot; without us, God will not." "God does not demand impossibilities; do what you can!" "Live as though your Judge were to meet you today, and you will not fear Him when He does come." "Prayer is capital drawing interest." "'Hard times! Troubled times!' these men are saying. But let our lives be good and the times will be good. We make our times; such as we are, such are the times." "There is nothing more unsatisfactory than a thing that rolls away; that is why money is made round, it won't stay still." The Italians still retain this in their proverb: "Money is round, it rolls away."

"Oh, the blindness and perversity of man! All that he has he wants to be good; himself he doesn't want to be good. Who wants to have a farm that isn't good? or a wife that isn't good? or a house that isn't good? or even a pair of shoes that aren't good? As if bad shoes could hurt you more than a bad life! When your shoes are bad you mend them, or throw them away and get a new pair; your life you will not mend." "Poverty is the load of some, and wealth the load of others, perhaps the greater load of the two. It may weigh them to perdition. Bear the load of thy neighbor's poverty, and let him bear with thee the load of thy wealth. Thou lightenest thy load by lightening his."

"Those who have nothing, but wish they had, are damned with the rich. For God does not consider what we possess but what we covet." "If you are suffering from a bad man's injustice, forgive him lest there be two bad men." "I do not know why it is more cramping to the soul to possess things it does not need than merely desire them. It is harder to get rid of what one possesses than not to desire what one has not got; the former is like losing a limb." "Out of God's gifts, then, we make gifts to God, and from us He receives what He first gave us. Our state of beggarhood would, unless He first gave us something, remain absolute emptiness." "Give with a heart glowing with generous sentiments; give as the fountain gives out its waters from the swelling depths; give as the air gives its vital breezes, unrestrained and free; give as the sun gives out its light, from the infinite abyss of its own nature."

"Spread your charity over the whole world if you will love Christ, for the members of Christ are spread over the whole world. What is the use of believing and blaspheming? You adore Him in the head, you blaspheme Him in the body. He loves His body. If you separate yourself of His body, the head does not for that matter separate itself from the body. In vain do you honour Me, the head cries to you from Heaven, in vain do you honour Me. It is as if somebody wanted to kiss your face while stepping on your feet. With his hobnailed boots he crushes your feet and tries to take hold of your head and kiss it; do you not interrupt his show of respect with the cry: 'What are you doing, man? You are hurting me!' Thus did our Lord Jesus Christ, before ascending into Heaven, recommend to us His body through which He was to remain on earth. He could see that many would honour Him in His glory, but He could see that their honours would be of no use, for they would have contempt for His members on earth."

A human touch is added to the astonishing number of St. Augustine's letters, sermons, books and confessions which have come down across sixteen centuries, when the reader knows that this writing was *all* he wanted to do; but the incredible interruptions of a bishop's widespread duties were perfectly cared for, also. As well as this stewardship of speech, contained in a couplet carved on his dinner table: "Who loves another's name to stain he shall not dine with me again."

Elsewhere in this book the continual generosity of St. Bridget has been mentioned; her history is one long row of baskets of apples brought to her, but given at once to nearby lepers; baskets of eggs, sent on to the sick. It was St. Patrick who said of her kind: "There are three orders of saints: those who are a glory on the mountain tops, those who are gleams on the sides of the hills; and those who are just a few faint lights down in the valleys."

The one saint with whom even a Protestant feels at ease is Francis of Assisi; by his humble rough habit, by his sermon to the larks, by his persuasion of the wolf of Gubbio, he seems so gentle and selfless that everyone loves him instinctively. It is a shock to come across his prayer: "O Lord God, if Thou art pleased to bestow gifts upon me, be Thou the Guardian thereof, for I have a great diffidence within myself; and I am a great robber, who may perhaps play the defaulter with Thee." There must have been joy among the angels of God just then! For they all knew perfectly well how he gave away his cloak the moment he saw a beggar shivering with cold: "Here, friend, here is thy cloak! I have kept it far too long from thee already." Which shows what he meant when he said: "Courtesy is Charity's own sister."

"Holy poverty," he explained, "is a treasure so high-excelling and so divine that we be not worthy to lay it up in our vessels; since this is that celestial virtue whereby all earthly things and fleeting are trodden underfoot, and whereby all hindrances are lifted from the soul, so that freely she may join herself to God Eternal." No wonder he could pray: "O Lord, so wean my mind from all that is under heaven by the fiery and sweet strength of Thy love, that I may be ready to die for the love of Thy love as Thou didst deign to die for the love of my love."

In the year 1270, Thomas Aquinas was saying something much more astute about money: "The art of acquiring money is subordinate to the art of using money, not so much by way of producing material for it as of providing tools for it. For money and every kind of wealth are merely economic tools." This might be a Wall Street broker speaking!

But, about the same year, see how differently Richard Rolle was talking from his hermit's cell in England: "I went about by covetousness of riches, and I found not Jesus. I ran by wantonness of the flesh, and I found not Jesus. I sat in companies of

worldly mirth, and I found not Jesus. In all of them I found Him
not; for He let me know by His grace that He is not found in
the land of softly living. Therefore, I turned by another way, and
I ran about by poverty, and I found Jesus, poorly born into the
world, laid in a crib, lapped in cloths. I went by sharpness of
suffering, and I found Jesus weary in the way, tormented by
hunger, thirst and cold, filled with reproofs and blame. I sat
by my love." And elsewhere he added: "Love cannot be lazy."
(A deepened force in all his words seems more moving in the
early English words; such as: "Thou sall strenkil mee lord with
ysope and .i. sall bee clensid: thou sall wayss mee and abouen
the snaw .i. sall be made white.")

After a modern Christian's more or less casual and undisci-
plined spending, it is wholesome to think through what it must
have meant for any saint to give up everything. Never to buy anything again. To eat only the meager meals provided in the religious
establishment where he or she lived. To abide by difficult hours.
To keep long silences. To live closely with persons who in
ordinary life might seem eccentric and undesirable. To think nothing of appearances. To have no mirror. It was a shock to learn
about St. Teresa of Avila, for instance, that as a nun she received
two serge habits (to last her lifetime) each weighing twenty-six
pounds. Obviously far too heavy for a Spanish summer. But not
nearly warm enough for constant kneeling on stone floors in
winter. Where does feminine pride go? And how quickly can it
be lost?

It is good to discover the saints' keener awareness of our
Lord's life made possible by feeling His crucifix hitting gently
against their knees at every step. This, *this,* was the Person whose
own simplicities and austerities seemed well worth the imitating.
The sound of bells at frequent intervals would call to prayer—
Matins, Prime, Tierce, Sexte, Nones, Lauds, Vespers, Compline;
then the beauty of old Plain Songs, the charm of old Psalms, the
long silences; and above all, the *Rule:* with no departures from
following it. The old thirteenth century "Ancren Riwle for
Nuns" is explicit and warmhearted, a stewardship of shared

concern: "At some time in the day or night think upon and call to mind all who are sick and sorrowful, who suffer affliction and poverty, the pain which prisoners endure who lie heavily fetted with iron; think especially of the Christians who are among heathen, some in prison, some in as great thralldom as an ox or an ass; have compassion for those who are under strong temptation; take thought of all men's sorrows; and sigh to our Lord that He may take care of them."

St. Catherine of Siena took this in deep earnest, for she was the one who went with a man afraid to die, and was the one who promised to receive his head after the execution—to comfort his fear beforehand.

It was St. Teresa who said of the clock: "It comforts me to hear the hours strike, for I feel that I have drawn a little nearer to God." "From silly devotions and gloomy saints, good Lord deliver us." "All my stock is a little hunger for Him." "Christ has no body now on earth but yours, no hands but yours; yours are the eyes through which look out Christ's compassion to the world, yours are the feet with which He is to go about doing good, and yours are the hands with which He is to bless us now."

She was gay and laughter-loving: "How I pity Satan—for he can never love anybody!" "Live your whole life, love your whole love!" "Christ did not call Himself 'the Custom' but 'the Truth.'" "My health is very bad, but God does so much through me that I laugh heartily at myself." "Sin is enmity against God! It is as if we said: 'Lord, I know full well that this action displeases Thee, yet I shall do it, nonetheless. I am aware that Thy eyes see it. I know perfectly well that Thou dost not want it, but I will rather follow my bent and fancy than Thy will.'" Her guitar is still to be seen in her cell in Avila, and she spoke of us all when she said: "Some people are full of the best resolutions, but never carry them out. They resemble the soldiers in a painting in a battle, who are in the attitude of striking the enemy, but never really strike."

It was another sixteenth-century Spanish saint who put into our spiritual bank a prayer to draw on, frequently: "Teach us, good Lord, to serve Thee as Thou deservest: to give and not to count the cost; to fight and not to heed the wounds; to strive and not to seek for rest; to labor and not to ask for reward, saving the knowledge that we do Thy will." Ignatius Loyola also added: "In this school we are taught to accept a rich poverty, a free slavery, a glorious humility." "Work as though all depended upon yourself; trust in God as though all depended upon Him."

We must not wish to become everything at once, nor to become saints in four days.

St. Philip Neri

Some become proud and insolent, either by riding a good horse, wearing a feather in their hat, or by being dressed in a fine suit of clothes; but who does see the folly of this? for if there be any glory in such things, the glory belongs to the horse, the bird and the tailor; and what a meanness of heart must it be to borrow esteem from a horse, from a feather, or some ridiculous new fashion! Others value themselves for a well-trimmed bearing, for curled locks, or soft hands; or because they can dance, sing or play; but are not these effeminate men who seek to raise their reputation by so frivolous and foolish things? Others for a little learning would be honoured and respected by the whole world, as if every one ought to become their pupil, and account them his masters. These are called pedants. Others strut like peacocks, contemplating their beauty and think themselves admired by every one. All this is extremely vain, foolish and impertinent; and the glory which is raised on so weak foundations is justly esteemed vain and frivolous.

St. Francis de Sales

*It is not by feet or change of place that men leave
Thee or return to Thee; rather in lustful, that is, in
darkened affections is the true distance from Thy face.*

St. Augustine

3 1

THE CHURCH THAT BEGINS
WITH BLOTTING PAPER

Blotting out the handwriting of ordinances that was against us,
which was contrary to us, and took it out of the way, nailing it
to His cross.   COLOSSIANS 2:14

Go into any post office. Take one long look at any limp old piece
of blotting paper lying on any counter. For this any Christian
can accept as more authentic than the latest Dead Sea Scroll,
dug up in damp and dangerous caves in the Holy Land. Since
what has the church ever been but a continual Money Order to
the World? a Registered Letter to the Saints that are scattered
abroad? an insured Parcel Post Package for the relief of widows
and orphans? an Air Mail Special Delivery which neither snow
nor rain nor hail nor dark of night has ever hindered from its
prompt delivery?

Architects may think that a church begins with a blueprint. But
a Christian knows that it begins with blotting paper—absorbing
all the sins of all its members, absorbing all the hymns and litur-
gies of all the writers of all ages, absorbing all the sermons of all
the clergymen, absorbing all the biographies of all the Christians
who have been turning the world upsidedown, absorbing all the

holy days and working days and birthdays of all its members, absorbing all the hopes and fears of all the years, merging them in the central Figure of that strange Man on the cross, who, by being lifted up, has kept drawing all men unto Him.

By the year 61, Pliny wrote of this absorption process: "This new sect has reached even the rural sections. There is nothing the matter with them except that they have a queer religion." And nothing seemed queerer than their attitude toward money, neighborliness and eternity. So queer, in fact, that a young Roman lawyer named Tertullian cried in surprise: "See how these Christians love one another!" For nothing could break this love of the fellowship, not even the cruel Law of Licinius: "A penalty was attached, to the effect that those who showed compassion were to share the fate of the objects of their charity, and that those who were humane to the unfortunates were to be flung into bonds and imprisonment, and endure the same suffering as the others."

By 1621 John Donne wrote of this same continuing absorption in one another:

The Church is catholic, universal, as are all her actions; all that she does belongs to all. When she baptizes a child, that action concerns me; for that child is thereby connected to that Head which is my head too, and engrafted into that Body whereof I am a member. And when she buries a man, that action concerns me: for all mankind is of one Author, and is one Volume. When one man dies, one chapter is not torn out of the Book, but translated into a better Language; God employs several translators: some pieces are translated by Age, some by Sickness, some by War, some by Justice; but God's hand is in every translation, and His hand shall bind all our scattered leaves again for that Library where every book shall lie open to one another.

On Stewardship Sunday how appropriate to substitute for the usual printed bulletin a blotter cut out in the shape of your own building, bearing on one side part of Paul's letter to the Colossians: 2:14-17 for a reponsive reading, together with the hymn:

> I love Thy church, O God, her walls before Thee stand,
> Dear as the apple of Thine eye and graven on Thy hand.

On the other side, the names of certain unforgettable Protestants whose contributions have been absorbed into the very walls of all Christian churches.

For this nineteen-hundred-year memory is our priceless treasure. Yet the heedless might consider the blotter pretty old and torn and stained by this time. It was Albert Schweitzer who said rather recently: "Civilization can only revive when there shall come into being in a number of individuals a new tone of mind, independent of the prevalent one among the crowd, and in opposition to it—a tone of mind which will gradually win influence over the collective one, and in the end determine its character. Only an ethical movement can rescue us from barbarism, and the ethical comes into existence only in individuals."

Chaucer has painted the portrait of one such:

> A good man was there of religion,
> And was a poor Parson of a town;
> But rich he was of holy thought and work;
> He was also a learned man, a clerk,
> That Christes Gospel truly would preach;
> His parishens devoutly he would teach,
> Benign he was, and wonder diligent,
> And in adversity full patient;
> And such he was y-proved ofte sythes,
> Full loath were he to cursen for his tythes,
> But rather would he given out of doubt
> Unto his poor parishens about
> Of his offering, and else of his substance;
> He could in little thing have sufficance . . .
> This noble ensample to his sheep he gave,
> That first he wrought, and afterward he taught . . .
> But Christes lore and his apostles twelve
> He taught, but first he followed it himself.

This "poor parson" has been absorbed into the blotting paper of every church everywhere. In Germany it was Martin Luther, of whom Thomas Carlyle wrote: *"The world and its history were waiting for the man."* But about himself Luther said a great many memorable things: "As Christ has given Himself to me, I must give myself as a sort of Saviour to all whom I meet"; "If anybody should knock at the door of my heart and ask: 'Who lives here?' I should never dream of saying: 'Martin Luther lives here,' but: 'Jesus Christ lives here.' " "Enable us rise above ourselves to Thee; and from Thee to go below ourselves in love and to remain always in Thee, and in love."

But with even costlier bluntness, Luther also said other sentences which sank deep into the blotters of his day: "Every man needs two conversions: the first of his heart, the second of his pocketbook!" "Goods do not make a man good; the fruits do not bear the tree, but the tree the fruits." "Wealth is the smallest thing on earth, the least gift that God has bestowed on mankind." "I have had many things in my hands, and I have lost them all; but whatever I have placed in God's hands, that I still possess." No wonder he could write:

> Let goods and kindred go, this mortal life also;
> The body they may kill: God's truth abideth still;
> His Kingdom is forever.

In one of his Expositions he wrote: "May God in His mercy save me from a Christian church where there are faint-hearted and weak people, the sick, and those who are aware of their sin, misery and wretchedness, and feel it, and who cry to God without ceasing and sigh to Him for comfort and help; and believe in the forgiveness of sins and suffer persecution for the Word's sake. Satan is a cunning rogue. Through his fanatics he seeks to make the simple-minded believe that the prayer of the Gospel is useless." This was in 1527; and it might seem as if this desire to dwell among sinners had been granted for he also wrote: "Our Lord commonly giveth riches to such gross asses to whom He affordeth nothing else that is good." "The god of this world is riches, pleasure and pride, wherewith it abuses all creatures and gifts of God."

By 1534 another name was being indelibly absorbed into the blotter of the church's past, for when he was only twenty-six John Calvin published his *Institutes,* with a complete outline of his theology: "No member of the Christian body holds his gifts for himself or for his private use, but shares them among his fellows. Nor does he derive benefits save from those things which proceed from the common profit of the body as a whole. Thus the pious man owes to his brother all that is in his power to give." Calvin himself ate only one meal a day, and lived up to the full symbolism of his coat of arms—the burning heart aflame and open bestowing hand. The Pope in Rome was heard to complain bitterly over Calvin's immense success in ruling the city of Geneva: "The trouble with that heretic is his indifference to money!" The Council of Geneva took it for granted that every citizen was also a disciple of the church, and the Council therefore censored harsh creditors, punished usurers, merchants who cheated clients, and clothmakers whose yardgoods proved too narrow were fined.

All the great historic churches have just such great historic handwriting blotted into their walls, absorbed into their memories, until eventually this remembrance of things past belongs to all churches alike. A kindred pride, for instance, in the way Susannah Wesley brought up her nineteen children on a pittance and a method: "If you would judge of the lawfulness or unlawfulness of pleasure, then take this simple rule—whatever weakens your reason, impairs the tenderness of your conscience, and takes off the relish of spiritual things, *that* to you is sin."

No wonder John Wesley would grow up to say:

I fear, whenever riches have increased, the essence of religion has decreased. For religion must necessarily produce industry and frugality; and these in turn produce riches. As riches increase, so will pride, anger, and love of the world. Is there no way to prevent this? There is one way, and there is no other under heaven. If those who gain all they can and save all they can will likewise give all they can, then the more they gain the more they will grow in grace and the more treasure they will lay up in heaven.

In an equally practical way Charles Wesley put his mother's method into his hymn:

> I want a principle within of watchful, godly fear,
> A sensibility of sin, a pain to feel it near.

About this same time, elsewhere in England, Deacon Ryland shouted down a young man who felt that Jesus Christ meant what He said about going and preaching and teaching: "Sit down, young man!" said the deacon, "if God wants to convert the heathen He will do it without your help or mine!" But William Carey would not sit down. And before long a few Baptists met in the Widow Wallis's parlor, taking up a collection in Andrew Fuller's snuffbox, the amount coming to thirteen pounds, two shillings, sixpence. Not really enough to send William Carey to India; but he went right on working at his old trade: "My business is to preach the gospel, I cobble shoes for a living."

After forty years in Bengal, with no vacation, William Carey wrote out this "AGREEMENT" with his two fellow missionaries: "Let us give unreservedly to this glorious cause. Let us never think that our time, our gifts, our strength, our families, or even the clothes we wear are our own. Let us forever shut out the idea of laying up a farthing for ourselves and our children. Let us continually watch against a worldly spirit, and cultivate a Christian indifference toward every indulgence. Rather let us bear hardness as good soldiers of Jesus Christ."

This tremendous self-forgetfulness is not isolated to India. For in Africa David Livingstone's words have been as indelibly absorbed into Christian history: "I will place no value on anything I have or may possess except in relation to the Kingdom of Jesus Christ." "Recall the 21 years, give me back all its experiences, give its shipwrecks, give it me surrounded with savages with spears and clubs, give it me back again with the club knocking me to the ground, give it me back, and I will still be your missionary!" Seventy-five years ago when this magnificent hero died, England buried him in Westminster Abbey, and the magazine *Punch* neglected its wit for one issue to print its own tribute:

Open the Abbey doors and bear him in
To sleep with king and statesman, chief and sage,
The missionary come of weaver-kin,
But great by work that brooks no lower wage.
He needs no epitaph to guard a name
Which men shall prize while worthy work is known,
He lived and died for good—be that his fame;
Let marble crumble: this is Living-stone.

One signature has been indelibly spreading over the past fifty years of the church's blotting paper—that of Walter Rauschenbusch. It was stirring to grow up in Rochester, New York; to have him slowly awakening the social consciousness of pulpit and pew alike; to remember the day when he called in the home and personally presented his paraphrase of I Corinthians 13:

If I increase wealth beyond the dream of past ages and increase not love, my heat is the flush of fever and my success will deal death.

Though I have foresight to locate the fountains of riches, and power to preempt them, and skill to tap them, and have no loving vision for humanity, I am blind.

Though I give of my profits to the poor and make princely endowments for those who toil for me, if I have no human fellowship of love with them, my life is barren and doomed.

Love is just and kind. Love is not greedy and covetous. Love exploits no one; it takes no unearned gain; it gives more than it gets. Love does not break down the lives of others to make wealth for itself; it makes wealth to build the life of all. Love seeks solidarity; it tolerates no divisions; it prefers equal workmates; it shares its efficiency. Love enriches all men, educates all men, gladdens all men.

The values created by love never fail; but whether there are class privileges, they shall fail; whether there are millions gathered, they shall be scattered; and whether there are vested rights, they shall be abolished. For in the past strong men lorded it in ruthlessness and strove for their own power and pride, but when the perfect social order comes, the strong shall serve the common good. Before the sun of Christ brought in the dawn, men competed, and forced tribute from weakness, but when the full day shall come, they will work as mates in love, each for all, and all for each. For now we see in the mirror of selfishness, darkly, but then we shall see the destinies of the race as God sees them. But now abideth honor, justice, and love, these three; and the greatest of these is love.

Phillips Brooks also has left on America's blotting paper his significant entry, beginning with the day when his father, in Litchfield, Connecticut, was living on $800 a year, with eleven growing children. He has recorded how his mother "sat opposite him murmuring in her sweet, refined, gentle, sad way that bills were due, that she had no more money; that, indeed, she did not see how they could get along; that for her own part she expected to die in the poorhouse. At that father dropped his hands to the table and his eyes sparkled as he said: 'My dear, I have trusted God for forty years and He never has forsaken me; I am not going to distrust Him now.' That waked me up; it was better than the catechism. It sank into me; and during my earlier life I went through perils of sickness and poverty and all forms of limitation, but I never lost sight of that scene and that sentence."

Bishop Brooks had begun by being a teacher; but both his pedagogy and his discipline were so poor that he was dismissed; and considered his future a probable failure also. So that when he found himself the best-loved and most famous clergyman in Boston, he knew what it meant to say: "You must learn, you must let God teach you, that the only way to get rid of your past is to make a future out of it. God will waste nothing." "Do not pray for easy lives. Do not pray for tasks equal to your powers. Pray for powers equal to your tasks. Then the doing of your work will be no miracle; but you will be the miracle. And every day you will wonder at yourself, at the richness of life which has come to you by the grace of God." "You ask what you can do? *You can furnish one Christian life!*" "You go to your saint and find God working and manifest in him. He got near to God by some saint of *his* that went before *him*, or that stood beside him, in whom he saw the Divine Presence. That saint again lighted his

fire at some flame before him. And so the power of the sainthoods
fills and animates the world."

The sainthoods in the blotting paper! The only warning is: we
need to hold up a mirror in order to read what the blotting paper
says; for now we see through a glass—darkly. But then?

Having been tenant long to a rich lord,
*   Not thriving, I resolvéd to be bold,*
*   And make a suit unto him to afford*
A new small-rented lease, and cancel the old.
In heaven at his manor I him sought:
*   They told me there that he was lately gone*
*   About some land, which he had dearly bought*
Long since on earth, to take possession.
I straight returned, and knowing his great birth,
*   Sought him accordingly in great resorts,*
*   In cities, theatres, gardens, parks, and courts.*
At length I heard a ragged noise and mirth
*   Of thieves and murderers: there I him espied,*
*   Who straight, Your suit is granted, said, and died.*
                    George Herbert, 1593-1633

All we have willed or hoped or dreamed of good, shall
*   exist;*
Not its semblance, but itself; no beauty, nor good, nor
*   power*
Whose voice has gone forth, but each survives for the
*   melodist*
When eternity affirms the conception of an hour.
The high that proved too high, the heroic for earth too
*   hard,*
The passion that left the ground to lose itself in the
*   sky,*

Are music sent up to God by the lover and the bard;
Enough that He heard it once; we shall hear it by and
by.

Robert Browning, 1812-1889

3 2

WHAT GIVES?
(being a brief anthololgy of Stewardship in Slang:
dedicated to Jennie Geddes)

There is not a word in my tongue, but lo! O Lord, Thou knowest
it altogether. Thou hast beset me behind and before, and laid
Thine hand upon me. Such knowledge is too wonderful for me.

PSALM 139:4-6

It has been a long while since Jennie Geddes flung her footstool
at Dean Harris in St. Giles Cathedral, and entered church history
with a bang. Her aim was superlative, and she made her point:
that no dominie in Edinburgh need read from the English Book
of Common Prayer—*common* indeed! As if braid Scots were not
a lot more common and bonnie and bracing to bid a body grip on
to God and the Gude Book. You took your fling, Jennie; and, in
the end, St. Giles honored you with a plaque on the church walls
(and another one for the poor Dean), even preserving your old
footstool in a museum. What a temptation, therefore, to fling
something at another dominie.

For we have a Dean, ourselves, three hundred years later!
Our Dean Weigle, surrounded by twenty-five distinguished

scholars, slaved long years before publishing an R.S.V., rather recently. The Introduction says of their Book: "It must stand forth in language that is direct and meaningful today. It is our hope and prayer that this Revised Standard Version of the Bible may be used by God to speak to men in these momentous times, and help them to understand and believe and obey His Word."

But Jennie! Jennie! who but you could appreciate that the man on the street speaks a still *more* common lingo than theirs—too broad and blunt for highbrows, perhaps; but just earthy enough and salty enough to catch the lowbrow between the ribs. Anyhow, in memory of your footstool we fling these footnotes in slang at our clerics, in this un-Revised, un-Standard Version: "in the hope and prayer that they may be used by God to speak to men in these momentous times."

1. ALL WET (The rains descended and the winds blew and beat upon that house; Matthew 7:25) Everybody knows how A. Phillip Goodrich gave his umbrella one rainy day to a ferryman in exchange for some much-needed cash. His pennies from heaven have made automobile history. But even better Christian history began one Saturday when a Filipino student in a strange American town stopped a Methodist on the street and asked how to get to the Catholic church the next morning—only to learn that it would mean a three-mile walk. But when Sunday dawned it was raining cats and dogs, too wet for even a Catholic to leave his boardinghouse. Until a knock at the door announced his Methodist acquaintance, standing there with an umbrella hooked over each arm. He feared the Catholic would get soaked through if he had no umbrella; he offered to go along, to show him the short cuts; he was much more fortunate himself, he said, his own church was at the corner. Overwhelmed by such friendliness the Catholic said: "Then why don't I go to your church with you?" He went, and he liked it. He went the second Sunday, and liked it even better. By the third Sunday, he was completely carried away. And within four years he was studying at Drew Theological Seminary to become a Methodist minister. By the time he told

this story to Gordon Torgerson on shipboard he had become Bishop Valencias of the Philippines with more than 113,000 other Methodists in his parishes. (But, of course, Jennie, any Protestant who never provides a second umbrella deserves to be called "all wet.")

2. BITING OFF MORE THAN YOU CAN CHEW (Which of you, intending to build a tower, sitteth not down first, and counteth the cost, whether he have sufficient to finish it; Luke 14:28) Up in Vermont a farmer's wife was very proud of her new sewing machine which her husband had just "chawed out" —for some tobacco has tags which are redeemable, and the machine was one of the premiums. Mrs. Bonham told how Frank just "chawed and chawed" until finally there were enough tags; but now that he was chawing out a grandfather clock, it was a question if he could ever make it!

3. BROTHER, CAN YOU SPARE A DIME? (So he paid the fare thereof; Jonah 1:3) Jonah, of course, spent his own dime and went on the wrong boat, headed the wrong way to accomplish the particular mission the Lord had in mind. But several generations ago, thousands upon thousands of Congregational boys and girls in Boston each spared a dime to build their own boat, *The Morning Star*, which then sailed among the South Sea Islands, carrying missionaries. Typhoons and tidal waves wrecked many a later ship, which other children in the world spared other dimes to rebuild. But three or four years ago, when the *Morning Star VI* sank, her skipper was Rev. Eleanor Wilson. She has been on a lecture tour to raise money from the present generation of Sunday School scholars around the world. An author was so fascinated by this modern Odyssey of a 65-year-old missionary that she wrote *The Lady Was a Skipper;* and although the new *Morning Star VII* began sailing on April 14, 1957, not all the necessary funds have been raised yet. This would seem to give a dime dramatic dimensions for teenagers, who now spare their dimes in less shipshape fashion in order to:

consume 190 million candy bars a week,
chew 230 million sticks of chewing gum a week,
drink 130 million bottles of pop a week,
eat 13 million ice cream cones a week.

4. BUMMING THEIR WAY (Lord, we have forsaken all to follow Thee, what then shall we have? Matthew 19:27) Probably Peter had left only an old fishing smack and a few torn nets, the same as James and John, who were mending their nets when Jesus called them. Peter's question almost sounded as if he had come along only for profit. The English word "saunter" is said to have grown out of the French phrase used by pilgrims traveling to the Holy Land in the Middle Ages; for if they knocked at doors en route saying: "À la Sante Terre," (To the Holy Land) almost any householder would feed them gladly, in order to gain merit in heaven. But when tramps and chislers saw how simple a way this was to get three square meals a day, they too began banging on doors, shouting noisily: "À la Sante Terre"; but with hands held out in so grasping a gesture that people said scornfully: "This one is just a Sante-Terrer! A saunterer!" And a generous word turned mercenary.

5. BUSMAN'S HOLIDAY (Even to your old age I am He; and even to hoar hairs will I carry you: I have made, and I will bear; even I will carry, and will deliver you; Isaiah 47:4) Obviously Blaise Pascal was one of the French Christians to whom God had entrusted all his fellow men. For early one morning on the streets of Paris he saw all the day laborers hurrying off to work in the same direction, and that same evening saw them all plodding wearily homeward on foot. "If only those poor people had some sort of a public carry-all to transport those going in the same direction," he sighed sympathetically. Then and there inventing the first omnibus! For as he himself said, later: "All the trouble in the world comes from not being able to sit quietly in one's own room to think things through. . . . God may not need my intelligence, but He certainly does not need my ignorance!"

6. CAN YOU "DIG IT"? (Then the steward said within him-

self: "What shall I do? for my lord taketh away from me the stewardship; I cannot dig; to beg I am ashamed"; Luke 16:3) Can you fathom why some desirable plum is taken out of your keeping? Why you are no longer considered a faithful steward of the loving-kindness of God? Has your sharing dwindled to an irreducible minimum? Are you such as Oliver Goldsmith described:

> A kind and gentle heart he had
> To comfort friends and foes;
> The naked every day he clad
> When he put on his clothes.

Or does Willie Loman's son (in *Death of a Salesman*) express this emptiness so that you *do* "dig it," when he said that he still felt temporary about himself?

7. COUNT ME OUT (The Lord shall count, when he writeth up the people, that this man was born here; Psalm 87:6) Not long ago a proper Bostonian lady mistook a milestone for a tombstone, by misreading the words: "*1 MI. from Boston*" into: "*I'M from Boston*." She smiled with satisfaction: "How simple! But how adequate!" Quite forgetting that a miss is as good as a mile; and that this headstone was nameless, dateless, graceless, traceless, faceless.

8. CUTTING A MELON (Better is a handful with quietness, than both hands full with travail and vexation of spirit; Ecclesiastes 4:6) A television program recently introduced an oil millionaire, after showing his colossal castle and mentioning his supercolossal fortune, estimated at $400,000,000. He admitted casually that often he cut his melons in making business decisions by flipping a coin, heads or tails, about whether to buy or sell, even if the deal was as high as a million dollars. In the interview he said his greatest goal in life was "to complete the Canada pipeline!" Albert Einstein would have preferred a *handful of quietness:* "Possessions, outward success, publicity, luxury—to me these have always been contemptible. I believe that a simple unassuming manner of life is best for everyone, best for the body and the mind."

9. DEAD BROKE (And when he had spent all . . . he began to be in want; Luke 15:14) An immigrant father, unable to read, took a letter from his son to the corner butcher shop, where the butcher boomed out the contents in loud blunt tones: "Hi, Pop. I'm sick, so send me some dough, for I'm dead broke, not a red cent left. Love, Josef."

The father began fuming: "Who does he tink I am? Mr. Rockefeller? He don't sound sick, one speck! Not one penny vill I send." But out on the sidewalk, his anxious little wife said, pleadingly: "Papa, perhaps butcher not so goot for reading English; I like better we let baker try read letter, also."

So they went into the bakery; and the baker who was a gentle little Italian put on his glasses, threw himself into character by putting pathos into every syllable: "Hi, Pop-a . . . I'm-a seeck-a, so . . . send-a me some-a dough-a . . . for I'm dead-a brrrooke-a, not-a one-a red-a cent-a left-a . . . Love-a, Yosef-a." Both parents burst into tears, but the baker patted their shoulders sympathetically: "He ees young-a man-a! He will-a recovaire queeck-a, so . . . why break-a the heart-a? For send-a the dough-a, try-a the telegram-a; one-a hour, and-a eet ees in-a his-a hand-a!"

So, once more, stewardship was a matter of interpretation.

10. DROP ME A LINE SOMETIME (Ye are our epistle, written in our hearts, known and read of all men; 2 Corinthians 3:2) An Australian magazine called *Stamp News* has an editorial entitled "Hypocrisy": "The United States in April broke all records for bad taste and hypocrisy by issuing an 8-cent stamp bearing the slogan: 'In God We Trust.' If one of the smaller nations—Switzerland, Denmark or Sweden, e.g., with a proven record of peaceful intentions had used this slogan, it would not have been out of place. Its use in trigger-happy America, however, is as incongruous as would be its adoption by the equally bellicose Soviet Union. Far from trusting in God the U.S. has shown only too clearly that it trusts nothing but its own ability to assemble a bigger, better and brighter stockpile of Atomic, Hydrogen and Cobalt Bombs than anyone else. The U.S. has deliberately turned its back on its Deity, and instead, embarked on a policy of lunacy

which could easily lead to the extermination of mankind. For it to use such a slogan on a stamp is a shocking piece of bad taste. The American clergy has not gone on record to protest about the stamp, but that will cause no surprise. Were any of them to raise their voice and speak the truth, they would immediately be branded as Commies and hounded from their pulpits by the Senate."

11. EXCUSE MY DUST (For He remembereth that we are dust; Psalm 103:14) Dust is dramatic stuff, indestructible and sacred and story-laden. So little, yet so big. Seemingly so local on our tabletops, yet actually a long long memory blown to us from out of Eden and Egypt, out of Babylon and Bethlehem and Bethany. In one speck of dust so small as to be beyond our naked vision, are more particles than there are inhabitants on our planet. Seemingly so still, yet moving in their orbits with a velocity that staggers the imagination. All women treat dust far too unlovingly: for it is poetry, and has much to tell. All men treat it too unheedingly: perhaps only Gandhi sensing the mystery of its history, for in New Delhi his words are engraved on the walls of the government radio station: "I want the cultures of all lands to be blown about my house as freely as possible. But I refuse to be blown off my feet by any of them." Ethics of the dust, this! A stewardship of the past and the present, passed on to the future.

12. FIFTY-FIFTY (Half of my goods I give to the poor; Luke 19:8) Zaccheus has outdone, outshone, outpledged and presumably outpaid the benevolence budgets of the churches in your town, none of which ever seem to elect an Even-Stephen as treasurer—to insure a fifty-fifty benevolence basis.

13. FIT TO BE TIED (Remember them that are in bonds, as bound with them; and them which suffer adversity, as being yourself also in the body; Hebrews 12:3) It is one thing to Christianize one's own nervous system; but quite another thing to practice John Woolman's being "baptized into the feelings of the people," with our Lord's compassion, "touched by every feeling of their

infirmities." An *economist*—planning carefully to bear one an-other's burdens; a *housekeeper*—saving out a loaf for the lonely exile; a *steward*—with twelve baskets full for the Stranger.

14. GETTING DOWN TO BRASS TACKS (And I will fasten him as a nail in a sure place . . . and they shall hang upon him all the glory of his father's house, the offspring and the issue, all the vessels of small quantity, from cups to flagons; Isaiah 22:23-24) *"Christians hold the world together"* said the Letter to Diognetus in the first century, and they are still the square pegs in round holes on which all our tomorrows will hang in our Father's house.

15. GO JUMP IN THE LAKE (Cast thy bread upon the water, for thou shalt find it after many days; Ecclesiastes 11:1) Some stories sound unusually neat and tidy. Such as the day when Winston Churchill was a child and fell in a lake on his parent's estate, and began to drown. But the gardener's son jumped in and rescued him. The parents were so grateful that they asked the young fellow what he wanted most in the world? "I'm saving up to become a doctor!" But the nobleman took care of all this train-ing in one generous gift, at once. Eventually—as Sir Arthur Fleming—this doctor became famous as the discoverer of peni-cillin; and eventually, when Sir Winston Churchill lay dying of pneumonia, the gardener's son again could rescue him, with penicillin! As the sundial says so sensibly: *"Today Is the Tomor-row You Worried About Yesterday."*

16. GOING DUTCH (Share ye one another's burdens, and so fulfill the law of Christ; Galatians 6:2) When Helen Frick was a debutante in Pittsburgh, her father asked her what she wanted him to give her as a coming-out present. She chose a valuable piece of ground worth half a million dollars to be given to the city for a public park, to be set aside for children. The wealthy millionaire gladly gave the land. The society girl gladly saw slum children playing safely, sharing her childhood memories of grass and trees and fresh air.

17. GOOD-BY NOW (It is expedient for you that I go away,

for if I go not away the Comforter will not come; John 16:7):
You must have noticed lately that something new has been added
to farewells, that wistful word: "Good-by *now*." As if parting were
such sweet sorrow. As if a hole would be left in your pavement,
a vacuum in your atmosphere, an empty chair at your table. But
that is not true! For "Good-by" means "*God-by-you*." The French
adieu also assigns you "*To God*," and the Spanish, "*Go with God*."
Your Giver of all good gifts has promised to be with you always.
Your inexhaustible banker of all resources stands ready to supply
all your need. Your Comforter who comforts your own discom-
forts expects that, in turn, you too will comfort the comfortless.

18. GYPPED (Will a man rob God? Yet ye have robbed me.
But ye say: "Wherein have we robbed Thee?" "In tithes and
offerings"; Malachi 3:8) A certain preacher upset the good women
of his church by objecting to the use in all their meetings of
"*The Robbers' Farewell*": "The Lord watch between me and thee
while we are absent one from the other." For Mizpah, he explained, meant a watch tower, with Esau keeping a sharp eye on
that scalawag Jacob, to see that he did not cheat him again, and
Jacob in jitters over the dirty job he had just pulled off. "In any
case, ladies," the preacher suggested, "when you do use this
benediction, remember to cultivate an equally uneasy conscience
over what goes into your church offering envelopes!"

19. HAND-OUTS (With Him the alms of a man is as a signet;
and He will keep the bounty of a man as the apple of the eye;
Ecclesiasticus 18:22) An Armenian storyteller always says of himself: "*God gave me three apples*," meaning one to reward the
narrator of the tale, one for the listener, and one for God in sheer
gratitude. Such a stewardship of thanksgiving as has filled this
"Twelve Baskets Full"—that nothing be lost.

20. HARD-BOILED BABY (Were they ashamed when they
had committed abomination? Nay, they were not at all ashamed,
neither could they blush. . . . For they have healed the hurt
of the daughter of my people slightly, saying: "Peace, peace";
when there is no peace; Jeremiah 8:11-12) There ought to be

background music at this point, "Has Anybody Here Seen Dinah?" For she was that hard-boiled Junior Miss who went out to see the daughters of the land; but it was a case of "Boy Meets Girl," with Prince Charming inviting her to "Have One on the House," after which they both "Acted Like Crazy"; with fade-out music of "Hail, Hail, the Gang's All Here" as her furious brothers stampeded on scene; after which the curtain went down to the riotous sound of "There'll Be a Hot Time in the Old Town Tonight." As modern as that; and straight out of Genesis; even including Jeremiah's statement that "they" have healed the hurt of the daughter of my people slightly. Of what are the stewards of law and order dreaming that heal so slightly the wounds made by certain movies, certain comics and certain television shows?

21. HERE'S MUD IN YOUR EYE (Their land is full of silver and gold; neither is there any end of their treasures; their land is also full of horses, neither is there any end of their chariots; Isaiah 2:7) Alexander the Great on his travels is said to have wandered to the gate of Paradise. But when he knocked and told the guardian angel his name, the angel asked: "And who is Alexander?" "Conqueror of the whole world!" "But this is the Lord's gate, only the righteous enter here." Alexander asked for some small token to prove that at least he had reached the outskirts of heaven. The angel tossed him a small fragment of a human skull, saying: "Weigh it!" Alexander showed it contemptuously to his wise men, who brought a pair of scales, placing the bone in one pan while Alexander laid all his silver and gold in the other pan—but the small bone outweighed them all. Alexander flung in all his crown jewels and diadems, but they flew upward like feathers against the bone; until one of the wise men tossed a few grains of dust on the bone. Up flew the scale! For the bone was that which surrounded the eye; and nothing can ever satisfy the eye until covered by the dust of the grave.

22. HE'S NOT ALL THERE (Where two or three are gathered together in my name, there am I in the midst of them; Matthew

18:20) This ought to be a perfect description of a Budget Committee at work. But the latest definition of a committee is a group of the Unfit appointed by the Unwilling to do the Unnecessary.

> Three thousand for my convertible,
> Five thousand for a piece of sod,
> Ten thousand I paid to be in a house,
> A dollar I gave to God.
> A sum to entertain
> My friends in endless chatter,
> And when the world goes crazy mad
> I ask: "Lord, what's the matter?"
> Yet there is one big question—
> And for its answer I now search:
> With things so bad in this old world,
> What's holding back my church?

(from the calendar of the First Christian Church, Mansfield, Ohio)

23. HOT AIR! (Their mouth speaketh great swelling words, having men's persons in admiration, because of advantage; Jude 16) On the mantle of the Quaker Hill Club in Pawling, New York, appear these words from the ancient Sanscrit: "He who allows a day to pass without generosity or enjoying life's pleasures is like a blacksmith's bellows—he breathes but does not live."

24. HOW'S TRICKS? (The heart is deceitful above all things, and desperately wicked: who can know it? I the Lord search the heart, even to give every man . . . according to the fruit of his doings; Jeremiah 17:9-10) In one of her lesser moments Gertrude Stein once said that a cousin of hers told her about money that it was always *there*, but the pockets change—it is not in the same pockets after a change, and that is all there is to say about money. But back in 1636, locked up in an Aberdeen prison for his beautiful beliefs, old Samuel Rutherford was much more perceptive than that: "By doing good with his money, a man as it were stamps the image of God upon it, and makes it pass current for the merchandise of heaven." "My faith has no bed to

sleep on but Omnipotency." "Of all created comforts, God is
the lender; you are borrower, not the owner. How little of the
sea can a child carry in his hand so little do I take of my great
sea, my boundless and running-over Jesus Christ." "I would seek
no more till I were in my country than a little watering and
sprinkling of a withered soul, with some half outbreakings and
half out-lookings of a revealed and believed-in Godhead. A little
of God would make my soul bank-full."

25. I'LL BE SEEING YOU (For now we see in a glass darkly,
but then face to face; 1 Corinthians 13:12) In the Phillips' translation this verse becomes: "We are like men looking at a landscape
in a small mirror." One interpretation being that He is our landscape, our world, our eternal Home, for in Him we live and move
and have our being. It was G. K. Chesterton who said that there
are two ways of getting home: one is to stay there, and the other
is to walk around the whole world until you come back! This
latter the steward's ranging roundabout, through all his stay-at-
home giving.

26. I'LL TELL THE WORLD (And the eleeven disciples
gaed awa intil Galilee, to a mountain whaur Jesus had trysted
them. And, seein Him, they adoored him; hoobeit, some swither't.
And Jesus, drawin nar, spak to them sayin: "Thar hae been gien
to me a' pooer in Heevin and on yirth! Gang ye tharfor, and mak
ye disciples o' a' the nations"; Matthew 28:16-19) Jennie Geddes
knew this verse; but since her day all sorts of Scotsmen have been
heeding that "Gang ye"—Robert Moffat, David Livingstone,
Alexander Mackay, Mary Slessor, Robert Morrison, John Williams, James Chalmers; and nobody "swither't" in telling the
world.

27. IS MY FACE RED? (Look not upon me, because I am
black, because the sun hath looked upon me: my mother's children were angry with me; they made me the keeper of the vineyards; but mine own vineyard have I not kept; Songs of Solomon
1:6) There was a time when all art and drama and music belonged to religion. But somehow we did not safeguard it in the

church—is my face red? Once all education, libraries, colleges, medical and nursing institutions belonged to the church, but somehow we shifted them over to the State, general Boards or the Red Cross—is my face red? Once all childhood, hunger, disaster, relief, were concerns for the Christian family, but we were so slow that the United Nations gets there sooner with more—is my face red? General MacArthur asked American churches to send two thousand missionaries to Japan at the end of the war, and we sent 200—is my face red?

28. IT DOESN'T ADD UP (The Lord added to the church daily such as should be saved; Acts 2:47) Emerson once said that life is not doing a sum, but painting a picture. Much the way Corot's parents were milliners and thought it ridiculous to have to support a grown son who insisted on painting pictures which nobody bought and which critics found fault with. But by and by a few critics noticed that after seeing Corot's strange misty-looking trees and rivers, suddenly nature itself began resembling Corot's strange woods! After he became very popular and very rich, he always kept a drawer full of money in a table near the front door, so that any poor peasant could step in and help himself. His parents were scandalized: "They will rob you out of house and home. Then what will you do?" "I will paint another branch!" Corot answered, confident that the God of all nature had plenty for peasants and painters. (But nowadays, it takes twenty-one church members seven years to add one new convert to the church.)

29. KISS YOUR MONEY GOOD-BY (Wasted his substance in riotous living, and when he had spent all . . . he began to be in want; Luke 15:13-14) In our last nineteen-billion-dollar Christmas it was possible to buy a $300 toy kangaroo which could be wound up to jump a few steps, then out of whose pouch a smaller kangaroo would pop. Or, for a poorer purse, there was an $11 duster made of nine genuine mink tails, for use in dusting off the tops of bars. This makes five hundred million dollars spent on dogs and dog licenses sound actually noble—the dog being alive,

faithful, and a better protector of home and purse than the family conscience seems to be.

Jennie Geddes might well present such purchasers with an old Scottish Collect: "From ghoulies and ghosties and long-legged beasties that go bump in the dark, good Lord, deliver us." For of what use is eternity to a man who does not know how to spend the next half hour? or to a woman who can kiss away a twenty-dollar bill for costume jewelry? or to a nation gambling away thirty billion dollars annually?

"What difference will it make if I become Christ's man?" asked the Pictish Druid King. And Brendan, the Celtic monk, said, long ago when the world was young: "If you become Christ's man, you will behold wonder upon wonder, and every wonder true."

30. LEAVE IT TO GEORGE (If thou count me therefore a partner, receive him as myself; Philemon 17) Nobody, however, can be a Christian by proxy. A man seeing a poor beggar said: "I certainly feel for him!" But a Quaker asked immediately: "Friend, has thee felt for him in thy purse?" For nobody can be a tither by proxy, or a donor by proxy. Although everybody has a "go" at it! As Sydney Smith wrote: "Man is certainly a benevolent animal. A never sees B in distress without thinking C ought to relieve him directly."

31. LEGAL-EAGLE (The Lord is our judge, the Lord is our lawgiver, the Lord is our king; He will save us; Isaiah 33:22) For all the people who keep saying that there ought to be a law against thus and so, Walt Whitman wrote a few lines:

> Were you looking to be held together by the lawyers,
> Or by an agreement on paper? or by arms?
> Nay—nor the world, nor any living thing will so cohere.

A wonderful Collect for Advent prays that with the same joy with which we welcome the Christ Child we may also welcome Him when He comes to be our Judge. It is too bad, really, that we have become too familiar with His own parable of the last judgment to hear it freshly any longer. But a more old-new,

difficult-simple, impossible-possible stewardship text occurs nowhere else in the Bible.

32. LIKE A SHOT IN THE ARM (They helped every one his
neighbor, saying: "Be of good courage." So the carpenter encouraged the goldsmith; Isaiah 41:6-7) This shot in the arm
happens happily every month in a suburb of San Francisco when
the Third Baptist Church in town sends a $100 check to the
Westlake Baptist Church in Daly City—the happiest part of the
story being that the Westlake Baptists are white and newly-orga-
nized, while the Third Baptist Church is made up of 3,000 Negro
members, whose pastor promised the white congregation that
they could count on this shot in the arm for fifty months. Some
things sound too good to be true—but the fact is that when
the Reverend Roy Milam from the white suburban church was in
town in the Third Church office, word came that a Negro boy
needed a blood transfusion, and the white pastor hurried to the
hospital to give it. As somebody has phrased it:

> Your Parish is His Body.
> Your Offering is His Hands.
> Your Prayer is His Heart.
> Your Sins are His Thorns.

33. LONG TIME, NO SEE (They sit before thee as my people,
and they hear thy words, but they will not do them: for with their
mouth they show much love, but their heart goeth after their
covetousness; Ezekiel 33:31) This whole passage shows the Lord
talking to the preacher about the two-timers in the congregation,
those Christmas-Easter apparitions who appear out of the blue
and then disappear into the woodwork: nonsupporters, noncon-
tributors, nonentities on the church roll whom only the smell of
pine and the scent of lilies fetches forth semiannually.

34. NO KIDDING? (Hath not God chosen the poor of this
world rich in faith, and heirs of the Kingdom which He hath
promised to them that love Him? But ye have despised the poor;
James 2:5-6) When Sadhu Sunder Singh went from his native

India to England, and from his ascetic life of Christian mysticism into formal church services, he said gently, of others: "The children of God are very dear but very queer, very nice, but very narrow." And about himself he said: "Now I have no desire for wealth, possessions and honor. Nor do I desire even heaven. But I need Him who has made my heart heaven. His infinite love has expelled the love of all other things. The heart is the throne of the King of kings. The capital of heaven is the heart where the King reigns." There was never any possibility of mistaking the utter simplicity of this saint who had given up ease and wealth and family to walk the world barefoot, in his yellow robe, telling and retelling the life of Christ.

35. NOT WORTH A FIG? (One basket had very good figs, even like the figs that are first ripe: and the other basket had very naughty figs, which could not be eaten, they were so bad; Jeremiah 24:2) Two anonymous gifts to aid political refugees came from Britain—totaling more than $20,000. The money was used by the World Council of Churches for the reception and care of homeless refugees. The Council wrote to the address given by the donor inquiring about the possibility of further gifts. The reply came from a woman: "There is no more money. I have tried to take Christ's teaching on money literally, disposing of the capital of my small fortune as occasion arose. The last check I sent you was the end of my capital. This has brought a wonderful sense of liberation, allowing me to work as a mill girl for eight months. There is a tremendous field for evangelization in the factories."

36. PAIN IN THE NECK (And when the ten heard it, they were moved with indignation against the two brothers; Matthew 20:24) Some people can always feel a thunderstorm coming by a crick in the neck, and the two Sons of Thunder were also a pain in the neck to the disciples when they discovered they wanted top seats, as if they were more V.I.P. than the others. Robert Browning once prayed: "Make no more giants, Lord, but elevate the race."

37. PIE IN THE SKY BY AND BY. (Thou fool, this night thy

soul shall be required of thee, then whose shall those things be which thou hast provided? So is he that layeth up treasure for himself, and is not rich toward God; Luke 12:20-21)

> Rags make paper,
> Paper makes money,
> Money makes banks,
> Banks make loans,
> Loans make poverty, and,
> Poverty makes rags.
>
> Old English proverb

38. ROLLING IN DOUGH (What is that in thy hand? Exodus 4:2) When Franco moved into the royal palace in Spain he had a wastebasket on each side of his desk—the first was labeled: "Problems that Need Immediate Solution"; the other label read: "Problems that Time Has Solved—Our Greatest Ally." The second one was really waste. But George Washington Carver reached into every possible wastebasket and salvaged enough to equip his laboratory by using plenty of ingenuity; he too had a sign—over his door: "God's Little Work Shop"; and although he never grew at all rich himself, his 300 discoveries of how the humble peanut could be used, put useless cotton plantations to new uses, and restored that entire southern economy. Dr. Gordon Seagrave haunted wastebaskets also, looking for discarded medical instruments for his Burma hospital; you may have read his book *Waste Basket Surgery* which shows what a determined doctor can do when rags are handy and riches are not.

39. SOME LOOT! (The earth is the Lord's and the fulness thereof; Psalm 24:1) Venobe Bhave has been one of the most picturesque saints on earth the last few years, covering more than 20,000 miles of India on foot in his famous Land-Grant Movement, stopping in every village to say to the landlords: "If you had four sons you would divide your wealth equally between them. Treat me as your fifth son! Give me a share of your land for the sake of *God-as-revealed-in-the-poor*." His own phrase for this remarkable outpouring of land is "LOOTING FOR LOVE." Thin,

emaciated, utterly dedicated, Bhave was fifty-seven when he started this enormous marathon in 1951; always subject to malaria, and with a duodenal ulcer. But people could feel the power pouring from him, the way Ram Chandra Reddi must have felt it when his was the first such grant, and he signed away one hundred acres for Venobe Bhave to distribute. It was unbelievably marvelous to have forty landless families called forward then and there, asked how they would divide their land? They went into an excited huddle, but came back with a remarkable decision—eighty acres would be plenty, two apiece; so Venobe could perhaps give their twenty extra acres to somebody else? For in looting for love, love proved contagious!

40. STICK 'EM UP! (The thief cometh not, but for to steal, and to kill, and to destroy: I am come that they might have life and that they might have *it* more abundantly. I am the good shepherd: the good shepherd giveth his life for the sheep; John 10:10) The following quotation from *The Spiro* Palo Alto, California, may help us realize the higher cost of the non-Christian way of life: "A quick bit of research revealed the following interesting comparisons: When a gun-toting youth on a rampage kills a man, it costs the state about $125,000 to send him through the courts to the electric chair. If he gets a life term he eventually costs double that amount. Thus one crime is equal in cost to a church building in which literally thousands each year learn something about the sacredness of life." (From the calendar of Park Avenue Christian Church, New York City.)

41. THANKS A MILLION (What shall I render unto the Lord for all His benefits to me? I will pay my vows unto the Lord now, in the presence of all His people. . . . I will offer unto Thee the sacrifice of thanksgiving; Psalm 116:12, 14, 17) An old English legend tells how God sent two Angels on earth to collect the heartfelt desires of His people, each Angel with a basket—one labeled THANK YOU, the other GIVE ME. To God's dismay, the Thank You Basket came back practically empty, whereas the Give Me Basket bulged with requests. Presumably

from persons who sing complacently: "Somebody Up There Loves Me." As if That Man Upstairs had pets. Well, Jennie Geddes, it may have been like this in Scotland, too, or why does your proverb say: "Ye come o' the M'Taks and no o' the M'Gies"?

42. THAT BURNS ME UP (Ye that put away the evil day, and cause the seat of violence to come near; that lie upon beds of ivory . . . that invent instruments of music; that drink wine in bowls, and anoint themselves with the chief ointments; but they are not grieved for the afflictions of Joseph; Amos 6:3-6) It is fascinating to find out what disturbed our Lord most deeply— social climbers desirous of "sitting pretty" ("Top Man on the Totem Pole"); adults who turned children away, as of no consequence; traders turning God's temple into a den of thieves; priests and Levites coming from worship in Jerusalem, yet passing by an afflicted soul on their road home to Jericho.

In *The Divine Liturgy,* the Eastern Orthodox fathers have this prayer for May 9: "Burn up, like thorns, all my transgressions; purge Thou my soul, and hallow my imagination: knit firm my bones and joints withal: shine into all the five senses of my body: fasten me wholly in the fear of Thee. Guard, shield and shelter me evermore from every deed and word which stains the soul. Cleanse, wash, adorn me: set me right, give me understanding, enlighten me. Prove me the habitation of Thy Spirit only, and in no wise the dwelling-place of sin."

43. WE NEVER HAD IT SO GOOD (We do not well: this is a day of good tidings, and we hold our peace; 2 Kings 7:9) Like everybody's delicious dream of finding money on the sidewalk, four lepers who had been starving in the siege of Samaria ventured into the abandoned camp of the Syrians, found it unbelievably stocked with marvels, and had the time of their lives gorging on all the food, hiding treasures in twelve baskets full. Until suddenly they became more model stewards and hurried back to town to share the surplus with the starving.

44. WHAT'S COOKING? (Whan Martha was unco pernickety aboot mickle servin, the Laird sayed: Martha, Martha, ye are put-

till't and fashed wi' a hantle o' things; Luke 10:41) Or, as Dr.
Fosdick said in a sermon: she began to get the meal, and then
the meal got her! To find *the one needful thing* becomes the
Christian's only "dish of tea."

45. WHITE ELEPHANT (By faith Moses refused to be called
the son of Pharaoh's daughter, choosing rather to suffer affliction
with the people of God than to enjoy the pleasures of Egypt for
a season; esteeming the reproach of Christ greater riches than the
treasures in Egypt . . . for he endured as seeing Him who is invisible; Hebrews 11:24-27) Gandhi called possessions "tying a
white elephant at my door." Embarrassing bulk blocking the way
in and way out, for as he kept saying: to have superfluities while
brothers lacked necessities was sin. Over a hundred years ago
Frances Schervier gave us a prayer about all this: "What is mine
through Thy gift let it be Thine through my gift."

46. YOU SAID A MOUTHFUL (The head cannot say to the
feet: "I have no need of you"; 1 Corinthians 12:21) Paul might
have written this verse to describe Dr. John Flynn, the pioneer
Presbyterian Inland missionary to Australia's vast and remote sand
desert areas. People lived on such inaccessible ranches, back
country, that they had always been totally isolated from schools,
hospitals and churches until John Flynn invented his pedal radio,
which anybody could pedal at home like a stationary bicycle, thus
producing enough power for a voice to be heard 500 miles away.
This meant immediate touch with doctors, nurses, teachers, preachers. Any ranch could become "the church which is in thy house,"
where sermons could be heard, lessons taught, symptoms diag-
nosed, treatments suggested, and the solitary made glad. In 1955
a new church was dedicated in Alice Springs to the memory of
this scientific steward of the loving-kindness of God.

47. YOUR JOHN HANCOCK (What I have written, I have
written; John 19:22) Only a few things about a person are his
very own—his soul, his fingerprints, his "John Hancock" which
can turn any checkbook into a prayerbook. Back in the days when
almost everybody was illiterate, a legal document was torn in

half, zigzag fashion, for if the two halves fitted together perfectly then the lawyer could say: "This indenture witnesseth." And, curiously enough, all later lawyers have kept on using this phrase for legal documents to this very day. The Christian steward sees that—like Pilate—whatever he writes is written for all time and eternity: "This is Jesus, the King of the Jews." And this steward is always echoing Pilate: "Do you not know that I have the power to crucify you or to release you?"

48. WHAT GIVES? (Give, and it shall be given unto you; Luke 6:38) In the spring of 1956 an Italian Catholic truck driver backed into and knocked off a beautiful old colonial pillar of the Featherbed Lane Presbyterian Church in the Bronx, New York. All very sad—since the church had no insurance, and the driver had none; also, most unfortunately, he had no driver's license, either. It seemed like an impasse. But compassionately, the Presbytery found the driver a job as janitor of another Presbyterian Church; and by having had no charges pressed against him, the janitor agreed to pay back the damages out of his salary across the following years. It was at this point that a Jewish woman suddenly stepped into the story, for she was overcome with astonishment at this pleasant Presbyterian co-operation with a Catholic, about which she had read in her daily paper. Nobody could have expressed her delight more impressively—for she entered a television quiz program; won $650; and promptly sent it to the pastor of the Featherbed Lane Church, toward the pillar, as a token that the rich and the poor *have* met together! and the Lord *is* the maker of them all! just as her own King Solomon said so wisely, centuries ago.

Noo, when Jesus was born i' Bethlehem, lo! Wyss Men cam frae oot the East . . . and lo! the starn whilk they saw i' the East gaed on afore them, till it stood whar

the wee bairn was. And whan they saw the starn, they were blythe wi' unco blytheness. And comin intil the hoose, they saw the wee bairn and his mither Mary; and loutin doon, worshipp't Him. And openin oot their gear they offer't till Him gifts—gawd, and frankincense and myrrh.

Matthew 2:9-11

Tak tent no to do yere gude warks i' the sicht o' men, that ye may be seen by them; else hae ye tint reward frae yere Faither wha is in Heeven. Whan, then, ye wad do a gude wark, dinna hae a bugle-horn soondit afore ye, as the pretenders div in kirks and merkits, that they may be roosed o' men. Truly say I t' ye, they hae gotten a' their reward! But whan ye wad do a gude wark, lat yere left haun no jalouse what yere richt haun is thrang wi'. That yere gude warks may be dune hidlins; and yere Faither wha sees i' the hidlin place, sal his ain self reward ye oot i' the licht.

Matthew 6:1-4

ACKNOWLEDGMENTS

For permission to quote the following, the author is grateful: to Harcourt, Brace and Company for the verse "In God We Trust", from *Good Morning, America* by Carl Sandburg; to the Rauschenbusch family for their father's paraphrase of 1 Corinthians 13; to Rev. Edward K. Ziegler for his Materialists's Version of the Twenty-third Psalm; to the David C. Cook Publishing Company for the use of portions of her own articles from "The New Century Leader" and "Adult Bible Class" ("The Gift Is Forever"; "Some of My Best Friends Are Tithers"; etc.); to The Christian Century for the poem by John Fremont Merrill, copyright May, 1949, Christian Century Foundation; to the Presbyterian Organization of Women's Work, for the three quotations by Jean Kenyon Mackenzie, from "The Glowing Ember."